A HISTORY OF
THE AUCTION

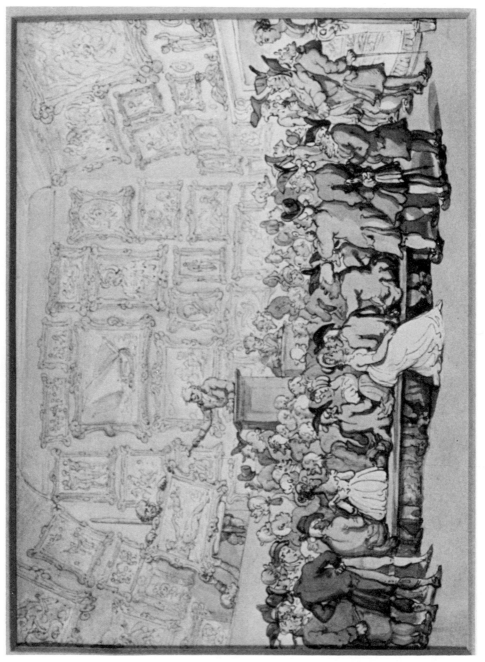

A Sale at Christie's—from a watercolour by Rowlandson. Photo courtesy Christie's

A History of
the
Auction

by
BRIAN LEARMOUNT

BARNARD & LEARMOUNT
1985

First published in Great Britain by
Barnard & Learmount

British Library in Publication Data

Learmount, Brian
A history of the auction.
1. Auctions—History
I. Title
380.1'09   HF5476

ISBN 0-9510240-0-0

Printed and bound in Great Britain by
Butler & Tanner Ltd, Frome and London

To Mary . . .

Contents

Illustrations

Acknowledgements

My grateful thanks for their invaluable assistance in the research for this book are due to Clive Bostle and Elizabeth Lee of the Buckinghamshire Library Service. My thanks also to John Hudisteanu for his occasional research and constant encouragement.

The enthusiastic co-operation of Jim Hillier of Messrs Buckland's was much appreciated as was his willingness to supply archive material for illustration.

For the rest of the illustrations and for access to library material my sincere thanks to—
Messrs Christie, Manson & Woods
Windsor Slough & Eton Express
The Estates Gazette
The Bibliotheque Nationale

For their assistance in the final production I am indebted to the Rationalist Press Association—specifically Nicolas Walter and David Stewart.

Introduction

'Going for a song' has become a much used and well recognised phrase since the media—and in particular television—realised the potential entertainment value of the art-auction business.

It is only during the course of this century that the auction rooms have become such a major component of the art world, and it is of course this involvement with the thoroughly speculative art trade that has made the salerooms and their staffs such a prime target for the media.

In these days of rapidly escalating values hardly a week passes without a major news item on television, radio, or in the newspapers, relating to this or that important work of art, at this or that well-known saleroom. The well-known saleroom is very likely to be Christie's or Sotheby's, who have both used the intense media interest in these events to some advantage, and who by virtue of their efficient publicity machines have succeeded in capturing the lion's share of the market.

For how long have the London salerooms dominated the auction in this way, what went before, where in fact did it all begin and how did it develop into the international business it is today? What was it that the auctioneers sold before the arts took command; cotton perhaps or tea, sugar or slaves?

Our research will show that long before the twentieth century connection with art, simply as an element of trade and commerce, the history of the auction had already spanned more than two thousand years. Even today's auction devotees might be surprised to learn that auctions were held in ancient Babylon before the birth of Christ, and that house contents sales were so popular in ancient Rome that more than one ancient Roman of high rank is recorded as having disposed of the family furniture by this method when times were hard.

The auction as a method of sale has always had a special fascination which derives, strange as it may seem, from the uncertainties associated with the process. The fact that no fixed price structure exists as in most other trading operations seems to lead the auction buyer to believe that he might get a low-priced bargain and the seller to believe that a high price might result, thus encouraging both to participate.

The excitement generated by each brief moment of suspense before the hammer falls on each lot applies to buyers and sellers and spectators alike, and is the same excitement whether it is a small local or large international sale. The man in the middle, the auctioneer, may take part of his profit from both buyer and seller, if he operates, as the London salerooms do, a 'buyer's premium' — a thoroughly modern phenomenon, or is it?

Throughout the seventeenth and eighteenth centuries the auctioneers adapted to the social and economic patterns of the time. They sold the imports of the new East India Company, they sold slaves and the products of the Industrial Revolution. The auctioneers were heavily involved in the notorious 'triangular trade' which, more than anything else, it may be argued, established them in the forefront of commerce, and provided the wealth which first allowed their diversification into the fine arts to begin.

The auction and the auctioneers came in for much criticism in the early nineteenth century in both England and America. Many abuses were claimed for the system, and much debate as well as a great deal of correspondence on the matter passed between the supporters and opponents of the auction, and involved both the American congress and the British parliament. In examining some more modern criticisms we will look at the influence of television on a multi-million pound industry with show-business connections.

We will also examine the activities and the operation of the dealers 'ring', groups of dealers who seek financial advantage by attempting to depress prices in the salerooms of the world. 'Ring' operations were made illegal in England in 1927, but prosecutions are rare, and the legislation is far from effective. Even those dealers who participate in today's auction rings might, however, be surprised to learn that their equally unscrupulous ancestors were doing precisely the same thing in eighteenth-century Paris and nineteenth-century England.

It was interesting to discover during this investigation just how much the salerooms and saleroom methods of the world varied, and to learn that one might bid by handshake or whisper, by push-button or by telegraph, depending on whether one was in Japan, Holland or the United States.

Our examination of the auction and its history will reveal some major differences and yet many remarkable similarities between the ancient and modern auction scene. The differences are on the whole historic; the auction has been principally over the years just another method of selling and distributing goods, and of course over the years the types of commodity disposed of by the auction method have changed. We will find when we seek for records of the auction and auctioneering styles that those details exist primarily in the records and chronicles of business methods and marketing techniques.

The similarities, on the other hand, may appear as the result of the search for the common thread, the link which has given the auction its fascination for so many years. It is without doubt this fascination with the subject, which stems from some very basic human characteristics, that has allowed the auction not only to survive for all those years, but to grow and prosper. Its success is based, therefore, not so much on its efficiency as a business technique as on man's unchanging and unquenchable desire to possess more than the next man, and to demonstrate publicly either his good taste or great wealth, or preferably both, in the pursuit of that which is unique or at least in short supply. The immediacy of the auction, the split-second to make up the mind before the hammer falls, when added to man's naturally acquisitive nature provides a formula which few are able to resist.

CHAPTER 1

The Early History

It will be necessary in the course of a consideration of the history of
the auction to deal with one or two popular misconceptions regarding
the nature of the auction. A mere passing acquaintance with the
present-day system might well lead one to assume, for example, that
auction as a method of business has always been primarily involved
with the sale of antiques and works of art, perhaps even as an entertaining diversion for those wealthy enough to be able to pursue the
acquisition of such things, or as a shop window for those dealers whose
business it is to make available a constant supply of art for wealthy
patrons too busy acquiring the wealth to have the time to personally
organise the trappings.

It is of course true that by far the largest part of the business
generated by the auction rooms of the world today is devoted to the
sale of collectables and fine art items. There are, however, even now
many other areas of trade which use the auction system and these
include the sale of cattle and fish, the sale of property and motor
vehicles and many others. It is true also that the further into the past
one descends in the search for the origins of the auction the more one
is likely to find the system being used simply as a method of trade, as
a means of disposing of large surpluses of commodities quickly and
efficiently, and with little or no emphasis on the fine arts.

Without a doubt the auction has a long and colourful history, and
like most things has, with the passage of time, changed and adapted
itself to meet the social and economic needs and conditions of each
period. Thus as present day associations, including criticisms and
abuses of the system, might properly reflect today's affluent and acquisitive society, so a study of the historic auction should reveal
glimpses of the social and economic attitudes of the times.

The earliest known reference to the auction comes to us from the
Histories of Herodotus. Herodotus was born between 490 and 480 BC
at Halicarnassus on the south-west coast of Asia Minor, and he has
described the history of his times to such great effect that he has been
called by Cicero and others 'the father of history'. In a section devoted
to a description of Babylonian customs at about the year 500 BC he
writes as follows:

In every village once a year all the girls of marriageable age used
to be collected together in one place, while the men stood around
them in a circle; an auctioneer then called each one in turn to
stand up and offered her for sale, beginning with the best-looking
and going on to the second best as soon as the first had been sold
for a good price. Marriage was the object of the transaction. The
rich men who wanted wives bid against each other for the prettiest
girls, while the humbler folk, who had no use for good looks in a
wife, were actually paid to take the ugly ones, for when the auctioneer had got through all the pretty girls he would call upon the
plainest, or even perhaps a crippled one, to stand up, and then ask
who was willing to take the least money to marry her—and she
was knocked down to whoever accepted the smallest sum. The
money came from the sale of the beauties, who in this way provided
dowries for their ugly or misshapen sisters. It was illegal for a man
to marry his daughter to anyone he happend to fancy, and no one
could take home a girl he had bought without first finding a backer
to guarantee his intention of marrying her. In cases of disagreement
between husband and wife the law allowed the return of the purchase money. Anyone who wished could come even from a different
village to buy a wife.

This early reference is interesting in more than one way. Not only
does it establish the earliest known date at which the auction system
was being used but it tells us something else. The fact that Herodotus
states that in the case of disagreement after the sale the purchase
money could be returned suggests that exactly as is the case today,
the sale was subject to certain conditions which were enforcable by
law. The account also leads us to consider what may be regarded as
another popular misconception, and that is the assumption that bidding at an auction invariably proceeds in an upward direction. The
word 'auction' is from the Latin 'auctio' which means increase. The
word auction therefore is largely presumed to describe a proceeding
at which the public are invited to compete for the purchase of property by successive offers of advancing sums. This is not always the
case. The form that the auction takes and the method of bidding may
vary from country to country across the world, and even in one
country—in England for example—methods have changed over the
years.

In the case of the example quoted by Herodotus it would seem that
in the first part the sale of the pretty girls involved an increasing bid
type of auction, but that when it came to the less comely wenches a
form of dowry was needed in order to unload them onto the less
discerning buyers. At this point the auction would take an inverse
form and rival bidders would make reducing bids until they reached

the minimum which one of them would be willing to accept in return for each unfortunate female.

In national and historical terms methods other than the ascending bid method include the Dutch or upside-down auction, auction by inch of candle and the Japanese method of simultaneous bidding. We will consider the detail of such methods together with any other variations on the theme as we reach them in our story. While there is every reason to suppose that the auction system was widely used throughout the ancient world, the precise extent of its use and the methods employed will never be known to us. The scant references available tell us that auction was a feature of the trade of more than one ancient civilisation, but detailed descriptions are rare, and after Herodotus we must move on to Rome in the search for evidence.

There is no doubt that auctions were used by the Romans in commercial trade. The word auction is of course a derivitive of the Roman word auctio, and whilst the available evidence concerning the type of bidding used is scarce, it would seem reasonable to assume that as auctio means increase the bidding proceeded by successive increase until the highest bidder was found. A study of the literature of the period reveals that the Romans, rather like the Greeks, had a word for it; and the titles of the various participants in the auction business are faithfully recorded. The 'dominus' was the seller—the owner of the goods to be sold. The 'argetarius' was the organiser of the sale, the businessman who put up the finance to cover the expenses of the sale, and the 'praeco' was the promoter of the sale, a sort of latter-day advertising agent who doubled up by acting as the auctioneer. The final figure in the auction action was the lucky highest bidder, known to his ancient Roman friends as the 'emptor'.

A forthcoming auction sale was advertised in two ways, a public announcement was made by the praeco or herald and written notices (proscriptio) were posted giving details of the sale. It is also recorded that sales were held in an 'atrium auctionarium', and it is considered likely that the goods to be sold were on view before the sale began in the same way as they are today. What small evidence that exists regarding the method of bidding would suggest that rather than a system of public outcry the sale, once under way, proceeded quietly with bids indicated by a nod or a wink.

It might well be that the Romans were also the originators of a type of auction sale highly popular in much more recent times, that is the house contents sale held 'on the premises'. It seems that the odd hard-up Roman would use the auction to sell off his furniture and effects. Caligula, for example, auctioned the furniture and ornaments belonging to his family to help him meet his massive debts, and it is reported that Marcus Aurelius—to cover a state deficit—held a furniture and effects auction which lasted for some two months.

The highly efficient Roman war machine, which so successfully colonised large parts of the ancient world, was responsible for providing further large-scale opportunities for the auctioneers. The many great victories achieved by the Roman armies produced vast quantities of goods of all kinds plundered from the various vanquished populations. Much of the booty was disposed of by the auction method, and many of those taken captive were sold in the same way to help supply the slave markets of the Roman world. Such, in fact, was the extent of the business generated in this way that Roman business agents accompanied the military expeditions in order to be on the spot when these auctions were held. The term used for such sales was 'sub hasta', or 'under the spear', a Roman version of 'under the hammer'.

Modern day travellers might be surprised to learn that the idyllic Greek island of Delos, legendary birthplace of Apollo, was the central slave market for both Greece and Rome. Its present solitude, disturbed only by the inevitable tourists intent on viewing the ruins of its glorious past, is in direct contrast to the feverish activity there must surely have been when the island was a major slave port dealing with the Greek and Roman as well as the pirate traders of the period. The slave auctions serviced the Roman empire in another way also, in that taxes were imposed on all sales of slaves in order to raise revenues. During the reign of Augustus the duty was two per cent, and under Nero it was enacted that the seller should in future pay the tax. From this we may deduce that previously it had been the buyer who paid, and if that is indeed the case then clearly the inventors of what was thought to be a modern phenomenon—the 'buyer's premium'—were the Romans.

All those outraged dealers, therefore, who today trumpet loudly about this 'iniquitous' surcharge, and who speculate publicly on whether the blame for its inception lies with Christie or Sotheby, or by collusion, with both, can now be assured that it was neither; and that all the modern arguments both for and against have, like almost everything else in creation, been argued before in another time, in this case around two thousand years ago. Nero's reversion was claimed to be a remission of tax, but Tacitus observed that it was a remission in name only, for the tax would continue to be paid by the buyer in the form of a higher price, required by the seller to cover the tax. Under Caligula, the tax, like almost everything else, was abolished.

A particularly interesting method of dealing with the estate of a debtor by auction is recorded in the 'Institutes of Justinian'. Under Roman law the debtor could avoid arrest by agreeing to abandon all his property to his creditors; and if he chose to do this, or if the debtor was dead or was in hiding so that he could not be summoned before a magistrate, then a particular course of action was initiated. The creditors were awarded a 'venditio bonorum' or compulsory sale which placed them in full possession of all the debtor's property. Once this had been done the sale of the goods was announced by advertisement, and after an interval of thirty days if the debtor was alive and fifteen if he were dead, a meeting of the creditors was called. At this meeting the creditors chose one of their number to conduct the business for them, and after a further short interval the conditions of sale were fixed under the supervision of the praetor.

Depending again on whether the debtor was alive or dead, there would be a final delay of either ten or twenty days, at the end of which time the goods would be put up for public auction. After the sale of the goods as a single lot, the successful bidder would be declared 'bonorum emptor', at which time ownership of the property would be officially transferred to him and he would legally assume the role and responsibilities of the original owner. From that moment on the new owner could sue and be sued exactly as the debtor could have sued and have been sued.

Another Roman 'first' may well have been achieved in 146 BC, following the military victory over the Achaeans. The consul, Lucius Mummius, ordered that the booty of paintings and sculpture should be sold by public auction in Rome. At the sale a painting of Bacchus by Aristides attracted a bid of 600,000 sesterces—an astonishing price for the time equivalent to almost 23,000 gold sovereigns. The successful bidder was Attala, King of Pergamum, but his joy of acquisition was short-lived. The Roman authorities, it seems, became highly suspicious that the high price was on account of some special virtue which the painting possessed, some magical power perhaps, of which they had not been aware.

In the event Attala never received his purchase. Like so many later treasures in so many other capitals the authorities refused the picture an 'export licence'. It was not allowed to leave Rome and in fact went instead to adorn a temple dedicated to Ceres.

The terrible tragedy which overtook Pompeii but which has proved to be such an enormous benefit to archaeologists and historians has also provided a small link in our auction chain. The name and even the image of one of the local auctioneers, together with wax tablets of his invoices, have risen again from the ashes of his ruined home in the immortal city. The bust of the auctionator Lucius Caecilius Jucundus, found during the 1845 excavations, is on public view at the Naples Museum.

Arguably the strangest but certainly the largest auction of all time took place during the period of Roman supremacy. In 193 AD the entire Roman empire was put up for sale by the Praetorian Guard. It was sold as one lot and there were only two bidders. The background to this extraordinary event is vividly described by Edward Gibbon in his *Decline and Fall of the Roman Empire*. Gibbon tells us that the Praetorian Guard, whose numbers had been gradually increased by successive Emperors anxious to preserve their total dominance over State and Senate alike, had come to realise the strength that their special position afforded them. He goes on:

> Such formidable servants are always necessary, but often fatal, to the throne of despotism. By thus introducing the Praetorian guards into the palace and the senate, the emperors taught them to perceive their own strength, and the weakness of the civil government; to view the vices of their masters with familiar contempt, and to lay aside that reverential awe which distance only and mystery can preserve towards an imaginary power.

Finally, with all the reverence laid violently aside, the guards murdered the emperor Pertinax. In the wild disorder that followed, Sulpicianus, the ex-emperor's brother-in-law and governor of the city, was sent to put down the mutiny. But he, despite witnessing the return of the murderers bearing the head of Pertinax impaled on a lance, determined to seize the opportunity to obtain the vacant throne for himself. He had scarcely begun to make his plea, when, Gibbon tells us:

> the more prudent of the Praetorians, apprehensive that, in this private contract, they should not obtain a just price for so valuable a commodity, ran out upon the ramparts, and, with a loud voice, proclaimed that the Roman world was to be disposed of to the best bidder by public auction.
>
> This infamous affair, the most insolent excess of military licence, diffused an universal grief, shame, and indignation throughout the city. It reached at length the ears of Didius Julianus, a wealthy senator, who, regardless of the public calamities, was indulging himself in the luxury of the table. His wife and daughter, his freedmen and his parasites, easily convinced him that he deserved the throne, and earnestly conjured him to embrace so fortunate an opportunity. The vain old man hastened to the Praetorian camp, where Sulpicianus was still in treaty with the guards, and began to bid against him from the foot of the rampart. The unworthy negotiation was transacted by faithful emissaries, who passed alternately from one candidate to the other, and acquainted each of them with the offers of his rival. Sulpicianus had already promised a donative of five thousand drachms (above one hundred and sixty pounds) to each soldier, when Julian, eager for the prize, rose at once to the sum of six thousand two hundred and fifty drachms, or upwards of two hundred pounds sterling. The gates of the camp were instantly thrown open to the purchaser; he was declared em-

peror, and received an oath of allegiance from the soldiers, who retained humanity enough to stipulate that he should pardon and forget the competition of Sulpicianus.

Eventually after some formality and a great deal of celebration the victorious Julian retired to his quarters to reflect on the days events. Gibbon records:

> Yet it was observed that, after the crowd of flatterers dispersed, and left him to darkness, solitude, and terrible reflection, he passed a sleepless night; revolving most probably in his mind his own rash folly, the fate of his virtuous predecessor, and the doubtful and dangerous tenure of an empire which had not been acquired by merit, but purchased by money.

Bearing in mind the Roman word for the highest bidder, it seems that here was an early example of a now familiar warning, 'caveat emptor' —let the buyer beware.

Very little is known about the auction in other ancient civilisations. It is reported that in seventh-century China the personal belongings of deceased monks were disposed of by auction. The monk who acted as auctioneer was expected not only to advise those bidding as to the general condition of the items, but also to offer a warning to his companions if he suspected that they were getting carried away and offering too high a price.

When finally in its turn the Roman empire crumbled, civilisation began the plunge into the abyss known as the Dark Ages. The sacking of Rome by the Barbarian hordes in 410 AD heralds a long pause in our search for evidence. It is at least highly unlikely that the conquerors of Rome auctioned off the booty in emulation of their vanquished foes, and it is almost certainly true to say that no evidence of continuing activity in the auction field exists in the next several hundred years. Further firm evidence for the auction story will not be found until the middle of the sixteenth century, from which time onwards the references will become more and more profuse.

It is obviously difficult when writing any history to fill in the gaps where the evidence is simply not available. The period of the Middle or Dark Ages is singularly lacking in record, and inevitably leads to speculative analysis based on detective work and the subjective interpretation of the individual. The major problem lies in establishing continuity between the end of the civilised ancient world and the beginning of the modern world when the records largely reappear. The problem is particularly acute in our case because the gap in the auction story is a long one. There may, however, be a satisfactory explanation for this which we will consider later.

In earlier times the distinct lack of source material for the period led many writers to the conclusion that there was in fact a discontinuance in many areas. It was believed that previously well-established social and cultural activities and attitudes simply and quite suddenly ceased, only to resume and flourish when 'rediscovered' several hundred years later. Modern historians, in general, are not of that opinion. They find it difficult to believe that attitudes and functions change at a particular moment in time, only to return in similar form at a later date. Denys Hay, professor of medieval history, is quite clear on the matter:

> The past is not a Christmas pantomime and seldom if ever deals in transformation scenes. Older attitudes and techniques persist unadulterated or only thinly diluted with the new.

Professor Hay is obviously not convinced that lack of evidence automatically assumes a lack of continuity, and so it must be in our story. It would seem reasonable to assume that an established practice common in Roman society would be transmitted by them to the several areas of the world under their control. This together with the evidence for an already long previous history of auctioneering must make it unreasonable to believe that the practice simply stopped at a particular moment in time. What we must not forget is that the auction was, at this time, simply a component in the trading system. A much more likely explanation, therefore, for the lack of evidence is that trade at this time simply declined to such a low ebb that the records have proved impossible to discover. Society in the Middle Ages did in fact become basically an agrarian society. The wealth of the period was based almost exclusively on the land and its product. Professor Hay sums it up in a sentence:

> Money and merchants always existed, it seems, even in the darkest part of the Dark Ages, but they were insignificant.

There is just one more question to answer as far as this part of the story is concerned. Why such a long gap in the evidence for auction activity, a gap stretching as far as the sixteenth century. After all the Renaissance was under way in Italy in the fourteenth century, and that part of history described as 'modern' was begun in almost all of the countries of Europe by 1500. Should we not then have expected to find trade resuming significant proportions much earlier, and does not the length of the pause lend weight to the discontinuity argument. Modern historical theory is again our salvation with a reasonable explanation. Europe in the fourteenth century suffered intermittant warfare, peasant revolts, serious famine, and the Black Death. All of these catastrophies, but particularly the last, resulted in the most serious depopulation. The fourteenth century was an age of economic decline, and the loss of skilled manpower in the towns forced a recession in industry and consequently in trade. Recovery was not achieved until the sixteenth century.

The thread of our story will continue from the second half of the sixteenth century, and will flourish from that point. That our subject conforms precisely to its historical context is an encouragement to the belief that auction is a function basic to trade in society, and that a universal spirit of competition in trading must assume its use in most if not all civilised societies.

CHAPTER 2

Europe 1550–1750

Some of the earliest evidence of a renewal of auction activity is to be found in documents in the possession of the French government at the Bibliotheque Nationale. The most ancient of these documents is an Act of 1556 which created a group known as 'Huissiers Priseurs' (Bailiff-Auctioneers). The Act laid down the duties of those nominated to the post, who were 'to have the exclusive rights to deal with and appraise and sell property left by death or taken in execution'.

What evidence there is of the sales themselves suggests that they were fairly impromptu affairs without cataloguing or prior viewing, and held quite immediately on the premises formerly occupied by the deceased owner or debtor. Bidding was almost certainly of the ascending type with items going to the highest bidder. The bailiff acted as auctioneer, but not in the same way as today's auctioneers operate, for he would engage the services of a 'crier' to seek out the bidders and to repeat the bids. The absence of a catalogue and the lack of previous viewing made it imperative that the auctioneer was left free to give glowing descriptions of the offered goods to the prospective buyers, while the crier loudly repeated the bidding.

It is fortunate that a fine piece of descriptive writing remains to advise us of something of the character of these sales and indeed of the Bailiff-Auctioneer. The piece is from 'Tableau de Paris', by Sebastien Mercier:

The business of the auctioneer becomes every day more lucrative. As luxury grows the more numerous become the necessities, the quiet struggle between ease and poverty causes a multitude of sales and purchases. Losses, bankruptcies, deaths, all are to the benefit of the auctioneers when reverses, variations of fortune, or change of place or circumstance call for forced or voluntary sales. There follow, as a matter of course, the little tricks of the trade. For instance, an auctioneer is often dealer and salesman in one, either on his own account or 'hand in glove' with the other dealers, and in his sales he knows how to work the oracle; that is to say, knocking down the article when it suits him according to his own private plans or those of his secret associates in the 'deal'. The fall of the hammer is an irrevocable decision, but oh, what an uproar before the final word. The auctioneer is compelled to have a stentor for a crier at his disposal. Nothing is heard but the everlasting shouts of the buyers, 'one sous, one sous' whilst the salesman, on his part, cries, 'once, twice, three times'. One would imagine that the article in question was to be sold on the instant, for the auctioneer always says 'for the last time, going, going'. But the crowd continue shouting 'one sous, one sous' and behold the object runs up a 'sous' at a time to a thousand livres beyond the first price. One sous has turned the balance. One sous has fixed the destiny of the article. The auctioneer, dressing in black, with his flute-like voice, and the crier in tatters, but full of 'eau-de-vie', whose voice makes the windows rattle. The ear is wearied with the constant and deafening repetition. The stentor's hoarse cry of 'silence' hardly rises above the confused murmur of the crowd, passing the articles from hand to hand, inspecting them or disdaining them according to fancy or requirement.

When you have been present at one of these tumultuous gatherings, the monotonous cries and the buzz remain in your ears for a full fortnight afterwards. This is how things are sold, from a picture by Rubens, down to an old coat out at the elbows.

In the auctions after death, the tinkers have the first chance, for the kitchen utensils take precedence, seeing that the defunct needs them no longer. The buyers of these pots and kettles thus come to mingle with purchasers of the diamonds, furniture and old lace.

The earliest reference to the word auction in the *Oxford English Dictionary* dates from 1595, but an earlier English reference is available from the proceedings of an action brought in the London courts in 1795. In a complicated legal argument regarding the definition of an auctioneer, evidence was submitted that 'by a charter of Henry the seventh, confirmed by Charles the first, the business of selling by auction was confined to an officer called an Outroper, and all other persons were prohibited from selling goods or merchandise by public claim or outcry'.

Thus we may assume that the auction system was in use in England at the end of the fifteenth century, but it is not to be until well into the seventeenth century that further hard evidence becomes available. That evidence confirms that the system is well established, and between 1660 and 1680 we discover not only several references which assume auctions to be quite common, but a record indicating that Conditions of Sale are already in use and a further indication that at least three different methods of bidding are in use in the various auction rooms.

It is generally believed that in the seventeenth century in England, as in France, auctions in the form of peremptory sales were held by order of the court. The first graphic descriptions of sales by auction, however, come to us from an impeccable source— *The Diary of Samuel Pepys*. The entry for November the 6th, 1660, reads:

> To our office, where we met all for the sale of two ships by an inch of candle (the first time that ever I saw any of this kind), where I observed how they do invite one another, and at last how they all do cry, and we have much to do to tell who did cry last. The ships were the Indian, sold for £1300, and the Half-moon, sold for £830.

Almost two years later the 'Diary' records a somewhat fuller description of another sale of ships, and by this time Pepys is getting to grips with the finer points of the auction. The entry is that for September the 3rd, 1662:

> After dinner we met and sold the Weymouth, Success and Fellowship hulkes, were pleasant to see how backward men are at first to bid; and yet, when the candle is going out, how they bawl, and dispute afterwards who bid the most first. And here I observed one man cunninger than the rest, that was sure to bid the last man, and carry it: and inquiring the reason, he told me that just as the flame goes out, the smoke descends, which is a thing I never observed before, and by that he do know the instant when to bid last.

These entries suggest that the disposal by the navy of obsolete sailing vessels by auction was a not uncommon practice, and Pepys's record indicates a growing familiarity with such events. Indeed his description in the second passage of the particular expertise displayed by one of the bidders must assume a history of such sales long enough at least to have allowed that expertise to have developed.

The particular method used in the auctions observed by Samuel Pepys was 'sale by candle', sometimes referred to as the 'English method'. Certainly the evidence shows clearly that it was a method of sale used in England for a very long time. The usual practice at such sales was to set up an inch of lighted candle, and the person who made the last bid before the flame went out became the purchaser. One could imagine, even without Pepys's brief description, that a certain amount of experience was an essential to successful bidding, and it may be confidently predicted that many a fierce argument developed over who indeed the final bidder had been.

There is no doubt that the 'candle' method was extremely popular in England at the end of the seventeenth century, even though, as we will see, certain new methods were on trial at the time. Evidence for its general use is found in an Act of William the third, dated 1698, which is an 'Act for settling the Trade to the East Indies.' The Act

laid down the conditions under which individuals might enter into
trade by importing merchandise from the East Indies. It also allowed
groups of merchants to import collectively in order to overcome the
limits on individuals, and as such was the vehicle instrumental in
forming what was to become known as the East India Company.

Total annual imports were subject to strict financial limits, and
certain types of goods were subject to quota restrictions. The Act set
out the penalties for exceeding these limits and established an inspectorate empowered to examine cargoes and to seize goods imported in
excess of the limits. The Act went so far as to prescribe the particular
method of sale to be employed for the goods imported. The Act
decreed:

> all Goods and Merchandizes, belonging to the Company to be
> erected, or any other Traders to the East Indies, and which shall
> be imported into England or Wales, pursuant to this Act, shall by
> them respectively be sold openly and publickly by Inch of Candle,
> upon their respective Accounts, and not otherwise; upon Pain that
> the same, or the Value thereof, shall be forfeited and lost.

The fact that here is a specific direction under the law to dispose of
goods by a particular method of public sale, must without doubt
indicate that such method was not only commonly in use at the time,
but had been established practice over many years. We gain some
indication of the span of years over which a form of the 'candle'
method has been in use when we learn that the earliest known reference to a public sale in England is a sale by candle of 1490, and that
even today in France new wines are sold by candle each autumn. We
will deal with the detail of that first reference later in this chapter and
with the French wines in a later chapter.

Obviously the greatest disadvantage of the candle method of sale is
its slowness, the time taken for each lot to be sold, waiting for the
candle to burn and the moment for bidding to arrive. In the case of
the sales observed by Pepys time was clearly not important with only
two or three ships to sell; and almost one hundred and thirty years
later a sale of timber at the Bank Coffee-House in Threadneedle Street
by the same method was concerned with only about fifteen lots. In
today's busy auction arena the average sale deals with around five
hundred lots in a day, and the modern auctioneer rattles along at the
rate of a hundred or more lots per hour. To cope with this present
pace the candle method would need to have been converted to elec-
tricity over the years. By the original method one could well imagine
that average modern sale taking a couple of weeks to complete, as
well as leading to endless disputes resulting in at best litigation and at
worst a punch-up.

It was almost certainly a need for greater speed which, in the

FOR
SALE
BY THE
CANDLE,
AT THE
BANK Coffee-House, *Threadneedle-Street*,

On *Wednesday* the 19th of *May*, 1790,
at FOUR o'CLOCK,
Immediately after Change is over;
The following GOODS,

Being Part of the Capital Stock of the Saw
Mill at Dartford, in Kent,
And removed to the *East Country* Wharf, at the
Paguants, for the Convenience of the Purchasers.

Consisting of

150000	Feet of ½ Inch Yellow Boards	
30000	Ditto of ⅞	Ditto
80000	Ditto of ⅞	White
50000	Ditto of 1	Ditto
30000	Ditto of ½	Ditto
12000	Ditto of Running, 2¼ inches thick, 12 to 22 feet long, and 6 inches broad	

Lying at Mr. Porter's Wharf, near the Albion Mills.

25	Ends of 4 Inch dry Beach Plank	
121	Ditto	3 Inch ditto
367	Ditto	2¼ Inch ditto

Lying at the St. Petersburg Wharf, uncleared at a former Sale.

144	Onega Deals, 18 Feet	3 Inch
113	Ditto	16	2½
120	Ditto	20	2
200	Ditto	12	1¼
240	Ditto Battens 20		1¼
240	Ditto	16	

CONDITIONS OF SALE.

I. THE highest Bidder (in due Time) shall be declared the Buyer, who must immediately deposit into the Hands of the Brokers, Twenty per Cent. in Part of Payment and One Shilling per Lot to the Brokers to bind the Bargain.

II. The Boards to be taken as they rise from the Piles, and the other Goods as they lay, with all Faults; the Boards at the Measurement raised on them, and to be cleared away within 14 Days from the Time of Sale at the Buyer's Expence, and the Remainder of the Purchase-Money to be paid on or before the Delivery of the said Goods.

III. If any Lot or Lots shall remain uncleared at the Expiration of the Time above limited, the Deposit shall be forfeited, the Goods re-sold, either by private or public Sale, and the Deficiency (if any) that may arise by such Re-sale, shall be made good by the Purchaser, who shall be answerable for Interest of Money, Risque of Fire, and every other Expence which may attend his not complying with the above Conditions.

Lastly. If any Dispute shall arise at this Sale, the Lot or Lots in Dispute shall be put up again, or be determined by the Majority of the Company. It is also expected, that every Purchaser will pay the Deposit before he leaves the Sale-Room; and that no Order will be given before the Remainder of the Money is paid.

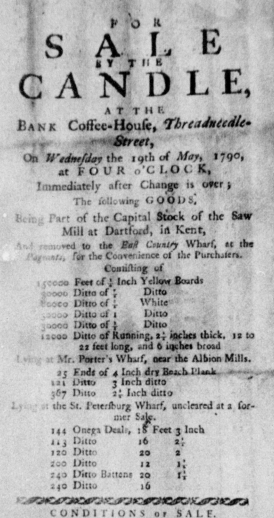

Advertisement for an eighteenth-century Sale by Candle. Photo courtesy Estates Gazette

late-seventeenth and eighteenth centuries, caused new methods to be introduced into the auction scene. As a new breed of auctioneer became involved in the new markets opened up by the increasing tempo of trade and the exotic imports from abroad, the quicker methods of sale began to take precedence over 'sale by candle', which although still used in a limited way was to diminish in popularity over the next hundred years.

It appears that the search for alternative methods was conducted with great fervour, and even included variations on the 'candle' theme. A 'dumb bidding' was a sale where the owner of the goods would place under a candlestick a reserve price which if not equalled by any of the bidders would render the proceedings void. 'Candlestick biddings' are also reported where each of the several bidders had no knowledge of what the others had offered. However, when the period of experiment was over and the smoke had finally cleared, it was the ascending bid method which emerged victorious. This is confirmed by the fact that most eighteenth century dictionaries define the word 'auction' as a sale by successive increasing bids, and while some still list 'sale by candle' it has become a separate and secondary reference. The first edition of the *Encyclopaedia Britannica*, published in 1771, lists both in this way, and an earlier publication, Samuel Johnson's *Dictionary of the English Language* says of the word:

> A manner of sale, in which one person bids after another, till so much is bid as the seller is content to take.

Clearly what was good enough for the Roman Empire was to be good enough for the English merchants, and quite a few not quite so important but fairly significant 'empires' were to go 'under the hammer' in the next two hundred and fifty years.

Whatever the method it is certain that by 1682 the auction had become a familiar event in London, for an issue of the *London Gazette* for that year refers to 'the daily attendance at the Auction-house'. Most of the sales of this period would be held in the fashionable coffee-houses, and already some of them would be dealing exclusively with books and paintings. Thus we may presume that the long association between art and the auction had its beginnings at about this time. Some evidence of this is contained in an obscure article by one Ralph James who although he quotes no references or authentication, records much detailed information said to relate to the sales of the period. It might well be that Mr James is quoting directly from rare contemporary catalogues, rare because they were produced only for use within the saleroom in very limited numbers, and were the only item of record associated with the sale at this time.

Mr James tells us that the principal auctioneers of the late seventeenth century were a Mr Gilleflower and a Mr Millington, and he quotes a 'curious address' inserted by Millington into a catalogue of a sale of Paintings and Limnings held at the Barbadoes Coffee-House in February, 1689. Part of the address reads as follows:

> When I first essay'd this way of Selling Paintings and Limnings by Auction, I propounded to myself the obliging of the Gentry, Citizens etc and to bring it into esteem and reputation, to make it familiar and acceptable, and withal an honest gain to myself. And as I am bound publickly to own, so I will upon all opportunities freely acknowledge, that the worthy Gentlemen, the Buyers, have both by their presence and custom, promoted and encouraged it. And that I may remove the Prejudices of some, and the Misapprehensions of others, as to the sincerity of the management, I have printed the Conditions of Sale with an additional one, that no Person or Persons shall be admitted to bid for his, or their own Pictures, for I will, and cannot omit to aver, that the Gratifying of my Customers with moderate Pennyworths in the things I sell, was one of the Principal motives that gave rise to the attempt, and it is the most probable way to continue it, which having (without vanity be it said) in some measures effected, I do not in the least repent, (that for your sakes, Gentlemen) I have hitherto extended and exercised my lungs.

Given that this account is accurate, it supplies several valuable pieces of information about the auctions of the period. Not only is it interesting to note that paintings are the sale commodity, but we learn that catalogues are being produced which contain printed conditions of sale. Limning, incidentally, is defined by the first edition of the *Encyclopaedia Britannica* as the art of painting in water-colours as distinct from oil painting. The fact that Mr Millington also points out that he has been exercising his lungs in pursuit of his occupation must surely indicate that his sales were conducted using the ascending bid system. If that assumption is correct then it adds a further element to our understanding of the period, for we already know that the candle method is much in use at this time. If we then add yet another variation by way of an extract from an announcement of sale believed to be of a similar date to the last, then it might seem reasonable to suppose that some experimentation with methods was taking place at the end of the seventeenth century. The extract is again supplied by Mr James:

> The goods will be exposed to sale, by way of Mineing, (a Method of Sale not hitherto used in England) on Thursday 12th, Friday 13th, and Saturday 14th of this instant March, at Mrs. Smythers Coffee House in Thames street, by the Custom House: The Sale begin-

ning each Morning precisely at Nine of the Clock. The
said Paintings are to be viewed from this day forward
until all be sold. Catalogues may be had at the place of
sale.

The statement that the method of sale was one 'not hitherto used in
England' suggests its importation from another country, and as the
method in question is based on descending bidding it may be presumed that the other country was Holland. In all probability the
auctioneer would put up each lot at a high price and gradually reduce
it until someone called out 'mine'. Such a method has long been
common in Holland, for so long in fact that the descending bid
method has become known as the 'Dutch auction'. It might even have
been that in the English version the business was not ended on the
cry of 'mine'. By combining methods on trial at the time it could be
permissible for another bidder to immediately offer an increase on the
price just accepted, and thereby cause the auction to revert to the
ascending bid method at that point.

Although we might speculate on this method or that, however, and
on which was the more popular, the very fact that there is evidence
of such a diversity of auction systems before the close of the seventeenth century is significant. Such diversity suggests a high level of
auction activity with several methods of sale being used and adapted
in order to deal with the disposal of a wide range of commodities. It
suggests a flourishing commercial sector with a good deal of competition, and entrepeneur managements seeking new and interesting
methods by which to sell their goods. It suggests that the auction is
here to stay, and that its influence will inevitably grow.

One, if not the first, of the major exponents of the auction business
was Christopher Cock. Certainly by 1735, and in all probability for
some time before, Cock was conducting business of a substantial nature through his auction rooms in Covent Garden. Peter Ash, in an
article for the Centenary Supplement of the *Estates Gazette* in 1958,
unearthed a good deal of information regarding the activities of
Christopher Cock through some painstaking research among newspaper advertisements of the early eighteenth century. What Mr Ash
was seeking particularly in his research was a record of the first sale
of property by auction. He discovered, in fact, that the sale of chattels
by auction preceded the auctioning of land and property, and he
concluded, at least from his own research, that many of the established
chattels auctioneers of the period moved into the property market as
it developed.

Such an argument is certainly sustainable in general terms, but it
should be pointed out that the early records are far from complete,
and cannot therefore tell the whole story. The earliest record of Cock's

activities is contained in the *Daily Advertiser* of the 25th of April, 1735, which announces three chattels sales at 'Mr Cock's Great Room, in the Piazzas, Covent Garden'. The style of the advertisement suggests that Cock was already at this time a highly successful auctioneer, and subsequent insertions in the leading newspapers of the day show him going from strength to strength. The *London Evening Post* of 8th–10th of March, 1739, carried an advertisement in which was announced a sale of bankrupt stock which also included the personal property of the unfortunate trader. The announcement reads:

> By Order of the Assignes of Mr Thomas Thorogood, late of Bedford-street, Covent Garden, Laceman, will be sold by Auction, on Thursday the 5th of April next and the following days, at Mr Cock's in the Great Piazza, Covent Garden.
>
> The most valuable Part of the said Bankrupt's Stock in Trade, consisting of the best Gold and Silver Lace, in Point d'Espagne, open and common Orrises, Threads &c for Robings of Gowns, Sacks, Petticoats, Mantels &c with great Choice of Embroider'd and Brocaded Waistcoats, and Short Aprons. Also great Variety of other rich Goods of which Catalogues will be deliver'd on Saturday the 31st of this Instant at the Place of Sale: and the Goods will be expos'd to View on Monday the 2nd of April, and the following Days, 'till the Hour of Sale, which will be each day at Eleven.
>
> N.B. In the first Day's Sale will be sold two Houses belonging to the said Bankrupt's Estate, situated at Paddington, and adjoining to the Church-yard.

A year later a *London Evening Post* advertisement of Cock's announces what appears at first glance to be a sale of property only which begins:

> By Mr Cock will be sold by auction on Whitsun Monday, at Three in the Afternoon The House and Lands of the Honourable General CROFTS, deceased, situated on Haley-Green, in the Parish of Warfield, in the County of Berks, in Windsor-Forest.

However, after describing the accommodation in some detail the announcement closes by adding an option to purchase the contents:

> Round the said House belongs about six Acres of Land, Part free, the rest Copyhold: which, with the said House, Out-houses, Gardens and Furniture if requires, will be put up in one Lot.
>
> N.B. The Situation is on healthy Soil, with pleasing

> Prospects every way, and joins to the Forest: it is but six Miles from Windsor, four from Bagshot, nine from Staines, and is always on excellent road.

Cock was the celebrity auctioneer of his day. He ran his business with great style and his clients included the Notables of the period. In February, 1740, he disposed of the household furniture of the Dowager Countess of Gainsborough, and a remarkable record remains in the form of a newspaper advertisement in which he announced the forthcoming sale of no less than ten houses, including two in Old Bond Street. Mr Ash, in his article, uses this advertisement as evidence in support of his argument that Cock was one of those originally chattels auctioneers who made the transition into property. Whilst it certainly appears to be the case that by the 1740s Cock was involved in the property business in a big way, it is nevertheless clear that he is not prepared to neglect the 'furniture and effects' side of the business either; for the same lengthy advertisement concludes as follows:

> On that and the following Days will be Sold by Auction.
>
> THE HOUSEHOLD FURNITURE in the main House, with two Diamond-Mills, a CHARIOT on Springs, lin'd with Crimson Velvet, complete, and a Town Coach. Also the Household Furniture, Silver, Plate, Jewels, China, a Wardrobe, and the Valuable Effects of HENRY BURY, Esq.: late Clerk of the Exchequer, deceas'd.
>
> The Goods &c may be View'd on Saturday the 5th and every Day till the Hour of Sale, which will begin each Day at Half an Hour after Eleven in the Forenoon precisely.
>
> Catalogues to be had gratis on Friday the 4th at the Place of Sale, and at Mr COCK'S, in the Great Piazza, Covent-Garden.
>
> The Conditions of Sale, with the Particulars of the Several Houses as above-mentioned, may be seen at the Place of Sale, or at Mr COCK'S.

From the evidence of these and many other advertisements there is no doubt that Christopher Cock was an auctioneer who, for his time, conducted business on an unprecedented scale. He was possibly the first of the major auctioneers, and his example may have led to an increase in auction activity and towards the establishment of the important auction houses of the later eighteenth century.

As previously mentioned, the purpose of the article by Peter Ash, which brought to light the activities of Mr Cock, was to discover the first auctioneer of land and real property. Whether or not Christopher Cock fits this bill is still a matter for speculation, for the evidence produced by Ash, while confirming Cock's growing interest in property sales, also shows clearly his continuing involvement in chattels sales. There is also another matter which might defeat Ash's argument even had he made out a satisfactory case in this instance. That matter is a reference—also mentioned earlier—to a sale by candle said to date from 1490. Some intermittent correspondence in *The Conveyancer* between 1927 and 1932 was concerned with sales of land by the more unusual auction methods. There were several such sales instanced in the debate as being of early origin, and whilst only one of those quoted claimed a particular date, the number of cases mentioned suggested that the sale of land by auction was accepted practice long before the sales recorded at the end of the seventeenth century.

A paragraph from the issue of May, 1932, is of particular interest for not only is it concerned with the earliest recorded public sale in England, but the method of sale is specified as being 'sale by candle'. It is worth quoting the paragraph in full:

> Church Acre, at Chedzoy, which actually measures 3r. 19p., was left in 1490 by one Yea, with instructions that the sale should take place every 21 years during the burning of the piece of candle. The proceeds were vested in the Rector and churchwardens for the time being, to be expended as they think fit upon repairs to Chedzoy church. In 1904 the land was sold for £68. A report in the Somerset County Herald of the auction in 1925 states that it was conducted at the Manor House Inn by Mr W.H. Tamlyn, snr., of Messrs. Tamlyn & Sons, Bridgwater, and the report continues: 'Biddings commenced at £20, and steadily increased in sums of £5 to £10, until £70 was reached. From then the biddings rose in £1 stages, the only offers being from Mrs Rose Leake, of East Bower, and Mr E.J. Fry, of Chedzoy. The latter had bid £78, but just before the final flicker Mrs Leake offered £80, and when the candle expired at 7.30, having burnt 23 minutes, the lady was declared the purchaser.

Whatever else we may deduce from that account, the one thing absolutely certain is that the twenty three minutes taken to sell that one lot is only acceptable as a business proposition if one lot is all you have to sell. The volume of business passing through the auction rooms in the early eighteenth century, and the subsequent rise of the pioneers of auctioneering as we know it would have been inconceivable had there not been significant changes in the modus operandi. Increasing trade at the end of the seventeenth century led to the experimentation with methods. The resultant improvements led in turn to a more stable and uniform system which was exploited to the

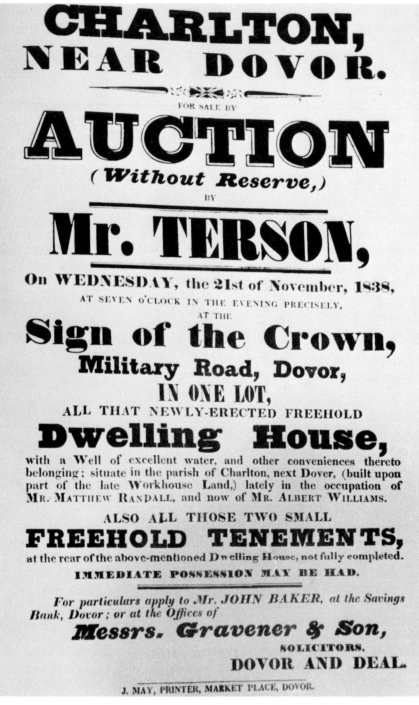

CHARLTON, NEAR DOVOR.

FOR SALE BY

AUCTION

(*Without Reserve,*)

BY

Mr. TERSON,

On WEDNESDAY, the 21st of November, 1838,

AT SEVEN O'CLOCK IN THE EVENING PRECISELY,

AT THE

Sign of the Crown,

Military Road, Dovor,

IN ONE LOT,

ALL THAT NEWLY-ERECTED FREEHOLD

Dwelling House,

with a Well of excellent water, and other conveniences thereto belonging; situate in the parish of Charlton, next Dover, (built upon part of the late Workhouse Land,) lately in the occupation of MR. MATTHEW RANDALL, and now of MR. ALBERT WILLIAMS.

ALSO ALL THOSE TWO SMALL

FREEHOLD TENEMENTS,

at the rear of the above-mentioned Dwelling House, not fully completed.

IMMEDIATE POSSESSION MAY BE HAD.

For particulars apply to *Mr. JOHN BAKER*, *at the Savings Bank, Dovor*; or at the Offices of

Messrs. Gravener & Son,

SOLICITORS,

DOVOR AND DEAL.

J. MAY, PRINTER, MARKET PLACE, DOVOR.

Property sale poster. Photo courtesy Estates Gazette

full by the entrepreneur auctioneers and culminated in the emergence of the eighteenth-century giants. In this context Christopher Cock stands at the cross-roads of the old and the new orders. He is more than simply the first major auctioneer, he is in fact the link between the auction world as it was and the auction more or less as we understand it today.

Once the form of the auction was firmly established those early auctioneers, and Cock in particular, soon realised the value of the advertising opportunities offered by the newspapers and periodicals— themselves newly established—as well as the benefit of permanent salerooms, essential to cope with the volume of business. Under the old system with just a few lots, anywhere had been good enough. In London in 1660 Samuel Pepys's office was the venue for a 'two lot' sale. By the 1690s the inns and coffee-houses had been pressed into service as venues; although presumably the auctions held there were never more than an incidental activity, a sideline to the normal business of the establishment. By 1735, however, we know that Christopher Cock was installed in his Great Room at the Piazzas, Covent Garden; a permanent address to symbolise the permanence of the auction system in trade and its influence on society from then onwards.

The transformation of the auction from a part-time to a full-time business was almost exactly parallelled in Paris. There the earliest auction locations are recorded as being the Bridge of Notre Dame and the Quai de la Ferraille, traditional outdoor locations. During the eighteenth century these ancient locations were superseded by the covered markets—the 'Grand Augustins', the 'Grands Cordeliers' in the rue du Battoir, and the hall of the Hotel d'Espagne in the rue Dauphine. Finally, as in London, the Parisian auctioneers opened rooms of their own for public sales, the most notable being Pierre Remy in the rue Poupee; Paillet, a picture dealer at the Hotel d'Aligre and Sieur Lebrun at the Hotel Lubert in the rue de Clery.

The 'first auctioneer', Christopher Cock, was both fortunate and shrewd. He was fortunate to have been in the right place at the right time, and to have chosen auctioneering as his profession in prosperous times when links between the auction and the sale of art and effects and property were being forged. He was shrewd enough to take full advantage of the situation with some eye-catching publicity and by courting the patronage of the nobility, an example which would be pursued vigorously by some later auctioneers.

Both Samuel Baker, founder of Sotheby's, and the first Christie, James, were involved in the auction business by 1750. Baker, a notable bookseller of the day, conducted his first auction of books in 1745, and in about 1749 the young James Christie moved to London to take up a position as assistant to a Covent Garden auctioneer. It would provide a nice link for our story if we could say that Christopher Cock was that Covent Garden auctioneer, but we simply do not know. There can be no doubt, however, that the pioneering experience of Cock and his contemporaries was a major factor in the rise to auctioneering fame of both Baker and Christie.

In just one respect Christopher Cock might have been most unfortunate. The fact that he was the first major auctioneer may well have proved fatal, in the end, to his own long term survival. Pioneers are most often not among those who gather the major benefit from their endeavours, and quite often, as is likely in this case, it is those following just behind who reap the greatest reward.

CHAPTER 3

The Slave Trade: The Caribbean and the American South

The success of the auctioneers in eighteenth-century London was based on the wealth newly generated by the increasing tempo of trade and commerce. Much of that increase was itself based on the development of the new trade routes to the East and West Indies, and to the settling and exploitation of the colonies in the Caribbean and the Americas.

Without doubt the largest and most profitable traffic engaged in by the shipowners and businessmen of the period was the trade in slaves. It is in fact a terrible irony that while the London auctioneers were busily building up their businesses to disgorge books and paintings and all the finer things of life to the new elite, the Dark Continent of Africa was being plundered for ever increasing numbers of slaves, most of whom were destined to be sold by auction in either America or the Caribbean. The 1771 edition of the *Encyclopaedia Britannica* says of 'slavery':

> Slavery is absolutely abolished in Britain and France as to personal servitude. Slaves make a considerable article of the traffick in America. The British south-sea company have, by treaty, the sole privilege of furnishing the Spanish West Indies with slaves.

Absolutely abolished it may have been in Britain and France, but nevertheless it was the British and the French seamen and traders who together were responsible for the movement and distribution of the majority of the negro slaves snatched from their African homes. The principal beneficiaries of the wealth thus generated, safe at home and far removed from the actualities of the slave traffic, were in no doubt that there was a price to be paid for their new-found comfort, but were convinced that the advantages were such that the end did in fact justify the means. The introduction to the letters-patent of the French East India Company read as follows:

The happiness of a people consists not only in a considerable dim-
inution of taxes ... but even more in the maintenance of commerce
which alone can bring into the kingdom an abundance that will
serve not as a means of luxury to the few, but as a blessing to the
many.

Commerce stimulates manufactures, by opening markets for their
products, and gives employment to a large number of people of
almost every age and sex. Overseas commerce is the means. It is
certain, both from sound reason and from the experience of our
neighbours, that the profit gained much outweighs the toil and
pain expended therein.

The extent to which the British and French traders believed that to
be the case may be judged by a study of the figures relating to the
numbers of slave ships using the ports of Liverpool and Bristol in
England, and Nantes and Bordeaux in France, during the principal
years of slave trading.

Liverpool's first slave ship sailed for Africa in 1709, and in the early
years the proportion of slavers to the total shipping of the port was
one in a hundred. By 1771 the figure had increased dramatically to
one in three, and in 1783 the port had 88 vessels trading in slaves. In
Nantes between 1715 and 1775 the vessels trading from the port
exported more than 229,000 slaves from Africa, an annual average of
3700, and the slave ships made up a fifth of the total shipping of the
port. In the 1780s the port of Bristol had 30 vessels engaged in the
slave trade, and the volume of West Indies trade handled by the port
was worth twice as much as the remainder of its business. Likewise
the sugar port of Bordeaux in 1720 had 74 of its ships involved in the
trade with the West Indies.

The enormous scale of this enterprise was crucial to the economic
progress of the 'civilised' countries. It was this 'triangular trade'—
consisting of the export to Africa of British manufactures to exchange
for slaves, the transportation of the human cargoes to the Caribbean
or America, and the return journey laden with the sugar or cotton or
other goods produced by the negro labour—which yielded the vast
profits which were re-invested into further industrial production and
development. The whole process resulted in an unprecedented level
of trade with the Caribbean territories which made them the most
valuable colonies the world has ever known.

The 'triangular trade' produced for the auctioneers a similar triangular benefit which allowed the auction to become established as a
major component of the escalating industrial and commercial scene.
In the first place the large and regular supplies of slave labour arriving
in the Caribbean and the Americas needed to be dispersed quickly
and efficiently, and auction soon became the popular method.

Secondly, the goods brought home on the return voyage were quite often sold by auction, indeed we have the evidence that in the case of the East India Company the sale of imported goods by auction was prescribed by statute. The excess of wealth generated by the 'triangular trade' was the factor which allowed the auctioneers to complete the third leg of their own 'triangle'. This surplus created a new clientele with the resources to indulge themselves in the acquisition of the finer things of life. The auctioneers were more than happy to oblige, and quick to take advantage of the new markets thus created.

It can be argued that the whole of this trading explosion stemmed from the commercial land management problems peculiar to the Caribbean territories and the American South. The tobacco, cotton and sugar crops suited to the soil and climate of the Caribbean were all labour intensive enterprises, and so it was in America. The crops considered best suited to the soil and climate of the South; tobacco, rice, and later cotton, could not be grown and marketed unless on a large scale. Thus with very cheap land and guaranteed markets the only real problem was a plentiful supply of cheap labour. In America as in the West Indies the answer lay in the importation of negro slaves from Africa. Many northern Americans were involved in the trading of slaves, but most of the cargoes were landed at Charleston or Savannah or some other Southern port convenient to the plantations where the negroes would be put to work.

Between the importer and the planter was a commission merchant who was responsible for sales and payment. He might sell publicly or privately, but as the value of the business transacted grew so the term auctioneer was increasingly added to the commission merchant's title. Many of the auctioneers and commission merchants were southern gentlemen of the upper classes, who, while engaging others to do the actual selling, grew very wealthy from their involvement with the trade. The extent of the trade and the profits can be estimated from some approximate figures given in Frederick Bancroft's book *Slave Trading in the Old South*. According to Mr Bancroft's information there were only about 300 negroes in Virginia in 1650, and yet by 1721 negro labour accounted for half of the total population of not only Virginia, but Maryland and South Carolina as well.

Although information relating to specific sales is difficult to come by before the end of the eighteenth century, there is a record of a cargo of 300 slaves from Africa being sold at Yorktown, Virginia, in 1736; while in 1737 in the same town a larger cargo of 490 was sold by Thomas Nelson, the grandfather of Thomas Nelson Junior, one of the signatories of the Declaration of Independence. Once newspapers have become firmly established, the hard evidence of the slave auctions becomes more easily obtainable through a study of the advertisements and announcements which they carried. The Charleston

A sale of slaves outside the Old Exchange in Charleston, South Carolina—from a

sketch by Eyre Crowe. From the Illustrated London News, 29th of November, 1856

City Gazette and Daily Advertiser of the 25th of February, 1796, contained no less than fourteen different advertisements relating to the public or private sale of a total of 288 slaves. The Fredericksburg *Virginia Herald* of the 5th of February, 1799, also contained a number of advertisements including the following:

> 15 likely young negroes belonging to the estate of William Bruce, then lately deceased, to be sold at auction.

Many of these sales, although so far removed from the chattels sales of London and Paris, would bear comparison with the peremptory sales for the discharge of debt common in Europe. When a Southern planter died leaving debts, or simply fell into financial difficulties, his slaves were likely to be the first of his assets to go under the hammer. We must remember that not only were slaves regarded quite simply as chattels to be bought and sold like cattle, but that of all the landowner's assets, his slaves were probably the one most easily and quickly convertible to cash. The *City Gazette and Daily Advertiser* also carried a notice of a forthcoming auction in an adjoining county:

> 25 negroes consisting of men, women, boys and girls, the property of James Dunlop, Jnr., of Great Britain.
> 18 negroes of the same kind, belonging to a Timberlake estate; and two good sawyers and a girl about 12 years old (together with two work-horses), all to be disposed of to the highest bidder to discharge the debts of their deceased Master, Reuben Thornton.

The same newspaper, in its issue of the 23rd of December, 1799, advertised that 12 or 15 men, women, boys and girls were to be sold for cash in front of a local tavern, and further stated that on the 13th of January, 1800 (if fair, if not the next fair day), the executor of one William Fauntleroy was to sell at the Westmoreland Court House:

> to the highest bidder, for ready payment, about 40 likely Virginia-born slaves, consisting of men, boys, women and children.

The plight of the negro family is highlighted by an announcement of sale by John F. Mercer, a personal friend and political ally of Thomas Jefferson as well as a sometime holder of high office in Virginia and Maryland. Mercer advertised for sale on the 10th of December, 1799, several families reserved from previous auction sales. In what appears to be a humane attempt to sell each family as a unit the notice states that should the families be purchased by private sale prior to the 10th the terms will be 'much moderated', and the public advised of their withdrawal from the sale in future advertisements. Otherwise, how-

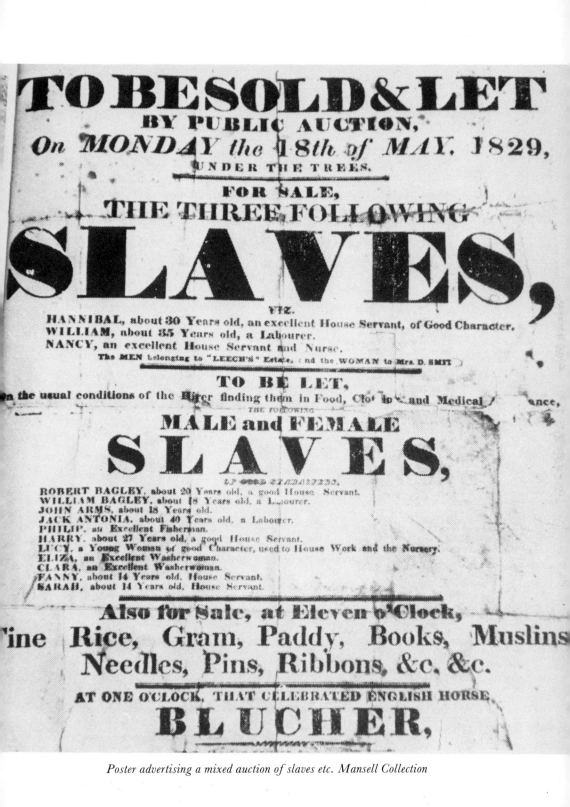

Poster advertising a mixed auction of slaves etc. Mansell Collection

ever, the group would be 'offered at public sale in such manner as the bidders may require'. Whether these families were kept together or separated like so many others we will never know, for although the advertisement remained unchanged until the 6th of December, indicating no takers until then, immediately subsequent copies of the newspaper are lacking in the Library of Congress files.

The last decade of the eighteenth century was a busy and profitable time for the slave traders. In this brief period in just two of the states for which statistics are available, the figures show the negro population of Tennessee rising from 3000 to more than 13,500, and in Kentucky from 12,000 to more than 40,000. In Tennessee the dramatic increase continued into the nineteenth century, for by only 1810 the figures for negroes had more than doubled again to 30,000. Some of the states, and in particular Virginia, specialised in breeding slaves for sale, and these domestic products, together with the regular shipments from Africa, resulted by the 1830s in a brisk interstate trade in negroes in which the auctioneers were heavily involved. The seasonal needs for labour, as well as the rising or declining fortunes of the planters, ensured a substantial traffic in slaves; and as that traffic increased so proportionately did the numbers of dealers, auctioneers and commission agents involved in the business.

The newspapers of the day reflected the scale of business and carried many columns of advertising relating to both the buying and selling of slaves. One such notice of a forthcoming sale advertised some:

> 15 or 16 likely young negroes to be sold at auction for cash (no postponements on account of the weather) at the front of the Orange Hotel.

The advertisement also gave notice that:

> gentelemen wanting good house servants of tried faithfulness will find this a good opportunity to supply themselves.

Competition among the auctioneers became intense, and the advertisements often indicate that demand at times exceeded supply, for on very many occasions offers to purchase negroes were the only notices to be seen. In Columbia, auctioneers Richard Wright and Edward Dyer were the leaders in their field, and in the 1830s Dyer was advertising as follows:

> A gentleman now in this city wishes to purchase for his own use (not for speculation) a cook, male or female, a carriage driver, not older than twenty five years, a seamstress and two or three boys and girls, accustomed to house service—the highest price now going will be paid.

This element of demand exceeding supply is not unusual among auctioneers or indeed in business generally, but in the case of the slave auctioneers resulted in a serious problem peculiar only to that particular business. The problem was what to do with the human merchandise coming in for sale but needing to be stored until there were sufficient numbers to make up an attractive catalogue which would encourage the buyers. The trouble with holding this kind of stock being that it must be accommodated securely and fed until sold.

There were in fact two types of dealer-auctioneer who each dealt with the problem in their own way. The established and respected city auctioneer set himself up with an auction room, or mart, in a main thoroughfare near the town or city centre. The mart would consist of a principal saleroom and a jail, a secure area where the negroes could be kept while awaiting sale. The astute auctioneers would quite often advertise the boarding of negroes in their private jails at nominal rates in order to attract business to the saleroom. In Richmond, Virginia, the *Tri-weekly Standard* announced that Hector Davis, 'auctioneer and commission merchant for the sale of negroes pledged his best efforts to obtain the highest market prices'. Davis also gave notice that he had a safe and commodious jail, where he would board at thirty cents a day all slaves entered for his sales—the small charge intended to win business from his rivals.

The other kind of slave trader was the itinerant dealer who moved from state to state or even from the North to the South gathering slaves as he went, until he reached a likely place to dispose of his collection. The slaves as they travelled would be tied or handcuffed in a line, and these human chains, or coffles as they were called, became a familiar sight snaking their way through the Southern countryside. Frederick Bancroft gives a graphic view of a slave coffle:

> The women with little children were carried in some vehicle. When more than a few, the men, handcuffed in pairs, fastened to a chain and followed by boys and girls, walked in double column, and the trader's mounted assistant brought up the rear. Thus, like a butcher's drove of hobbled cattle, they shambled into the streets and avenues of Washington and often passed close to the Capitol.

After walking for many days the slave coffle would arrive at its destination with its constituent parts in a dirty and ragged condition. Before the sale, however, like a valuable piece of furniture in some other faraway auction, the merchandise would be restored. A good wash, a meal and even some bright clean clothes would attract the attention of the bidders and might improve the prices considerably. In Richmond, Virginia, a Jewish clothier named Levy was the local specialist supplier of clothing for the negroes about to be sold, and

Eyre Crowe, who accompanied William Makepiece Thackeray on a lecture tour in 1853 described the slaves waiting to be sold thus:

> huddled close together, neatly dressed in gray, young negro girls with white collars fastened by scarlet bows, and in white aprons.

The conditions under which the negroes were accommodated and sold depended very much on the individual auctioneer. In the marts of the major auctioneers conditions generally would be quite reasonable, although saleroom arrangements were aimed at the encouragement of the patrons rather than the comfort of the slaves. The merchandise would be made available for inspection on two or three days prior to the sale at the jail which was annexed to the auction mart. During the days on view the negroes would be examined most rigorously for physical defects, and questioned closely regarding any special work skills which they might possess.

One of the very few conditions of sale was a guarantee of normal health and physical soundness. Should the auctioneer fail to notify any such physical defect, a case for misrepresentation could be made and he would be liable to a suit for a breach of warranty, actual or implied. Caveat emptor was, however, the golden rule, and it was simply a part of the everyday business of slave trading to examine the goods carefully. The negroes were almost invariably stripped and prodded and examined for sores or signs of previous ill-treatment. Another writer, William Chambers, witnessed just such an event and recorded it in his book *Things as they are in America*:

> About a dozen gentlemen crowded to the spot while the poor fellow was stripping himself, and as soon as he stood on the floor, bare from top to toe, a most rigorous scrutiny of his person was instituted. The clear black skin, back and front, was viewed all over for sores from disease; and there was no part of his body left unexamined.

At the other end of the scale the general dealer-auctioneer, lacking his own premises, would rent an empty shop or warehouse. Contemporary descriptions tell us that these were usually bare, dirty places with coarse carved benches or chairs sufficient to seat about fifty people, with at one end a platform and a screen. The auction day would begin at 9.30 or 10.00 a.m. On the days when several sales were scheduled in the same general area, it was usual as a matter of courtesy, as well as sound business, to organise them into a consecutive sequence. On mounting the platform the auctioneer would almost always employ a rapid patter technique which included exaggerated claims regarding the quality of the lot that he was selling, in much the same manner as a cattle auction. In order to obtain the best bids for labourers, youth and strength were emphasised, for servants reliability, and for young women health and child-bearing prospects. When disposing of good-looking girls the auctioneer would often indulge in broad or suggestive humour which would have been considered quite improper on any other occasion. Thomas Hamilton, observing slave auctions in New Orleans wrote:

> When a woman is sold he (the auctioneer) usually puts his audience in good-humour by a few indecent jokes. . . . Show your neck, Betsy! There's a breast for you; good for a round dozen before she's done child-bearing.

If business on any particular day was not sufficiently brisk and prices generally below expectations, many of the principal lots might be withdrawn, or bought in. This conforms with normal practice in the auction right up to the present time, and seeks to protect the reputation of the saleroom as well as maintaining a price-level. William Chambers observed the sale of a woman with three young children all under the age of three years. The porter was asked to hold up 'the fine healthy baby' while the auctioneer drew the attention of the crowd to the woman 'still young, with three children, all for 850 dollars'. The bidding, however, was sluggish, and the lot was withdrawn. On a day when more than one auction was taking place, as soon as the first had finished a crier would shout 'this way, gentlemen', and the entire company would follow him to a neighbouring mart where the next consignment was waiting to be knocked down. This pattern would be followed until all the day's business had been completed.

The 'Old Exchange' or Custom House in Charleston has the reputation of being one of the most historic buildings in the South, and it is certainly a landmark in the history of slavery. From colonial days to the mid-nineteenth century, in the open air just outside this building, hundreds if not thousands of slaves were sold annually to the highest bidder. It was there, on the 7th of January, 1852, that J.J. Ampere, a member of the French Academy, witnessed on one spot a public sale of negroes, and on another, at the same time, the sale of a horse and an ass. In his book *Promenade en Amerique* he described his observations as 'une scene hideuse', and found it difficult to believe that the auctioneer moved in polite society.

The auctioneer involved might well have been Thomas Norman Gadsden. The Gadsdens were an old Southern family of high social standing, and the thoroughly respectable occupations of other family members included John, a lawyer; Christopher, a Bishop; and James, a soldier and planter as well as president of the South Carolina Railroad and Minister to Mexico. It has already been said, however, that slave trading was a highly profitable business engaged in by many of the upper-class families, and it was almost certainly the same Thomas

Gadsden who is referred to in the work *Observations on American Slavery*, by R.L. Carpenter, an English clergyman. Carpenter watched an auction in Charleston on the 9th of April, 1850, and stated that it was conducted:

> by a slave merchant I met the evening before. Of course my acquaintance did not officiate in person, any more than the high-sheriff would act as hangman; meaner men are found ready to do the work.

Despite the undoubted influence of Gadsden and others, however, serious objections were eventually raised to the continuation of the sales outside the Old Exchange. The reason for the objections was simply that the large crowds attending the auctions often overflowed into adjacent streets and obstructed the traffic. With the abolition movement growing it was felt that such scenes were bound to attract the unwelcome attention of Northern and foreign travellers, and eventually a city ordnance was approved forbidding the sale of negroes, horses, carriages etc. near the Old Exchange after the 1st of July, 1856.

One of the South's largest and most notable sales took place in Charleston on the 9th of January, 1860. The sale was held at Ryans mart and jail, a venue which had replaced the previous location at the Old Exchange. As a result of the death and debts of the previously mentioned General James Gadsden, the soldier-planter member of the family, some 235 choice slaves were offered for sale on the 9th of January, if time enough, and if not the sale to continue on the 10th.

For about a week before the sale the negroes were subjected to inspection at the auction mart. Each individual wore a number which corresponded with a description in a printed catalogue giving details of age, occupation and any other information considered to be relevant. According to the *Mercury* newspaper of the 10th of January, 174 negroes went under the hammer on the first day fetching an average of about 700 dollars a head. The sale continued on the 10th until all were sold, the total for the Gadsden slaves being 176,000 dollars at a final average of 750 dollars for every negro. Two other groups of slaves were sold at the mart on the 10th of January besides the remainder of the Gadsden group, and the records show that the auctioneers final calculation for just two days trading was 329 negroes sold for almost a quarter of a million dollars.

The brief period around 1859-1860 appears to have been the zenith of the slave auction sales. The well-established auctioneers of each major Southern city seemed to be constantly competing to produce bigger and more spectacular sales with ever increasing numbers of negroes being catalogued. There is a remarkable similarity between the newspaper coverage of these events then, and the sort of media coverage given today to the important sales of the major auctioneers. Fairly extensive advertising for these large sales attracted a good deal of editorial comment on the spectacle they produced, and the auctioneers gathered much free publicity in this way. Whether the auctioneers had grown so prosperous that they could afford to indulge in this show-business type of operation which even further enhanced their reputations, or whether towards the close of the era of slavery there were simply more negroes on the market is not clear; perhaps something of both is the answer.

One of the best recorded sales of this kind was a sale at Savannah, Georgia, conducted by that state's best-known auctioneer, 'Captain' Joseph Bryan. By comparison with the Charleston sale just described, this epic was bigger and better and even slightly earlier, being held on the 2nd and 3rd of March, 1859. At least ten Southern newspapers from Richmond to New Orleans carried advertisements for the sale. The *Charleston Courier* announced:

> FOR SALE. LONG COTTON AND RICE NE-
> GROES. A GANG OF 460 NEGROES, accustomed to
> the culture of Rice and Provisions; among whom are a
> number of good mechanics, and house servants. Will be
> sold on 2d and 3d of March next, at Savannah by ...
> JOSEPH BRYAN. TERMS OF SALE—One-third
> cash; remainder by bond, bearing interest from day of
> sale, payable in two equal instalments, to be secured by
> mortgage on the negroes, and approved personal
> security ... The negroes will be sold in families, and
> can be seen on the premises of JOSEPH BRYAN in
> Savannah, three days prior to the day of sale, when
> catalogues will be furnished.

In the event Captain Bryan's premises must have been considered inadequate for a sale of such magnitude, for the venue was soon changed to the Race Course some three miles outside the city. Editorial comment in the *Savannah Republican* of the 28th of February stated:

> LARGE SALE OF NEGROES—Upwards of four hundred ne-
> groes, of both sexes and all ages, are now quartered at the Race
> Course, in charge of Capt. J. Bryan, of this city. The sale will
> commence Wednesday next, and probably continue for some days.
> This is probably one of the largest lots of negroes ever offered in
> the State, and it therefore presents many inducements to purchas-
> ers.

The negroes were brought to Savannah by rail and driven out to the Race Course, where they were housed in sheds used during race meetings. There was no furniture of any kind, and they sat and slept on the floor. The *Republican* for the 28th of February confirmed that viewing would take place on several days before the auction:

> SALE OF 440 NEGROES—Persons desiring to inspect these Negroes, will find them at the Race Course, where they can be sen from 10 A.M. to 2 P.M. until day of sale . . . J. BRYAN, Johnson's Square, Feb. 26.

No doubt very many of the large numbers of prospective buyers who had descended on the city for the sale were indeed desirous of inspecting the merchandise and were assisted in their appraisal by a sixteen page catalogue prepared by the auctioneers. The catalogue gave only the briefest of descriptions as for example:

  99—Kate's John, aged 30; rice, prime man
118—Pompey, 31; rice, lame in one foot
345—Dorcas, 17; cotton, prime woman
346—Joe (Dorcas's babe and the only member
      of her family present) 3 months

The day of the sale dawned wet and windy, but the *Republican* reported that 'the attendance was very large and from all portions of the State and the States adjoining'. By ten o'clock the slaves were assembled in the grand-stand of the Race Course, an enclosure about a hundred feet by twenty. The auction was held in an adjoining room which had one side open to the elements, and as the crowd of prospective buyers pressed round the platform on which the auctioneer and his clerks were accommodated, the wind howled and the rain poured in.

'Captain' Bryan, like most respectable Southern auctioneers, did not actually sell negroes himself. That, in this case arduous task, fell to T.J. Walsh, considered one of the best auctioneers of slaves in all Georgia; a large good-humoured man who claimed to have sold perhaps tens of thousands of negroes in his time. Many of the lots in the sale were family groups, and were sold as such. The method of bidding in the case of families was on a pro rata basis. A family of five, for example, valued together at 5000 dollars, might attract an opening bid of 500 dollars, and be knocked down finally at say 900 dollars. The actual bid price for the lot, therefore, being 900×5, that is 4500 dollars.

The sale lasted for two days, and the final facts and figures of the event make interesting reading. While there are minor variations in the published accounts, the enormous public interest and significant press coverage of the sale allows us to assume that the basic facts are substantially correct. The statistics show that 126 of those sold were under ten years of age, 182 were more than ten but less than thirty,

88 were over thirty but under fifty and 40 were over fifty years. The 436 sold over the two days fetched an average price close to 716 dollars apiece. The highest price for a man was 1750 dollars, the most for a woman 1250 dollars, and Anson and Violet, numbers 111 and 112 in the catalogue, were sold for 250 dollars each—being old and infirm. The sale total was a little over 300,000 dollars, and the conclusion of this memorable event was marked, at least by Captain Bryan and his friends and acquaintances, with baskets of champagne.

While the champagne corks were popping in Savannah, Mortimer Thomson was on his way back to New York with something of a coup for the abolitionists. Thomson, a special correspondent for the *New York Tribune*, had attended the sale incognito and had even joined in the bidding to help conceal his identity. His lengthy account of the sale was published in the *Tribune* on the 9th of March, 1859, and reprinted in a 28 page pamphlet by the American Anti-Slavery Society. It supplied many of the details reproduced here.

The inhumanity of slavery was attracting the attention of the world at large through the writings of the many foreign travellers moving across America. Although the Southern whites, with their blinkered vision, could not understand what the fuss was about, nowhere was the inhumanity better demonstrated than in the auction advertisements for mixed sales which included negroes. The *Southern Recorder* for the 16th of March, 1852:

> to the highest bidders two negroes, Nelson, about 32 years of age, Rachel, about 45, a sorrel mule, about seven or eight years old, a roan mule, about eight years old, and one two-horse wagon.

The *Memphis Weekly Avalanche* for the 13th of December, 1859, advertised to be sold near Huntsville, Alabama, in January, 1860, to the highest bidders:

> 136 slaves, 47 head of mules and horses, 54 head of cattle, the oxen, stock hogs, killing hogs and 90 head of sheep.

The *Southern Argus*, on the 18th of January, 1855, reported:

> In front of Ferguson & Wilkinson's auction store, Norfolk, were sold 3 horses, 2 carts, 1 fine buggy, 20 cases of boots, 6 or 8 casks of hams, 5000 cigars, and a likely negro girl 19 years old with a likely boy child of 18 months.

As the slave era drew to its conclusion, so more and more the accounts published by the writers and commentators passing through the Southern states directed the attention of their readers to the repulsive nature of the trade and of the people involved in it. William Howard

Russell, while visiting Montgomery, Alabama, in May, 1861, penned this description for his book *My Diary North and South*:

> The auctioneer, who was an ill-favored dissipated-looking rascal, had his 'article' beside him, on, not in, a deal packing-case—a stout young negro badly dressed and ill-shod, who stood with all his goods fastened in a small bundle in his hands, looking out at the small and listless gathering of men who, whittling and chewing, had moved out from the shady side of the street as they saw the man put up. ... The chattel character of slavery in the States renders it most repulsive ... A man in a cart, some volunteers in coarse uniforms, a few Irish laborors in a long van, and four or five men in the usual black coat, satin waistcoat and black hat, consti-tuted the audience, whom the auctioneer addressed volubly: 'A prime field-hand. Just look at him—good-natured, well-tempered; no marks, nary sign of bad about him, nine hunthered—only nine hun-ther-ed and fifty dol'rs for 'em'. Why its quite rad-aklous. Nine hundred and fifty dol'rs, I cant raly—thats good. Thank you, sir. Twenty-five bid—nine hunthred and seventy-five dol'rs for this most useful hand.' The price rose to one thousand dollars, at which the useful hand was knocked down to one of the black hats near me. The auctioneer and the negro and his buyer all walked off together to settle the transaction, and the crowd moved away— 'That nigger went cheap', said one of them to a companion, as he walked towards the shade—'Yes, sirr! Niggers is cheap now—thats a fact.'

From amongst the myriad of Southern auction marts, ranging in quality from adequate to disgusting, one venue stood out like a bright star—the 'French Exchange' in the Rotunda of the St Louis Hotel in New Orleans. A long arcade led directly from the street to the Ro-tunda which was some eighty feet in diameter. Pillars fifty feet high supported an ornamental ceiling with a dome, and the walls were painted with murals. The floor was of marble, as was the bar, which at the time was said to be the finest and largest known. Opposite the bar were six small platforms on which were marble desks for the auctioneers, and about them on busy days all the bric-a-brac of the auction room.

New Orleans was as different from most other Southern cities as the French Exchange was from most other auction marts. New Or-leans was glamour and gambling, music and entertainment, and it is not surprising to discover that in the slave auctions of the French Exchange plantation negroes were not much in demand. The auc-tioneers here disposed of a wide range of items including wine, furni-ture, books, paintings and, quite literally, negroes of a different colour. Most of those sold would be young, good-looking girls of a very light colour, some almost white. They would command very high prices according to the quality of their appearance, and any special skills which they possessed would be craft skills such as seamstress or hairdresser. Many, however, were simply regarded as sex objects, for these 'fancy girls' as they were termed, were very much the status symbol of the Southern gentleman, a visible sign of affluence.

With the ending of the Civil War in 1865 the slave trade ceased and the negroes were freed. At the French Exchange in New Orleans, at the auction marts of Savannah and Charleston, the cries of the great slave auctioneers were heard no more. The memory, no doubt, lingered on, and will continue to linger on, for the unique character of this unsavoury but significant branch of the auction family has left us with an equally unique legacy.

These objects which were once merely goods, chattels and numbers in an auctioneers catalogue, quite suddenly found themselves to be once again members of the human race, able to speak and write and thus record for us and for posterity, moving accounts of their personal experiences on the auction block. Many of these accounts were gathered together by Julius Lester and published in 1968 in his book *To Be a Slave*. As a conclusion to this chapter on the slave auctions, some of these rememberances are reproduced here. The original source will be found in the bibliography.

Every first Tuesday slaves were brought in from Virginia and sold on the block. The auctioneer was Cap'n Dorsey. E.M. Cobb was the slave bringer. They would stand the slaves up on the block and talk about what a fine looking specimen of black manhood or womanhood they was, tell how healthy they was, look in their mouth and examine their teeth just like they was a horse, and talk about the kind of work they would be fit for and could do.

MORRIS HILLYER
Library of Congress

When he go to sell a slave, he feed that one good for a few days, then when he goes to put 'em up on the auction block he takes a meat skin and greases all round that nigger's mouth and makes 'em look like they been eating plenty meat and such like and was good and strong and able to work. Sometimes he sells the babes from the breast, and then again he sells the mothers from the babes and the husbands and wives, and so on. He wouldn't let 'em holler much when the folks were sold away. He say 'I have you whupped if you don't hush'. They sure loved their six children, though. They wouldn't want nobody buying them.

JENNY PROCTOR
Botkin, p. 91

My brothers and sisters were bid off first, and one by one, while
my mother paralyzed with grief, held me by the hand. Her turn
came and she was bought by Isaac Riley of Montgomery County.
Then I was offered. My mother, half distracted with the thought
of parting forever from all her children, pushed through the crowd
while the bidding for me was going on, to the spot where Riley was
standing. She fell at his feet, and clung to his knees, entreating him
in tones that a mother could only command, to buy her baby as
well as herself, and spare to her one, at least, of her little ones. This
man disengaged himself from her with violent blows and kicks ...
I must have been then between five and six years old.

HENSON, pp. 12–13

When I was fifteen years old, I was brought to the court-house, put
up on the auction block to be sold. Old Judge Miller was there. I
knew him well because he was one of the wealthiest slave owners
in the county and the meanest one. He was so cruel all the slaves
and many owners hated him because of it. He saw me on the block
for sale and he knew I was a good worker so when he bid for me
I spoke right out on the auction block and told him: 'Judge Miller.
Don't you bid for me, 'cause if you do, I would not live on your
plantation. I will take a knife and cut my own throat from ear to
ear before I would be owned by you.

DELICIA PATTERSON
Library of Congress

I saw slaves sold. I can see that block now. My cousin Eliza was a
pretty girl, really good-looking. Her master was her father. When
the girls in the big house had beaus coming to see them, they'd ask,
'who is that pretty gal?' So they decided to get rid of her right
away. The day they sold her will always be remembered. They
stripped her to be bid off and looked at. I wasn't allowed to stand
in the crowd. I was laying down under a big bush. The man that
bought Eliza was from New York. The Negroes had made up
enough money to buy her off themselves, but they wouldn't let that
happen. There was a man bidding for her who was a big Swede-
lander. He always bid for the good-looking colored gals and bought
'em for his own use. He asked the man from New York, 'What you
gonna do with her when you get her?' The man from New York
said, 'None of you damn business, but you aint got money enough
to buy her'. When the man from New York had done bought her,
he said, 'Eliza, you are free from now on'.

DOC DANIEL DOWDY
Botkin, p. 155

CHAPTER 4

Europe 1750–1900

The second half of the eighteenth century saw the rapid growth of the auction business continuing, particularly in London and Paris. In London much of the business was still conducted in the coffee-houses, and towards the end of the century it was Garraway's coffee-house in Cornhill which was the principal venue.

Even so, the long and steady climb towards the monolithic auction enterprises of the present day had already begun in more ways than one, for as early as 1745 Samuel Baker, the London bookseller destined to be the founder of the great auction house which would become known as Sotheby's, had his first auction sale of books. Just five years later James Christie began the apprenticeship which would lead him to the establishment of his own business in 1766, the beginning of a line leading directly to the other great auctioneering institution.

These two premier exponents of the art and perhaps craft of auctioneering have, over such a long period of time, survived not only the trials and tribulations of an expanding but sometimes unpredictable business, but have each managed to resist the extremely competitive nature of the other. The fact that they have not only existed but prospered virtually cheek by jowl would perhaps suggest some special attributes which merit special attention. Between them they have written a sizeable chapter of auction history, and will be the subject of a later chapter in this history of the auction.

We will look here at just one facet of the early history of the book auctions initiated by Samuel Baker, and that is his list of 'conditions of sale'. The fairly sophisticated list of conditions shows clearly that by the mid-eighteenth century sales by auction were not only well established but well organised, and that the ascending bid method was in the ascendancy. Baker's conditions in full were as follows:

1. That he who Bids most is the Buyer, but if any Dispute arises, the Book or Books to be put to Sale again.
2. That no Person advances less than Sixpence each bidding, and after the Book arises to One Pound, no less than One Shilling.

3. The Books are in most elegant Condition, and supposed to be Perfect, but if any appear otherwise before taken away, the Buyer is at his Choice to take
or leave them.

4. That each Person give in his Name, and pay Five
Shillings in the Pound (if demanded) for what he
Buys, and that no Book be deliver'd in Time of Sale.

5. The Books must be taken away at the Buyer's Expence, and the Money paid at the Place of Sale,
within Three Days after each Sale is ended. Any
Gentleman who cannot attend the Sale, may have
their Commissions receiv'd and faithfully executed
By their most Humble Servant
Samuel Baker

It is reported that by 1766, when James Christie set up on his own,
there were about sixty auctioneers operating in London, selling everything it is said from art to hay. We can be sure that by 1779 the
auction had become a thoroughly acceptable element of the social
and commercial scene, for the measure of its success was that it had
attracted the unwelcome attention of parliament, which in that year
approved, 'An Act for granting to his Majesty certain Duties on Licences to be taken out by all Persons acting as Auctioneers; and certain
Rates and Duties on all Lands, Houses, Goods, and other Things,
sold by Auction.' The wording of the Act suggests that duties previously imposed on goods for sale had been avoided and become
difficult to collect, and that some auctioneers appointed to sell effects
by order of the court and in bankruptcy had acted fraudulantly in
some cases, thus depriving the exchequer of revenue.

This Act was intended to ensure that all auctioneers were licenced
and made accountable for the payment of the duties, and in order
that none escaped the net the definition of auctioneer within the
legislation was precise. It stated:

'No one shall exercise the trade or business of an auctioneer, or
seller by commission, at any sale of any estate, goods, or effects of
any kind whatsoever, by outcry, knocking down of hammer, by
candle, by lot, by parcel, or by any other mode of sale at auction.'

The cost of the licence was twenty shillings in London and five shillings elsewhere. The licence was renewable annually ten days at least
before the expiry date, and the penalty for selling without a licence
was a fine of one hundred pounds in London and fifty pounds outside.

The duties to be levied on the sale of goods by auction included
threepence in the pound on freehold and leasehold lands, farming
equipment, ships and vessels; and sixpence in the pound on all fix-

tures, furniture, plate, jewels, books, pictures, horses and carriages, and all other goods and chattels whatsoever. From the 5th of July, 1779, these 'Rates and Duties' were declared to be 'a Charge upon every Auctioneer immediately from and after the knocking down of the hammer'.

In London every auctioneer taking out a licence was required to give security by Bond in the sum of two hundred pounds, to ensure that he would within twenty eight days after each sale deliver at the Chief Office of Excise an exact and particular account in writing of the total amount bid at each sale together with the price of each item sold. He must at that time pay the monies due to His Majesty, and he or his clerk at the sale must make oath to the truth of the sale account. Failure to deliver an account or the submission of a false statement rendered the licence void and the Bond forfeit.

There were exemptions to the Act and these included any sale by order of the court or exchequer in England, Scotland or Wales; goods imported by the East India and Hudson's Bay Companies, goods distrained for rents and tithes, and goods sold under the authority of the Sheriff for the benefit of creditors.

The Act concluded, however, that certain procedures should be followed 'for the better preventing frauds which may be practiced by Auctioneers selling Estates, Goods, or Chattels, under the Authority of Sheriffs, or under direction of assignees under a Commission of Bankruptcy'. Every auctioneer so selling was now required to produce a catalogue of sale signed by the Sheriff as a guarantee that all the catalogue entries were truly the property of the debtor or bankrupt. A Sheriff or auctioneer who allowed any other property to be included in such a sale was liable to a fine of twenty pounds.

When *The Times* newspaper began publication in 1788 it immediately became a vehicle for the auction advertisements of the day. In a newspaper of only four pages it was common to find half of the back page devoted to such advertisements, and particularly interesting to note that the selection of sales were classified under two separate headings, 'sale by auction' and 'sale by candle'. There was a clear distinction in that the 'candle' sales dealt almost exclusively with imported goods such as wines and spirits, textiles and provisions; whilst the 'auction' sales were principally for property, furniture and effects – as well as one or two categories unusual by today's standards. Between January and March, 1788, the selection of sale by candle notices carried by *The Times* included:

At the HAMBRO COFFEE-HOUSE, Water Lane,
Tower-street
TO-MORROW, the 13th FEBRUARY, 1788
THE following GOODS Viz.

One Hundred and Seventeen Puncheons exceeding fine old JAMAICA RUM, bonded under the King's Lock.
Samples to be seen at the Broker's on Monday 11th to the time of sale.

At the New York Coffee-house in Sweetings-Alley, Cornhill.
THIS DAY, the 20th, instant, at Five o'Clock
WITHOUT RESERVE
A Large and Valuable Quantity of EAST-INDIA and BRITISH MUSLINS, with sundry RUSSIA and other LINEN DRAPERY GOODS.

On the same day at Mr Croft's warehouse at no 40 Meade Street could be had at four o'clock, 'the genuine stock in trade of Mr Thomas Marsden, man's mercer, draper &c., of Cloth Fair, assigned for the benefit of his creditors.' The Hambro Coffee-house was, meanwhile, well and truly back on the bottle with a sale of wines which included two hundred and sixty four dozen of old red port. 'The wines to be seen and tasted to the time of sale.' An unusual variant of the sales of imported goods were the Custom-House sales. Most of these appear to have been concerned with the disposal of sub-standard merchandise seized by customs officers in the course of their duties. Goods which did not conform to the standards laid down in the regulations, in particular wines and spirits, could not be held in stock by the retailers, and it was the practice, therefore, to sell the goods in small lots sufficient for private buyers.

CUSTOM-HOUSE LONDON
By Order of the Honourable Commissioners of His Majesty's Customs,
In pursuance of an Act of Parliament of the third year of his present Majesty,
On WEDNESDAY the 27th, and THURSDAY the 28th of FEBRUARY, 1788,
At Three o'Clock in the Afternoons of the said Days, In the Long Room, Custom-house, London, THE FOLLOWING GOODS, which are allotted in small quantities for the better accommodation of the several dealers, as well as private persons, who chuse to become purchasers.
FOR HOME CONSUMPTION
Brandy, Rum, Geneva, Arrack, Cordial Water, Tea, Coffee, Wool, Vessels, Boats, Materials of Vessels, refused Wine, Tobacco Ashes, Thread, Gauze, Orange, Cranberries, Elastic Bottles, Pelts, Squirrel Tails, large

French Looking Glass Plates, and Glass for optical use. Also such goods as have remained in his Majesty's Warehouse upwards of three months, not cleared, or the duty paid, viz. Pictures, Prints, Books, Paper, Stockings, Snuff, Steel Guns, Lead Bugles, and sundry other sorts of goods, as mentioned in the catalogues.

CLEAR OF ALL DUTIES

The Vessels, Boats and materials of Vessels to be viewed at the Tobacco Ground, near the West Dock, Rotherhithe; the Tobacco Ashes at the Tobacco Warehouse, Tower Hill; and all other goods at the Custom-house, London, on Monday the 25th, from nine to one in the forenoon, where catalogues will be delivered.

Similar sales were regularly held by His Majesty's Customs at the multitude of Customs Warehouses scattered around the British coast.

CUSTOM-HOUSE ARUNDEL
On THURSDAY, the 17th Day of APRIL, 1788
At Two o'Clock in the Afternoon

The following GOODS which have been seized, and legally condemned.

Brandy — 64 ⎫
Rum — 18 ⎬ Gallon, for private Families only.
Geneva—421 ⎭

Apart from the seized cargoes the Custom-houses had another line of merchandise which cropped up occasionally. They also disposed of the salvaged cargoes of ships which had been wrecked at sea or driven aground and written off.

AT ROTTINGDEAN
On WEDNESDAY the 23rd JANUARY, 1788,
At Eleven o'Clock in the Forenoon,

A Considerable Quantity of SALT FISH and OIL, being part of the cargo of the Anna Maria, stranded at the said place; together with the Ship's materials, for paying the salvage expences. The whole may be viewed the Morning of Sale.

CUSTOM-HOUSE CHICHESTER
By Permission of the HONOURABLE COMMISSIONERS of his MAJESTY'S CUSTOMS AND SALT DUTIES.
DUTY FREE
On WEDNESDAY the 6th of FEBRUARY next,
At Eleven o'Clock in the Forenoon,

ABOUT Seventy TONS of ALICANT SALT, being
part of the Cargo of the Swedish Snow Amphitrite,
lately stranded on the coast of Sussex.
The above salt is Warehoused in Selsea, near the beach,
and may be ship'd at a very trifling expence. Samples
may be seen in Selsea as aforesaid by applying to Mr
Francis Whitcomb, on the day of Sale at the Custom-
house in Chichester.

In the case of the sales by auction of property, furniture and effects,
it was common at the time to hold the sale 'on the premises'. The
advertising indicates that very few of the London auctioneers had
their own salerooms, and in all probability most operated from a
small office or even a private residence. Garraway's, Hambro's, the
New York and Bank Coffee-houses were used by all the principal
auctioneers of the day, but an examination of all the auction notices
appearing in *The Times* for the first quarter of 1788 shows that a good
eighty per cent of sales by auction were to be held on the premises of
the owner of the goods.

By Mr GREENWOOD
On the Premises
On THURSDAY next, the 24th Instant

The Neat and Genuine HOUSEHOLD FURNI-
TURE, Linen, China, Wines, Fire-Arms, Brewing and
Garden Utensils &c. &c.

Of a GENTLEMAN deceased

At his late Dwelling-House, opposite the Church at
Hammersmith, near the Fulham Turnpike.
To be viewed on Tuesday, and till the Sale, which will
be punctually at Twelve o'Clock.

By SAMUEL BURTON
On the Premises, no 21, Colebrooke-Row, Islington,
THIS DAY, the 12th of FEBRUARY

ALL the entire, genuine and Very Genteel Household
Furniture, valuable fixtures, and other Effects of

A GENTLEMAN leaving off housekeeping

The whole of which was new within Twelve Months,
and in excellent Condition.
To be viewed this day ... The Sale begins at Eleven
o'Clock.
Descriptions of the Furniture may be had by Catalogue
on the Premises, and of Mr Burton, Auctioneer and
Undertaker, no 128, Houndsditch.

The most notable feature of these advertisements is that the traditional use of the persuasive adjective is already much in evidence, as is the use of capital letters to stress the important features of the sale. This emphasis was not reserved solely for the goods, it was important to signify that the previous owner was a GENTLEMAN, and that if he was not in fact DECEASED there was some other very good reason for the disposal. What these advertisements were trying to say was that here was a rare opportunity to obtain something from the possessions of someone with infinitely better taste than the reader could ever hope to possess; that the goods might be obtained at a most reasonable price, and that there was no truth whatsoever in the rumour that the owner was only selling because the stuff was falling to pieces. Two good examples of the art are as follows:

By Mr ROBERDEAU
On the PREMISES, Charing-Cross
By order of the EXECUTORS
TO-MORROW, and FRIDAY, at
Eleven o'Clock

The Genuine HOUSEHOLD FURNITURE, Plate, Jewels, Linen, China, Pictures, Books, and other valuable effects of Mr HUGH HUGHS, Mercer, deceased, comprising prime Bed and Bedding, excellent mahogany articles in Wardrobe, Bookcases, Drawers, Chairs, Card, Pier, and Dining Tables, with circular ends; Pier Glasses, Carpets, 600 ounces of serviceable Plate, Gold Watch, Diamond Rings, a Cabinet Picture from the late Mr Seymour's collection, never before brought to sale; a well chosen library, a Forte Piano, by Ganor; a fine tuned Harpsichord in a Mahogany Case, and other articles.

May be Viewed TO-MORROW, and Catalogues had of Mr Roberdeau, No 6, Talbot-court, Gracechurch-street.

By Mr FORFUR
On the Premises, near the Assembly House, at
Clapham, in Surrey,
On THURSDAY, March 20th, and the following day,
at Eleven o'Clock,

All the Genteel HOUSEHOLD FURNITURE, 400 Ounces of Fashionable Plate, a brilliant Diamond Ring, fine Table and Bed Linen, a well-chosen Library, China, &c., of EDWARD GEORGE KEEPE, Esq., retiring into the Country.

Some of the advertisements give just a hint of an element of sharp

practice by some auctioneers. The need to state that a picture was
'never before brought to sale' as well as the name and situation of the
vendor, suggests that at least some members of the buying public were
becoming suspicious of the 'genuine' nature of some of the items
offered. It is entirely possible that a number of unscrupulous auctioneers were feeding 'trade' items into a deceased vendor's house contents sale in order to obtain an optimum price. Evidence to support
such a possibility might lie in the footnote to the following advertisement which appeared in *The Times* on the 12th of March, 1788.

By Mr BURTON
THIS DAY
(ON THE PREMISES)
No. 16, King-street, Tower-hill

The Genuine STOCK IN TRADE of Mr THOMAS
ROBINSON, Haberdasher and Laceman (who has retired from that branch of business); consisting of Thread
and Black Laces, Valencienne Edging, plain and
worked Muslin, Lawn, and Silk Handkerchiefs, Rib-
bons, Modes, Perfumes, Silk, Thread, Tapes, Cottons,
Table Cloths, Hose, with sundry articles. Also a part of
the Household Furniture, Paintings on Copper, and
about five Chaldrons of Coals.

   To be Viewed, when Catalogues may be had at the
Place of Sale, and of Mr Burton, Auctioneer and Undertaker, No. 128, Houndsditch.

   N.B. Not an article in this Sale, but is the sole property of Mr Robinson.

Another in the category of the somewhat unusual was a sale at the
New Lloyd's Coffee-house of just one lot, the Brigantine 'Mary',
British built in 1786, of 215 tons, under the command of one George
Davidson. The vessel may—to quote the advertisement—'be sent to
sea at a trifling expence, provisions excepted'. The provisions might
well have been obtained of Mr Burton, who was selling by order of
the assignees of Mr Joseph Symes, Hog-Butcher, 'The Genuine Stock
in Trade; consisting of Sixty Bacon Hogs, dried.'
   The public passion for fur items of all kinds was also well under
way, and large quantities of imported skins were finding their way
into the auction rooms. Looking at the numbers involved in just one
such sale and considering that it was to be at least a hundred and
fifty years before conservation would be much in the public mind, it
is almost surprising to discover that any of the species quoted have
survived at all. Skins sold at the New York Coffee-house in February,
1788 included:

140,300 Racoon, 15,700 Bear, 67,000 Martin, 28,000 Otter, 9,700 Wolf, 6,300 Fisher, 7,700 Cat, 20,500 Mink, 9,000 Fox, 480 Wolverin, 240,000 Musquash.

Although the names Christie's and Sotheby's are universally recognised as the principal London auctioneers, we should not forget that there are in fact four major auction houses based in London, all of which were founded in the eighteenth century. In 1793 William Charles Bonham and George Jones opened a small gallery in Leicester Street, and Bonham's was born. Like the other members of the London quartet Bonham's have, since those early days, moved their headquarters more than once, but unlike their competitors have maintained their saleroom as a family business, handed down from father to son.

The last member of the quartet became established in 1796. In that year Harry Phillips resigned his post as head clerk to James Christie, and on the 23rd of April held his first sale of, 'Neat and Elegant Household Furniture'. Like so many of the other sales of the period the sale was 'on the premises at Crown-street, Westminster', for it was not to be until late in 1797 that Phillips was to take the premises at 73 New Bond Street which the firm was to occupy for almost a century and a half. Precisely why he left Christie's employ is not ascertainable, but Phillips clearly had the personality of an irrepressable super salesman and it is likely that he had come to the realisation that he was good at his job, but unlikely to make his fortune working for Christie.

It is also true to say that his departure from the Christie camp coincided with a lean spell of business at Christie's, and there might well have been differences of opinion over the organisation of the firm. A study of the auction advertisements in the *Morning Post* newspapers for 1801 shows Phillips picking up some fairly important business, and it might be true to say that for some years after branching out on his own he was reasonably successful at beating Mr Christie at his own game. His advertising shows a lively mind and an innovatory approach to the business. He was the first to advertise admission to view by catalogue only, and to charge one shilling for catalogues— twice as much as others—refundable to purchasers at the sales.

By Mr HARRY PHILLIPS

On the Premises, No 72, South Audley-street, on THURSDAY, the 26th Instant, at Twelve o'Clock, and following Days,
PART of the SUPERB HOUSEHOLD FURNITURE, magnificent French Plate Pier and Chimney Glasses, of peculiar magnitude, four brilliant Cut Glass

Chandeliers, Parisian Or Moulu Lamps, Candelabras, and Girandoles, mechanical and musical Or Moulu Clocks, fine Bronzes, Marbles and Alabaster, in Figures, Vases, &c. Etruscan Ware, Cabinet Pictures, and Drawings by Du Croz, Tapestry Hangings, an extensive Dinner and Desert Service of old Seve Porcelane, and an assemblage of elegant Cabinet and ornamental China, of the Seve and Dresden Factories, Biscuit Figures, choice Wines, comprising fine old Port, Madeira, Sherry, and French Wines, Library of choice Books, and variety of valuable Effects, the property of
His Excellency Chevalier D'ALMEIDA,
Ambassador from the Court of Portugal (leaving England)
The Furniture comprises Drawing-room Suites in rich crimson and yellow Damask in Sofas, Chairs, Squabs, and Curtains, near 300 yards of Damask Hangings, large Carpets, sets of Mahogany Dining Tables, rich Cotton Furnitures, elegant Commodes, Consoles, with scarce Italian slabs, mounted in Or Moulu, Book-cases and Ecretoires, Work Tables, and every useful and ornamental article of Furniture. May be viewed three days preceding the Sale, by Catalogue only, to be had at One Shilling each, to be returned to purchasers, to be had as above; and at Mr Phillips Estate and Auction Office, New Bond-street.

It is easy to see that Harry Philips gave his advertising all he had got, spelling mistakes included, and when the house contents were hard to come by he showed his entrepeneur spirit by selling whatever was to hand.

By Mr HARRY PHILLIPS
At his Great Room, New Bond-street, THIS DAY and following days, at Twelve o'Clock, THE most Superb Assemblage of UNIQUE ELEGANCIES ever imported from Paris and Italy.
NOVEL TRANSPARENT LAMPS, decorated a-la-Chinois and a-la-Greque, formed to disperse an agreeable tinge of light imimative of Moon-light.
Alabaster Vases ... &c. &c.

Phillips was to see great success as an auctioneer and was to conduct many notable sales dealing with the affairs of some of the important people of his time. He was to sell, for example, the Bruton Street possessions of George 'Beau' Brumell, as well as chattels the property of the defeated Napoleon, brought from St Helena. Other notable clients included the Duke of Roxburgh, HRH the Duke of Kent, Lady Hertford, Prince Talleyrand, and as he would have said himself, &c., &c.

In 1823 Phillips sold the contents of Fonthill Abbey on behalf of the wealthy author, politician and collector William Beckford. It was a marathon thirty day event to which society flocked with a passion described by *The Times* as 'Fonthill fever', and there was yet another thirty day spectacular to come when he sold for the Duke of Buckingham what his advertising described as 'The Important and Highly Estimable Collection of the entire Property of a Nobleman of High Rank.'

Phillips had taken the art of the superlative adjective to new heights, but his colleagues in the auctioneering fraternity were never far behind. The *Morning Post* advertisements of 1801 positively glow with the warmth of the descriptions, and all of the furniture and effects offered are invariably 'Neat' or 'Valuable', 'Elegant' or 'Fashionable', 'Superb, Genteel, Unique', but above all 'Genuine'. All of these remarkable goods were at least 'the Property of a Gentleman' or a 'Person of Rank', or even 'a Gentleman retiring to the Country'. There was also the 'Gentleman, leaving off Housekeeping, at his house, the top of the Market-place, Brentford', as well as 'a Person of Distinction' who shall be nameless, and poor old 'Mr Fox, Cabinet-maker, a Bankrupt', who shall not.

Among the more unusual items advertised for sale at the turn of the century was a 'solid mahogany kneading trough, and a fourteen bushel baker's oven, etc.', to be had at London Docks, Wapping, and for coal merchants, 'four capital young seasoned draft horses, an excellent coal waggon and two coal carts together with hay and corn'. On offer at Garraway's on the 4th of February, 1801, was:

> ONE SIXTEENTH PART, or SHARE, of and in that long-established and well-known Daily Newspaper, called, THE TIMES, which Sixteenth Share has, for many years, produced the owner upwards of Four Hundred Pounds per annum, clear of all deductions and expences, and the Paper is at this time in the highest estimation and request.

For the very early nineteenth-century collector of natural history specimens there occurred a rare opportunity in a sale conducted:

> By Mr KING
> At his Great Room, King-street, Covent-garden, TO-MORROW and Two Following Days at Twelve o'Clock, A MISCELLANEOUS ASSEMBLAGE OF

ARTICLES, comprising Minerals, Shells, and Insects;
several Mathematical Instruments, a Cabinet, containing about 400 Roman, Greek, and English, Silver and
Copper Coins; old China; a curious carved Ivory Cup
and Cover; Mahogany Cabinet, with sliding glass drawers, filled with Insects, &c. from China, many of them
rare, an Indian Gun, inlaid with Gold &c.

May be viewed till the Sale; and Catalogues had at
the Room.

During the first quarter of the nineteenth century the auctioneers
were able to benefit once more from revolutionary progress. The
smoke discharged from the factory chimneys of the Industrial Revolution was clearing to reveal a new element in society, a new and
affluent middle class, determined to make its mark on the brave new
world. The seemingly endless cycle of mechanical invention stimulat-
ing increased industrial production leading to greater investment in
new machinery, produced further unprecedented growth and un-
dreamed of wealth.

A significant proportion of the wealth generated by this new middle
class was re-invested by them on the trappings necessary to display
their new status. They became great consumers not only of the domestic product, but of the imported luxury goods and the fine houses and
fine art which had previously been the preserve of the aristocratic
upper classes.

The commercial world needed to respond quickly to the new consumer demands in order to speed distribution of the ever increasing
range of merchandise available. No businessman was better placed for
such a rapid response than the auctioneer. With his gavel and his
notebook he was ready for business at the factory gate, in the market
place, coffee-house or auction room. It had always been characteristic
of the auctioneers to respond immediately to attend to the affairs of
the bankrupt or the executor, and so it was now. The volatility of the
new industrialisation process produced failure in almost as much proportion as success, and the auctioneer was on hand to redistribute the
possessions of those who became the victims of the new order.

As trade continued to expand outwards from London, the auctioneer was everywhere to be seen following the middle-class revolution out into the countryside, and by the middle of the nineteenth
century many of the major provincial auctioneers and estate agents
were established.

In Paris the old patterns continued to the end of the eighteenth
century. The traditional locations continued to be used except in the
case of the sales by order of the court when the sale would be 'on the
premises'. Sebastien Mercier leaves another memorial in his *Tableau*

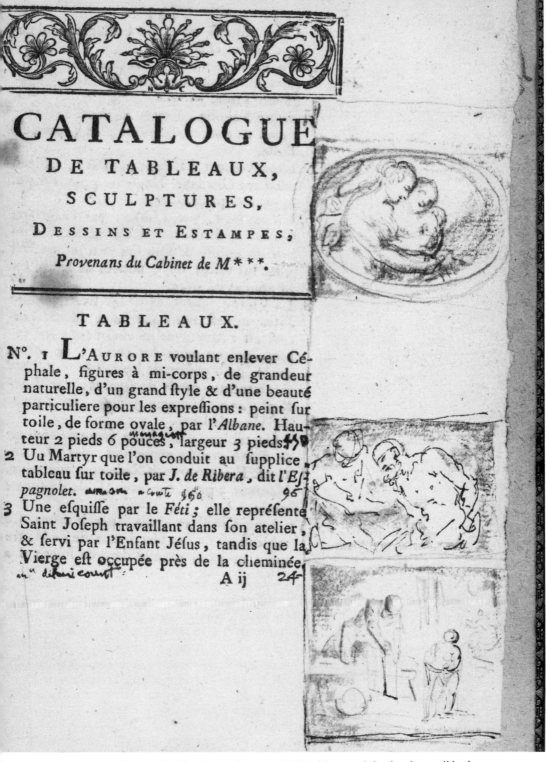

CATALOGUE

DE TABLEAUX,

SCULPTURES,

DESSINS ET ESTAMPES,

Provenans du Cabinet de M***.

TABLEAUX.

N°. 1 L'AURORE voulant enlever Cé-
phale, figures à mi-corps, de grandeur
naturelle, d'un grand ftyle & d'une beauté
particuliere pour les expreffions : peint fur
toile, de forme ovale, par l'*Albane*. Hau-
teur 2 pieds 6 pouces, largeur 3 pieds.

2 Un Martyr que l'on conduit au fupplice,
tableau fur toile, par *J. de Ribera*, dit l'*Ef-
pagnolet*.

3 Une efquiffe par le *Féti*; elle repréfente
Saint Jofeph travaillant dans fon atelier,
& fervi par l'Enfant Jéfus, tandis que la
Vierge eft occupée près de la cheminée.

A ij

Frontispiece of an early French catalogue—c1745—illustrated by hand, possibly by
Saint-Aubin. Photo courtesy Bibliotheque Nationale Paris

de Paris', designed to remind us, if we need reminding, that nothing that we can find in human nature is new. Writing of the auctions by order of the court he describes the 'Bande Noire' (Black Gang), which without any doubt is the direct eighteenth century forbear of that principal problem of generations of auctioneers—the 'ring'. Mercier says:

> In these auctions there is a private feature for which one must always be on the alert, this is called 'La Graffinade'. It consists of a 'ring' of dealers who do not outbid each other in the sales, because all those who are present at the sale are interested, but when they see a private buyer anxious for the article, they bid up and raise the price against him, supporting the loss, which becomes a small matter when divided amongst the members of the 'ring'. These sharpers thus become masters of the situation, for they manage matters so that no outside buyer can bid above one of their own ring. When a thing has been run up sufficiently high to prevent any outside bidder making a profit, the ring meets privately, and the article is allotted to one of the members. This arrangement accounts for the high prices which surprise so many persons of experience. The ring does not wish the article to reappear in the auction room, lest it should fall to a price lower than that at which they pretend to have acquired it. This conspiracy against the purse of private persons has driven from the auction room a large number of buyers, who prefer to be cheated by one member of the gang rather than the whole crew, who, according to the popular expression, 'are stiff in the back and joust in a style to scare the bravest of bidders'.

The workings of the modern 'ring' will be described in detail in a later chapter, and the similarities revealed will show what a remarkable record this account of Mercier's is. Despite the menace of the 'Bande Noire', however, the Paris auctions continued to flourish; but it was not until 1780 that the famous 'Hotel Bullion' was opened, and not until 1817 that it had become the focal point of the principal auctioneers of the city.

Between those dates, of course, France was racked by Revolution, a conflict with its roots in a class struggle that was aimed at a massive redistribution of the country's wealth. It was a Revolution in which the fine arts were denigrated, and in which the values of such items changed dramatically. We may be sure that the auctioneer's hammer was tapping away constantly during this period in an effort to assist in this financial re-organisatiion. It has even been stated in some sources that 'abuses and frauds were committed under the ivory hammer of the auctioneers', and that certain sales 'facilitated the disappearance of objects derived from illicit sources'. There is no direct evidence to support these charges, so innuendo will have to do.

The tradition of the Parisian auctioneers of moving in concert from one auction location to another had its origins in the street and market auctions of the late seventeenth and early eighteenth centuries. It was a tradition which was not to be abandoned despite the move into the slightly more sophisticated indoor salons of the nineteenth century. A tradition so strong, in fact, that it persists to the present day.

The artist Boilly has left for posterity a painting of a sale in progress at the Hotel Bullion in which the prospective buyers examine a painting while the auctioneer and his crier watch for bids. The Hotel Bullion depicted in the painting, in the rue Jean-Jacques Rousseau, remained the auction building of Paris until 1833, when the business moved to the Place de la Bourse at the corner of the rue Notre Dame de Victoires. With the transfer went the congregation of auctioneers and the name, for the new location became the new Hotel Bullion. While the name was the same, however, the new accommodation appears to have been somewhat less than adequate. In an article for the *Connoisseur* magazine in 1902, the famous French writer Octave Uzanne said of it:

> For nearly twenty years, auctions, both great and small, went on in this uncomfortable, aged and decrepit place, where one was sadly hustled and squeezed, in spite of the annexation of some additional rooms from adjoining buildings.

Uzanne goes on to describe a notable picture sale which took place in this, in his opinion, far from notable saleroom.

> The most noted auction which took place in this wretched old second-hand emporium was that of the gallery of the Duchess D'Orleans in 1852, which opened up a new phase in the market value of the works of contemporaneous painters, such as Eugene Delacroix, Descamps, Ingres, Paul Delaroche, and Ary Scheffer, who, for the first time, obtained values which until then had been reserved for the leading foreign artists

In England the rise of the provincial auctioneers continued, as did the resolve of the London salerooms to improve the quality of their business by selling only good house contents and fine art. That is not to say that the country auctioneers did not have their moments, but there was a distinctly rural flavour about many of the auctions outside London. The *Windsor and Eton Express & General Advertiser* was first published on Saturday the 1st of August, 1812. The strength of the country auctioneers at that time was more than adequately demonstrated by the fact that in the first as well as subsequent editions of this weekly newspaper, half of the front page was devoted to local auction advertisements.

Mr Crockett of Windsor was selling the 'Household Furniture and unredeemed Pledges', the property of Mr Spink, a pawnbroker, silversmith and salesman of the High Street, Windsor. The unredeemed pledges included 'watches, plate, beds and wearing apparel'. The largest proportion of the advertised sales were, however, associated with agricultural pursuits. In a period just prior to the establishment of the weekly markets, it was the practice, it seems, to sell standing crops, cattle, farming equipment and newly felled timber by auction 'on the premises'.

> Fine Growing Crops of WHEAT, OATS, and BEANS
> TO BE SOLD BY AUCTION
> By Mr J. BARTON
> On the Premises, on Wednesday, August 5th, 1812, at Two o'Clock in the Afternoon, THIRTEEN ACRES of Wheat, SIX ACRES of Beans, and SIX ACRES of Oats (more or less), situated at Arbor-hill, by the turnpike-road leading from Windsor to Slough and Salt-hill, Catalogues to be had of Mr Barton, and at the Place of Sale and the Principal Inns in the neighbourhood.

Mr Batten was advertising a sale to take place on the 8th of September:

> at Eleven o'Clock precisely, at the CAVALRY BARRACKS at Hounslow.
> NINETEEN strong, bony, active HORSES, belonging to His Majesty's 10th Light Dragoons; and also several high-bred BLOOD HORSES, belonging to Officers on Service.
> To be viewed on the morning of Sale, the above Horses are in high condition, and are well worth the attention of Gentlemen, for Carriages, Curricles, Farmers, Post and Coach Masters &c.

Local bankrupts provided the usual crop of sales. Mr Fennell was selling 'for the benefit of the creditors, the stock in trade of Mr John Pitt, of Datchet, Bucks, Carpenter', while Mr Barton, at his auction rooms in the central part of Eton, and by order of the Sheriff of Berks., was attending to the furniture and effects of Nathaniel Hunt, Victualler. The said effects including 'a four-pull beer engine and pipes, 40 bushels of coals, 50 dozen of porter, ditto of empty bottles, and 7 dozen of pewter quarts, pints, and beer pots'.

When the local auctioneer had the pleasure of receiving instructions to dispose of a major house contents, he was inclined to make the most of it. This inclination led him to include anything and everything of value in his catalogue, and his advertising could reveal some rather exotic lists of 'outside effects' tacked on to the end of the descriptions of the principal items. On Thursday the 15th of October, 1812, Daniel Smith was offering to the highest bidder:

> a pair of excellent, young Carriage Horses, and two saddle ditto; two handsome Milch Cows, a Chinese Sow in Pig; a Bee-house, with seven hives of Bees; a rick of Hay; garden rollers and implements, ladders, greenhouse plants, manure and numerous Valuable Effects.

It is clear that competition was becoming fierce amongst auctioneers everywhere, and by way of announcing his great success, and for the encouragement of further patronage, Mr Smith was pleased to give an advance notice of his impending good fortune:

> Notice of Sale of His Majesty's Flock of PURE MER-
> INO SHEEP, and capital Farming Stock at KEW and
> RICHMOND,
>   By order of the Trustees of His Majesty's Personal
> Property,
>   Mr DANIEL SMITH has the honour to announce
> that the SALE BY AUCTION of the above celebrated
> and extensive Flock of Pure Merino and Ryeland
> Sheep, together with the whole of the Excellent Live
> and Dead Stock on His Majesty's Farms near Rich-
> mond, will take place early in the Spring; of which
> particulars will be given in subsequent advertisements.

The less fortunate Mr Stevens at his repository at the Red Lion Inn, Staines, was meanwhile reduced to advertising for anything which might improve his prospects:

> It is particularly requested that the earliest Intimation will be given
> of the Property intended for Sale, as Books for particularising the
> same are opened at the Repository, and at Mr Stevens's FURNI-
> TURE WAREHOUSE AT STAINES, MIDDLESEX.

Others were inclined towards making what almost amounted to special offers in order to attract the necessary business:

> MR HENRY BURDEN Appraiser and Auctioneer (once more
> resuming the Profession) Most Humbly and Respectfully solicits his
> Friends and a generous Public for their Patronage, tendering to
> them his best abilities, with a strict attention to their Interest, a

punctual and early settlement of his sales, united with a REASON-
ABLE COMMISSION; on these principals he hopes to merit support.

Even the hallowed halls of England's premier seat of learning were
no refuge, it seems, from the auctioneer's hammerings:

ETON COLLEGE, BUCKS.
400 PAIRS OF BLANKETS TO BE SOLD BY AUC-
TION
By Mr BARTON, without reserve,
On THURSDAY, December 8th, and following Day,
at his AUCTION ROOMS; beginning at Eleven
o'Clock Each Day.
400 PAIR OF SUPERIOR QUALITY BLAN-
KETS; Mr Barton warrants them perfect for texture,
weight of wool, and sizes; few opportunities occur so
beneficial to the Public, and so appropriate to the Season.

At about this time the auction business was breaking up in London,
but only in the sense that the growing band of dealers in real property
had come to the conclusion that the coffee-houses could no longer
cope with the volume of auction business of every kind being transacted. As a result the first metropolitan auction mart for the sale of
property was opened in 1808 at the corner of Bartholomew Lane with
a frontage on Throgmorton Street. The building, described then as
'a specimen of elegant architecture', contained a basement with vault
and offices, and a ground floor with a saloon, coffee-room and offices.
A mezzanine floor provided galleries overlooking the saloon, and the
two upper floors each had three salerooms.

Many notable properties were sold in this building including at one
time the West Indies estate of a sugar planter, complete with the
slaves; and on another occasion Shakespeare's house at Stratford-on-
Avon.

By 1843 it began to seem as if everything in creation was destined
to come under the auctioneer's influence. The great range of goods
offered including fine paintings, well chosen libraries, the property
and furnishings of gentlemen, or otherwise, deceased or otherwise, led
to such a crescendo of hammering as rattled the very foundations of
the commercial world.

In the country you might wish to purchase of Mr Burton 'three
stout dung carts and several 'mines' of manure', but if that prospect
was a little overpowering Mr Barrett , on behalf of Mr Francis, could
supply you with 'five pair of fumigating bellows'. If all else failed one
could always pop along to Kempton Park to sample as well as view

the selection of choice wines offered by Hoggart and Phillips on behalf
of Mr Fish, deceased, who had obviously been trying to drink up to
his name to the extent of:

> 350 dozen fine flavoured Port, 20 dozen curious East
> India Madeira, 40 dozen Sherry, 40 dozen Claret, a
> few dozens of old Hock, 50 dozen of Lisbon, two pipes
> of excellent Port in the wood, three hogsheads of ales
> and table beer.

Almost as a demonstration of the all encompassing scope of the country auctioneer, Mr Tebbott of Windsor was selling in April, 1843,
Bulbrook Farm near Bracknell, literally lock, stock and barrel. The
sale was by order of the Sheriff of Berks., and included the lease of
the 118 acre farm—8½ years unexpired, the household furniture including a pianoforte by Broadrip and Wilkinson, and the farming
stock to include manure and firewood as well as two acres of turnips.

The Royal Estates were also heavily involved in the auction and
producing in their progress some rather unusual advertising— at least
by present day standards.

WINDSOR GREAT PARK
TO BE SOLD BY AUCTION
ON THE PREMISES
On Thursday, the 27th of April, 1843
About 4000 large Chestnut, Beech, Birch, Oak, Larch,
Scotch, and other Fir Trees and Poles, now lying in
Chapel Wood, and the Wick Nursery, which are worth
the attention of Contractors, Carpenters, Timber Dealers, and others, Catalogues, with conditions of sale, to
be had in due time on application to John Smith, wood-
man, who will show the lots; also at the Inns in the
neighbourhood.

Just a glance at the newspapers of the mid nineteenth century reveals
the popularity of the auction system, and nationwide in England very
large numbers of auctioneers must have been involved in trade. The
fact does not seem to have escaped the attention of the government of
the day, who, seeking to lay down a few ground rules and at the same
time raise a little revenue, introduced in 1845 the 'Auctioneers Act'.

Under the Act every auctioneer in any part of the United Kingdom
was required to take out a licence costing ten pounds and renewable
annually on the 5th of July. There were a number of specific exemptions, for example the sale of goods seized under a distress warrant for
arrears of rent up to £20 could be conducted by the bailiff without
a licence. The exemptions apart, however, failure to produce a current
licence on demand rendered the auctioneer liable to a fine of one

hundred pounds or one month in prison. The Act also required the auctioneer, before commencing any sale, to affix or suspend a ticket or board in clear view at the place of sale, to describe his full christian name(s) and surname and place of residence. The new legislation was, in the same way as the earlier Act, designed to make the auctioneers more accountable and in that way to limit malpractice.

The sort of Victorian preoccupations which produced the Great Exhibition in 1851 also created a market in the field of natural history collecting which some in the auction business were not slow to exploit. In the 1840s, Stevens Auction Rooms began to specialise in natural history specimens and offered a wide range of shells and fossils, butterflies and insects—even the eggs of the Great Auk, soon to be extinct. By the 1850s the public taste for live exhibitions led the firm to explore the previously uncharted region of live animal sales. From the organisational point of view the sale arrangements must have been at least difficult and possibly dangerous. A November 1855 edition of *Punch* summed up the problems quite nicely:

> We do not understand how the sale is to be managed or how Mr Stevens of King Street proposes to knock down the elephant. ... We should not be surprised if while the auctioneer is soliciting advances upon the Tiger, the Tiger were to make a sudden and unexpected advance upon the audience; and there are some lots that will hardly be under sufficient restraint to enable the porters to display them.

It was reported, however, that the sale was a great success, and that no serious injuries were sustained by either porters or prospective buyers.

Across the channel in the country areas things continued in the traditional ways. A story published in the *Daily News* of the 29th of December, 1881, described events in the small French fishing village of St Baptist, and in particular the return of the fishing fleet.

> Next morning the ships all come in with the tide, each racing to get in first, because the first fish sold usually brings the highest price. It takes but little time to drop anchor, pop the fish—already arranged in baskets—into the small boat, and pull to shore. As the boat's head grates on the beach a crowd of chattering, gesticulating folk press round to bid for the fish, which is neatly spread on a sort of basketwork tray, something like a hamper lid turned upside down. On the tray, there will be, perhaps, fifteen or twenty pairs of soles, or three dozen 'vives', or sixteen fine red gurnets, or mullet, or plaice, or turbot, or what-not. Large quantities of disagreeable coarse-looking skate are also sold, and fetch a good price. There is much excitement over the bidding. The captain sells the fish by

auction, putting the highest price on the basket to be sold, and gradually lowering it till some one closes with an offer. A girl stands near the captain, and with wonderful accuracy and neatness enters in a note book the kind of fish in each basket, whom sold to, and how much for. The bidding, the arguments, the jokes, are all in a patois very difficult to understand.

In November all the boats leave St Baptist and come to the English coast for the winter. They fish off 'Toorchay' (Torquay) and 'Plymut' (Plymouth), and run across twice a week to some big French port to dispose of the fish. At Easter the boats return to St Baptist, the village comes to life again, and joyful are the meetings between man and wife, father and children, mother and son, after a long winter's separation.

The account is interesting as a contemporary description of a continental fish auction, and also for confirming, as it does, that it was common practice for the continental fleets to fish off the English coast. Presumably the boats would at times put in to the English ports also to sell their catch, in the same way as they did at home. This would go a long way towards explaining how the continental auction system came to be introduced into some, but not all, parts of the British fishing industry. The most notable example of a diversity of systems is to be found in the North-East of England where the descending bid—Dutch—method is used in the fish markets of Hull, whilst the ascending bid—English—method is used in Grimsby, just across the Humber estuary.

Many of the principal provincial cattle markets were established from the mid nineteenth century onwards. The enormous popularity of these weekly markets sprang from the duality of their function in the community. They were obviously the place to transact business, to sell farm stock and produce, and to buy and replace equipment; but they were also social occasions, meeting places for the exchange of news and gossip. All these functions had previously been fulfilled by the rural fairs and the village centre gatherings for the purpose of barter, but these were less frequent events, and the weekly market with its guaranteed regularity and its attraction to farmers and dealers from a wide area, must have stimulated agriculture and agricultural communities like nothing else before.

The new markets replaced the old agricultural system of auction which took place on the premises. In that type of sale the crops and cattle and equipment were sold where they stood, and the auctioneer and the buyers moved from one sale location to another. Once the weekly markets were established it was the auctioneer who remained in the fixed position, and the cattle and produce were brought in by the seller, auctioned off, and carried away by the new owner.

The advantages of the new system were considerable, not least that the farmer no longer had to wait until he had accumulated sufficient stock for a viable farm sale, or until the next village fair. He could now feed small parcels of goods into the market to be included in the large weekly collective sales, and in effect could obtain his working capital as and when required.

We have looked at the environs of Windsor and Eton in order to demonstrate the substantial amount of auction activity that existed in a quite small local area. In fact a particularly good example of the rise and progress of a rural auctioneering family—typical no doubt of very many more throughout the land—is available for inspection in the same general area today. Having diversified very slightly, the firm of Buckland & Son, with offices in Windsor and Slough, proudly announces 'established over 150 years'. Today's business is in estate agency, in occasional auction sales of arms and armour, and in the operation of the weekly Slough Cattle Market, which the firm opened in 1850 and has run ever since. The firm's history may indeed be very similar to that of many of the great provincial auctioneering families of England, some of which have succumbed over the years to misfortune of one kind or another, but quite a number of whom have carried on 'for more than 150 years'.

Thomas Buckland was a farmer from the village of Wraysbury, near Windsor, who became a land agent and valuer, and founded the firm in 1826. The success of those like Thomas Buckland can be attributed to either a little bit of luck or a shrewd eye for an opportunity, or both, for in this case it seems that Thomas was shrewd enough to take advantage of his bit of luck at least twice-the luck being the coming of the railway.

When the Great Western Railway was driven through the area Thomas Buckland's services as agent and valuer were much in demand, and during those agriculturally disruptive years he did in fact handle the valuations and compensation claims for most of those affected in the local area. When that operation was successfully completed he settled down to gaining some solid experience in the auction field, selling everything from livestock to bedsteads.

In 1850 he put together his experience of the auction and his faith in the railway and opened the Slough Cattle Market on land alongside the Great Western in William Street, Slough. There it was to remain for well over a hundred years, and when the market finally closed in 1961 it was because Slough was by then a booming industrial town, and because the similarly booming cattle market was moving to new and modern premises in a more rural location.

For all of the nineteenth century, both before and after the setting up of the market, Buckland's would sell pigs and poultry on one day, furniture and fittings on another. They were favoured now and again with instructions to conduct sales on behalf of the Royal Estates, and did in fact conduct the first public sale ever held within Windsor Castle when timbers from Saint George's Chapel were auctioned off during refurbishment. The present partners have in their possession a fine collection of early sale catalogues associated with the firm, and the title pages of some are reproduced here. Brief reference to three of these old catalogues will demonstrate clearly the scope of the firm's activities.

On Thursday the 22nd of January, 1852, in Egham, Surrey, at eleven o'clock they were selling, 'Genuine Household Furniture and Fine Old Prints'. The total for the entire contents including chests of drawers, linen et al was just £70, and the title page carried at its head the immortal line:

The Property of a Lady deceased, on the Premises, in the High St.

It was farming stock at Wexham, Bucks., on Tuesday the 7th of July, 1846, at twelve o'clock, and the catalogue included the following lots:

1. Two corn bushels, and peck measure
4. Six hay forks, and 3 small rakes
6. Dung fork, shovel, and pickaxe

Lot six might be described as catering for the specialist in the field, by providing a tool for every occasion. This sale, complete with the livestock comprising pigs, poultry, horses and cows, and including six and a half acres of beans, realised in total just over £315.

In common with markets the length and breadth of the country, a notable feature of the auction year was the Christmas sale when all manner of produce, and particularly poultry, was on offer for the festive season. Such sales became the more notable for the auctioneers in the Windsor area upon receipt of the Royal command. On the 12th of December, 1894, Buckland & Sons were proud to announce:

The Prince Consort's Flemish Farm
A Xmas sale of fat stock belonging to HM the Queen
ON WEDNESDAY, DECEMBER 12, 1894
at One o'Clock precisely
Carriages will meet the Trains at both Windsor Stations

The general changeover to the sale of livestock by auction in the weekly markets was followed by the inevitable legislation on the subject. The 'Markets and Fairs (Weighing of Cattle) Act' of 1887 decreed that an auctioneer 'must not sell cattle at any mart where cattle are normally sold unless facilities for weighing are provided, and must not offer for sale cattle fit for immediate slaughter unless weighed and the weight disclosed to intending purchasers at the time of sale.'

1887 was also a significant year for the increasing use of the auction

WEXHAM, BUCKS.

CATALOGUE OF THE LIVE AND DEAD

FARMING STOCK,

Wh'ch will be Sold by Auction, by

MR. BUCKLAND

At Eleven for Twelve o'Clock, upon the Premises,

ON TUESDAY, JULY 7, 1846,

By Order of the Proprietor, Mr. Francis Groom, who is retiring from business. Comprising

FOUR USEFUL CART HORSES,

Two cobs, used for driving, capital young mare, 5 yrs. old, fit to ride or drive;

THREE FINE COWS, & CALVES,

AND TWO BREEDING SOWS;

RICK OF WHEAT,

WITH THE STRAW,

Rick of Beans, Stump of Old Meadow Hay,

TWO GOOD IRON AXLE WAGGONS,

Several 6-in.-wheel dung carts, market and spring ditto, chaise and harness, ploughs, harrows, land rollers, winnowing machine,

RICK AND LOAD CLOTHS,

Quantity of Hurdles, and other useful Farming Implements.

May be viewed the day previous, and morning of Sale, and Catalogues may be had on the Premises; George Inns, Uxbridge and Colnbrook; Crown, Slough; Angel and Crown, Staines; and at the Offices of Mr. W. T. Buckland, Land Surveyor and Auctioneer, 41, High Street, Windsor, and Wraysbury, Bucks.

W. WILLMORE, PRINTER, WINDSOR.

WINDSOR

CATALOGUE OF

The Valuable Well=Seasoned

TIMBER

and BUILDING MATERIALS
used in the Reconstruction of

ST. GEORGE'S CHAPEL

INCLUDING ABOUT

4,000ft. Run 9in. x 9in. Pitch Pine Baulks

And 6in. x 6in. Ditto

Large Quantity of Deals

In various sizes—9in. x 3in., 7in. x 4in, 7in. x 3in., 7in. x 2in.,
5in. x 2½in. and 4in. x 2in.

1in. & 1½in. Tongued & Groved Floor Boards

1in. White Deal Floor Boards, Match Boarding, Tongued and Groved
Boarding in Sheets, Oak Stained Panelled Pews, Centres, Trestles, Etc.

WHICH

MESSRS.

BUCKLAND & SONS

Are instructed to Sell by Auction in

THE HORSESHOE CLOISTERS, WINDSOR CASTLE

On THURSDAY, 23rd OCTOBER, 1930

At 1.30 o'clock.

Catalogues may be obtained of—

MESSRS. BUCKLAND & SONS, *Auctioneers & Surveyors*
SLOUGH, WINDSOR & READING ;
also 4, Bloomsbury Square, London, W.C.

EGHAM, SURREY.

CATALOGUE OF THE

GENUINE HOUSEHOLD

FURNITURE,

FINE OLD PRINTS,

And Effects, to be sold by Auction, by

MR. BUCKLAND

The property of a Lady deceased, on the Premises, in the High Street,

ON THURSDAY, JAN. 22, 1852,

AT 11 O'CLOCK.

FURNITURE Comprises Mahogany 4-post, Tent, and other Bedsteads, Looking Glasses, Toilet Stands, clean Beds, and Bedding; Venetian, Brussels, and Kidderminster Carpets; Dining, Loo, and Card Tables; Mahogany Sideboard with Cellaret; Wine cooler, Escretoire, &c. Chimney Glasses and Ornaments; fine old Prints, &c., &c., and the usual assortment of

KITCHEN AND CULINARY UTENSILS

May be viewed the day previous, and Morning of Sale, and Catalogues with Conditions had at the Catherine Wheel, Egham; Angel and Crown, Staines; Swan Inn, Chertsey; at the place of Sale, and at the Offices of the Auctioneer, Windsor.

ANDREWS, PRINTER, GUILDFORD.

THE PRINCE  CONSORT'S

FLEMISH FARM,

WINDSOR PARK.

CHRISTMAS SALE OF FAT STOCK,
BELONGING TO HER MAJESTY THE QUEEN.

MESSRS.

BUCKLAND & SONS

Are honoured with instructions to Sell by Auction, on the Premises, as above,

ON WEDNESDAY, DECEMBER 12, 1894,

AT ONE O'CLOCK PRECISELY,

15 Devon, Hereford, Highland & Shorthorn

BULLOCKS;

400 Prime Hampshire Down, Highland, Clune and Half-bred

SHEEP;

AND

100 BACON HOGS & PORKERS,

Of great weight and quality; the whole of which have been fed expressly for this sale.

Carriages will meet the Trains at both Windsor Stations.

*Catalogues may be obtained at the White Horse and Black Bull Hotels, Metropolitan Cattle Market,
London; of Mr. Tait, Shaw Farm, Windsor; and of Messrs. Buckland & Sons, Auctioneers, Land*

method on the continent. In Holland for example until that date dealers in the country's extensive fruit and vegetable trade would either buy the produce direct from the grower when ready, or would advance money on crops still under cultivation. More often than not the grower had need to resort to the 'money in advance' system, and consequently suffered the disadvantage of a fixed price return on his crops, often below prevailing market values.

The story is told that in the year 1887 an event occurred which was to revolutionise the entire Netherlands agricultural and horticultural industries. On a morning in midsummer a bargeload of vegetables arrived at the quay at the inland harbour of Broek op Langendijk in Northern Holland. The owner of the barge, a grower called Jongerling, would normally have sold direct or on commission to the waiting dealers; but on this particular morning business at the quay was so brisk and the throng of buyers so keen, that he could not easily decide which dealer to sell to. It is claimed that another boatman at the quay suggested that he might solve the problem by inviting the highest offer from the interested buyers, and that what followed was in fact the first auction sale of produce in the Netherlands.

Coincidentally it was on the 1st of May in the same year, 1887, that the first auction sale of fish took place in Germany. Earlier the German fishermen had sold the fish themselves, but this had meant long stays in port and an inevitable loss of production. Handing over the selling to a middleman, although satisfactory in releasing the fishermen to fish, sometimes led to the wholesaler taking an advantage when fixing the price paid to the fishermen. Occasionally whole catches were left to rot because individual fishermen refused to accept the going rate.

In an industry where supply and demand, and particularly supply, were subject to significant fluctuation, auction was eventually seen to be the best answer. That first auction in 1887 took place in Hamburg, and further auction centres were later established in Geestemunde in 1888 and Bremerhaven in 1892.

In the spring of 1852 the Paris auctioneers were once more on the move, this time from the Hotel Bullion to a new building erected on the site of the old opera house, now the rue Drouot. The newspapers of the day pronounced that the building was 'sumptuous and fully in harmony with the growing importance of the wielders of the little hammer'. A short time later, however, it was reported that the place was referred to by some as the 'Temple du Bric-a-Brac', and that waning enthusiasm for the accommodation was responsible for the abandonment of a proposal to decorate the walls with portraits of illustrious auctioneers and the niches with the busts of the great dealers and collectors. Finally it is said that within only ten or fifteen years of construction all enthusiasm was extinct, and everyone was

complaining of the dirty state of the building and the inadequacy of
its accommodation.

Octave Uzanne's article for the *Connoisseur* contains a savage attack
on the facilities provided by the Hotel Drouot towards the close of the
nineteenth century. His account of saleroom conditions at the time is
sometimes hilarious, graphically illuminating, and in all probability
fairly accurate. Having begun by stating:

'I need not discuss the heaviness, ugliness, and discomfort of this
building, which for forty long years has neither been enlarged,
cleaned, nor improved' ... he goes on to discuss in the greatest
detail all the imperfections of the building and to give his opinion
of the conditions there.

'We deserve something better than this wretched, uncomfortable
hole, a veritable rendezvous for vermin and microbes, where bron-
chitis lays in wait for victims in the draughty corridors and open
doorways, and where typhus hovers round in the nauseous, vitiated
atmosphere.

Then again, what curious and unclean folk one has to rub
shoulders with in the motley crowd of humanity one finds there. In
vain one anoints oneself with the oil of democratic love and puts
on the armour of social charity over one's delicacy. One must
sometimes go a step further and call to one's aid the prophylactics
of disinfectants to assure oneself against the cutaneous caresses of
innumerable parasites of roving instincts.

The public would, moreover, gladly welcome any facilities for
controlling articles put up for sale, and would greatly appreciate
the exclusion of objects emanating from shops and from interloping
dealers. It would hail with delight the suppression of "The Black
Gang", the contact with which alone often suffices to scare away
the most courageous lovers of art. There is a further question of
hygiene affecting "sales after death" which calls for attention and
definite settlement in any future scheme. One is justly astounded
that in any age when antiseptic methods are often carried to the
extremes of a mania, it is possible to warehouse and disperse in
public sales stuffs and linen (often from the very rooms where
disease and death have walked) without any attempt at purifica-
tion.

But unfortunately the auctioneers, whose means are so considerable, are not likely to pull down their building, and we are likely
for a long time to have to put up with the Hotel Drouot in its strait
corset of solid masonry.... Built originally for the quiet, jog-trot
days of Louis Philippe it has become to-day ridiculously behind all
progress, and is practically as much out of fashion as the old corn
market.'

HOTEL DES VENTES. MOBILIER

In England and much of Europe the auctioneers were well organised
and ready for the challenge of the twentieth century. In London
Messrs Christie, Sotheby, Bonham and Phillips were preparing to slice
up the art market cake, and the property dealers had moved to a new
Auction Mart in Tokenhouse Yard, opened in 1867, and reputed to
have become known 'wherever the English language was spoken and
in not a few places besides'.

In the provinces the country auctioneers were managing very nicely
on the bread and butter of property sales, spread occasionally with a
little jam from the proceeds of the periodic chattels auctions. The
tapping of the auctioneer's gavel was to be heard in all quarters
knocking down fat cattle in the markets, fresh fish on the quayside,
ripe vegetables in the Netherlands and anything from pots and pans
to paintings by Rembrandt in the chattel salerooms the length and
breadth of Europe. There was just one exception to this general progress towards the modern world, at least according to Uzanne. The
Hotel Drouot, he asserted, was not fit even for the nineteenth century
let alone ready for the twentieth. He concluded his article with a
blueprint for an auction building with facilities fitting to the capital
city of France. His 'crie de coeur' went as follows:

> What we want to-day is a large building, capable of satisfying all
> modern requirements, the design for which should be put up for
> public competition; a monument on noble lines and of immense
> proportions, such as can be found in the principal cities of the
> United States, notably in Philadelphia. This new 'Hotel des
> Ventes', open to air and light, well arranged, easy to clean, with
> facilities of access and ample installation, should be both elegant
> and comfortable. It should, moreover, be regulated by the same
> unswerving rules for all: rules which place the private amateur on
> the same footing with the dealer, and render impossible the exist-
> ance of monopolies in the hands of 'Black Gangs', and the stifling
> of the voice of the private collector.
>
> Each saleroom should be arranged in the form of a half circle
> with high, graduated benches, permitting a full view of and free
> access to the articles on show. There should also be a certain num-
> ber of paid seats at the disposal of genuine collectors, arranged near
> the auctioneer's pulpit, giving perfect freedom for the movements
> of the porters, the criers, and the expert, and thus avoiding the
> crowding of the store rooms with the fearful mob of curious folk,
> hustled hither and thither by the fierce elbowings of the attendants,
> as at present.
>
> I would also suggest, as a further facility for action in the auction

Frontage of the auction rooms at the corner of rue Drouot and rue Rossini in about 1852.
Photo courtesy Bibliotheque Nationale Paris

rooms of the future, the employment of a corps of small, sharp boys, going and coming, carrying the cards and payments of the buyers, and making themselves useful for all kinds of communications between the auctioneer and the 'room', passing round small articles, collecting deposits, guarding seats temporarily vacated, handing catalogues to those who need them; helping, in short, the outside public to compete on equal terms without mortification with the rascality of the 'Black Gang'.

The auction rooms in this ideal 'Hotel des Ventes' should, on the occasion of great sales, be opened on several successive days and evenings, arranged like a picture gallery, with chairs and benches, thus providing Paris with a veritable museum of decorative art, constantly renewed, giving amateurs and critics opportunities for a quiet view, far from the crowds in the other rooms where auctions are going on.

Sales by order of the Court, and all the wretched outcast lumber of the 'Mazas' of to-day, should be isolated in separate out-houses, where people could gather in clean rooms, carefully disinfected each day and purged of the microbes emanating from the previous day's rubbish.

Finally, since I am sketching a programme which is never likely to be adopted, I would ask that in the centre of the new 'Hotel des Ventes' there should be a glass-covered court-yard for the conveyances of the visitors, lavatories, a station for messengers, a poste restante, and a telegraph and telephone office, a writing and refreshment room, and, in a word, all that constitutes the art of living without fatigue, and all that is demanded in a place where one stays awhile and gets ruined, and excited and soiled, and jostled and heated; where people experience, in short, as many sensations as are provided by the vast halls of Monte Carlo, and sometimes as many mortifications as are to be met in the busiest gambling saloons.

Such are the reforms I would fain hope for, nay, which I would implore; reforms dictated by the most ordinary common sense, in spite of the parsimony and the routine of the gentlemen who wield the hammer. But this cry of distress will remain unheeded, and the art lover in Paris will, for a long time yet, have to put up with the insalubrity and the misery of the Hotel Drouot.

Uzanne's closing words were to prove more prophetic than even he could have imagined. The grimy old Hotel Drouot was to remain in the condition that he had so vociferously deplored for the better part

---

An art sale at the Hotel Drouot from a drawing by Gustave Dore. Photo courtesy Bibliotheque Nationale Paris

of the century just begun. Uzanne's words were written in 1902; had his plea for a modern showpiece auction building been heeded then, Paris might have been able to compete on more favourable terms with London in the coming battle for the title 'art capital of the world', a battle in which the auction rooms were to play so significant a part.

CHAPTER 5

The 19th Century Auction Wars in the United States and England

The notoriety achieved by the slave auctions of Southern America has caused them, in historical terms, to be regarded as the dominant feature of auctioneering activity in nineteenth-century America. There is no doubt, as we have already discovered, that the period of slavery was an important though nasty chapter in American history, and its influence should not be minimised. It must be understood, however, that much else was going on in the field of auction, in America, at the same time; and that one event in particular, taking place in the first quarter of the nineteenth century, did not achieve the wide publicity that it might have done because of the dominant slave trade interest. This event, lasting from the end of the war of 1812–14 until about 1830, was itself a kind of war—an auction war waged by the domestic traders on the one hand and the importers and auctioneers on the other.

The war with England which lasted from 1812 to 1814 was itself overshadowed by Napoleon's simultaneous and more spectacular exploits in Europe. The British merchants, never slow to seize an opportunity, saw in this rash of conflict an equally spectacular prospect for future trade. A number of factors were once again about to conspire to the advantage of British commercial interests, and once again the auction system was to be a major beneficiary.

A principal factor in this new equation was that while Britain and France were dominant in sea power and therefore trading power, it was the British who had through the revolution in industry concentrated on the manufacture of cheap goods for the mass markets. This was in sharp contrast to the French manufacturers, who continued to incline towards the production of luxury items, and the French anyway were heavily involved in factor number two, the Napoleonic Wars. France's problems and Britain's industrial production gave the British merchants a unique advantage in world trade, and those

merchants were shrewd enough to have observed a third factor which
was to enable them to press that advantage home.

The American government, prior to and during the war of 1812–
14, had pursued a policy of restriction which amounted to a blockade
in reverse. American ships were discouraged from entering European
ports and this policy effectively shut off a large part of the foreign
supply. The consequent deprivations brought about a strong demand
for goods in America, and in particular the kind of mass produced
consumer goods which the British had in plenty. In anticipation of a
major trading coup the British merchants set up well stocked depots
in the British possessions nearest to America such as Halifax and
Bermuda, and quietly awaited the cessation of hostilities. They also
observed, while waiting, that when prizes were taken at sea during
the conflict there had grown up a practice of selling the cargoes by
auction for speedy disposal. These large sales and the high prices
obtained attracted the attention of buyers and sellers alike, and gave
them the habit of attending public sales.

As one war ended the other immediately began as the British traders
pounced on their prey, determined to squeeze the last dollar from the
opportunity. They chose the auction as the quickest and most convenient method of sale, and the choice was more than justified by a
report in the 'Review of the Trade and Commerce of New York'
which declared that a British merchant or manufacturer by selling his
goods at auction could sell three times as much as could the American
importer, and at no greater expense.

Thus the battle lines were drawn, and although the real complaint
of the domestic merchant was against the large scale dumping of
cheap British goods on to the American market, it was in fact against
the auctioneers that this venomous campaign was directed. The main
reason for attacking the auctioneers was, of course, that it was the
speed of the auction system which allowed the foreign importers to
overwhelm the domestic trade, but there may have been a secondary
but largely unspoken reason which lent weight to the protests. Many
Northern Americans were far from being proud of what was happening in the South, and as early as 1808 a federal statute had banned
the importation of slaves from Africa. Certainly by 1818, when the
penal clauses of the legislation were strengthened, the primary slave
market had virtually ceased to exist. We know only too well, however,
that the domestic slave trade, sponsored by the breeding States, was
to continue and to grow for half a century yet. The Northern Americans were well aware of this, as they were aware of the fact that
much of the slave dealing was conducted by the auction method. It
might well have been a disquiet with what was happening in their
own country in the name of commercial progress that helped to direct
so much anger towards the alien importers who acquired wealth with

such apparent ease, and yet used the same auction system which brought their own countrymen into such disrepute.

The opponents of the auctioneers claimed that goods bought at sales in the coastal towns were transferred to the interior by itinerant dealers and offered for sale by auction day after day and even night after night in rooms adjoining the local retail stores. It was argued that these operations tended to disrupt and destroy the local retail trade as well as disturbing the regularity and dependability of commerce and industry generally, and that as a result prices fluctuated wildly and speculation was fostered.

The quality of the goods sold by auction was also the subject of much discussion, and it was alleged that inferior merchandise was being injected into the market by the auctioneers. It is certainly true that the Industrial Revolution was making cheap, mass produced goods available to everyone, and that the demand for these goods meant that the established trade channels in the prime markets such as America simply could not cope with the new burden of distribution. A completely new market structure was required, old methods and traditions had to be revised, and the auction facilitated this change of custom by breaking rigid trade channels and creating new outlets. The enemies of the system attempted to resist these changes by claiming that the auctioneers were corrupt, and that much of the merchandise offered for sale was of an inferior quality specially made for the auction.

The first phase of the anti-auction movement in America was to last until 1824, and one of the methods used against the auctioneers was the boycott. Unfortunately, like so many boycotts both before and since, the tactic was not spectacularly successful, to say the least. In fact the United Dry Goods Association of New York demonstrated in 1821 the virtual impossibility of persuading all the members of just one organisation to observe a boycott on an aspect of trade which was of undoubted benefit to many of them. The association, after unanimously adopting a resolution to boycott the auctioneers, discovered that in practice very few of its members respected the instruction, and quickly repealed the resolution to save face.

Similar boycott attempts were also unsuccessful, as were all efforts to legislate against the auctioneers. More than one attempt was made to introduce legislation, and in 1824 a bill was twice read but not acted upon. Between 1825 and 1827 activity subsided and interest waned; it was, however, to be merely the calm before yet another storm.

1828 saw a flood of petitions to Congress from widely scattered towns and cities, all complaining bitterly about the alleged outrages committed by the auctioneers. It might have seemed at first glance that the allegations were well founded in view of the wide and apparently unconnected geographical spread of the complainants, but in fact on close examination it becomes clear that there was a good deal of orchestration involved, and from more than one source.

One of the principal conductors in what turned out to be an extremely well orchestrated campaign against the auctioneers was Henry Niles, who took over an established trade journal of the period—the Weekly Register—and made it his own to such effect that it became *Niles Weekly Register*. The journal became the main organ of the anti-auction movement and Niles regularly attacked the auctioneers as part of his general policy of supporting domestic industry and trade. His general attitude may be judged from his comments in the edition of the 12th of April, 1828, when he described the auction as:

> The grand machine by which British agents at once destroy all regularity in the business of American merchants and manufacturers. It is probable that at least four fifths of the late and present excessive importations of British goods are on British account— these are forced on the consumption by the auctions.

On the 2nd of May in the same year an anti-auction meeting held in New York appointed several committees to help promote the movement's aims, and it was the 'correspondence committee' formed at that meeting which was largely responsible for organising the petitions to Congress.

Another committee appointed by the meeting occupied itself with setting down the arguments against auctions, with the result that before the year was out it had published a lengthy pamphlet entitled *Reasons why the Present System of Auction ought to be Abolished*. The pamphlet went into some detail regarding the evils of the auction system and listed nineteen principal arguments which may be summarised as follows:

1. Auctions are a monopoly; and, like all monopolies are unjust, by giving to a few, that which ought to be distributed among the mercantile community generally. A single auction house might do as much business as would support fifty respectable firms in private trade, each consisting of two partners, maintaining two families, and two or three clerks.
2. The commission under which an auctioneer acts is believed to be unconstitutional. It never could be intended that the business of selling goods, which is the occupation of a merchant, should be confined to a few individuals, to the exclusion of all others.
3. Auctions tend to concentrate the whole trade of the country in a few large cities, to the extinction of all other wholesale markets. And, even in these cities, the advantage is nearly confined to the auctioneers themselves.

4. Auctions are destructive to domestic manufacturers who have acted under a great and dangerous mistake, in ascribing their difficulties to foreign competition.

5. Auctions have been destructive to the regular American importers, of whom we must now speak in the past tense, as nearly all of that most respectable body have, as is well known, been driven from their occupation.

6. Auctions injure consumers generally, by enhancing prices. It is a great error to suppose that goods are sold cheaper at auction than at private sale. The principal buyers in New-York have been consulted, and they affirm, with one accord, that they purchase, on an average of one year, cheaper at private than at public sale. ... Both foreign and domestic manufacturers prepare, on purpose for auctions, goods defective in every respect—in length, width, quality, colour, and pattern; which no reputable house would venture to import, and to offer at private sale—and which would be dear at any price. Our country has, in consequence, become the great mart for the old stocks, and refuse fabrics, of England, France, Germany, and other parts of the world where unsaleable goods accumulate. Even when a fraud is occasionally discovered—the owner is generally kept out of view—the auctioneer is not responsible—some compromise is quietly submitted to—or wholly refused on some technical informality, and all exposure of the guilty party is prevented.

7. Three or four States, by imposing a duty on sales at auction, make all other States tributary to them, in direct violation of their rights of sovereignty.

8. Auctions give dangerous facilities for the sale of contraband goods. The Chancellor of the Exchequer in England, not long since, stated in Parliament that, notwithstanding the army of custom-house officers and soldiers, and the fleet of armed vessels .... prohibited articles could be easily introduced from the continent at an expense of only fifteen per cent including a guarantee of their safe delivery   In this country then, how easy it must be, to bring in any quantity of foreign manufactures ... They can be instantly sold by public sale, and the mantle of oblivion covers the whole, as it is a well known part of every auctioneers business to conceal the name of those who employ him.

9. Auctions have been found, by the experience of other countries, to be pernicious to internal trade.

10. Auctions, by creating an unnatural competition, unconnected with the want of the market, cause more goods to be sold than ought to be, or than otherwise would be sold.

11. Auctions produce all the pernicious effects of gambling.
12. Auctions facilitate fraudulant bankruptcies.
13. By means of auctions any rash or embarrassed individual may, by sacrificing at public sale a quantity of any article beyond what the demand requires, destroy all regular sales of that article for many months.
14. Auctions have introduced an extraordinary system of injustice in the appropriation of the funds of insolvent debtors.
15. Auctioneers form a moneyed aristocracy influencing the banks.
16. Auctions produce, from their very nature, the gross fraud of fictitious bidding.
17. Auctions sell more goods than they advertise beforehand.
18. By indulging in exaggerated description, auctions tend to destroy a regard for the truth.
19. All of the foregoing results in the deterioration of the morals of mercantile men.

In another pamphlet, published at about the same time and entitled *Remarks upon the Auction System, as Practised in New York,* the author claimed to quote specific examples of auction malpractice.

At what are called piece or shelf sales, which form nine-tenths of auction sales,—one minute or even less, and scarcely ever so much as two minutes, is all the time usually allowed to a large company of perhaps two hundred buyers, to examine, in the twilight of an auction store, amidst noise and confusion, goods which they never saw before. The worse the goods—the shorter will probably be the time given.

It was not by any means, however, a one-sided conflict. An examination of the complaints against the auctioneers by Congress produced an 'Auctioneers Memorial'—a strong statement in support of the honesty and honour of the auctioneers. That statement remains a matter of record in the Annals of the Congress of the United States.

Your memorialists are engaged in an extensive business, whose general influence upon other branches of trade has of late become a subject of much controversy. Your honorable bodies were, at your last session, petitioned, by those who consider the interests of commerce as unfavorably affected by the great extent of auction sales, to adopt such restrictive measures as would tend to limit or suppress them ... Your memorialists respectfully request the indulgent attention of your honorable bodies to a brief exposition of the general nature of their business, and of their manner of conducting it; and to the correctness of their representations they pledge their individual and collective respectability. Your honorable bodies will perceive, from the detail of their general practice, that there is nothing to warrant the charges of fraud and deception which have been urged against sales at auction, and that, in yielding to popular impressions derived from the objectionable mode of conducting the business which formerly prevailed, the opponents of the trade must have overlooked its actual importance and respectability...

... The auctioneer is not only legally and by common practice responsible for the correctness of his merchandise, but it is deemed a point of honor and of common justice to expose every art by which the interests of the purchaser would be sacrificed; and it is no uncommon thing for the buyer to acquire the first information of fraud from the auctioneer himself. The security to the purchaser is, however, necessarily subject to limitation; and public notice is always given that claims of all kinds must be made within a specified period. Immediate redress is obtained for deficiences and damages reported within that time. ...

... Ample time is given during the sale to examine accurately every article as it is offered; and the purchaser, in every respect, is secured against error and imposition, by an open and unlimited display of the merchandise, and by the public proclamation of every circumstance known to the auctioneer which may tend to enhance or depreciate its value ... The dressing, the glazing, and decorations employed in the preparation of inferior British manufactures for this and other markets are so notorious that they do not deceive the most inexperienced....

It is objected against auction sales that they have produced a revolution in the commerce of the country, and originated the difficulties which it is said now oppress it. Your memorialists would respectfully urge that the decline of business may be attributed to more probable and evident causes than the extension of auction sales which has, in fact, resulted from the same circumstances that produced the decline in our commercial prosperity, and has tended greatly to relieve the general distress....

From these considerations, your memorialists respectfully remonstrate against the imposition of legislative restrictions upon a business whose advantages have been carefully thrown into the shade, while none but groundless objections have been urged against it. Public sales, in their general character, are no longer the resort of the necessitous, who are compelled to the sacrifice of property by the pressure of distress. Buyer and seller now meet on neutral ground for their mutual advantage; auctions are employed as the most secure and convenient medium for the sale and purchase of merchandise at the current market rates; and any addition to the present charges, however trifling, so far from being a productive source of public revenue, would force the business into another channel, introduce the practice of selling inconsiderable samples at auction, by which the prices of large parcels at private sale would be regulated, encourage frauds on the revenue, and operate directly as a tax upon the yeomanry of the country.

As well as this stern rebuke from the auctioneers and their supporters, most of the nineteen arguments of the original pamphlet were answered in a counter production with the lengthy title—*An Examination of the Reasons why the Present System of Auctions ought to be Abolished: as set forth by the Committee of New York Merchants opposed to the Auction System.* These papers were originally published in the *Boston Daily Advertiser* in 1828.
On the question of the auction being a monopoly:

> The answer which a friend to the auction system might make, would be, that in this quarter auctioneering is not a monopoly, and that a licence may be obtained for a small sum by any man who can give a reasonable security for the payment of the State duty.

On the statement that a single auction house does as much business as would support fifty private firms:

> We imagine this is somewhat exaggerated, but it matters not whether it is or otherwise. It no doubt affords a good reason why commission merchants and dealers should wish to get rid of auctions, but at the same time it is one of the strongest arguments which can be urged in their favour, because it shows what a saving of labour and expense auctions occasion ... in the former case only some two or three families would require support from the profits, while in the latter, the profits must be high enough to support one hundred families, two or three hundred clerks, and some three or four hundred apprentices and labourers.

As far as crushing the middle ranks by dividing the population into very rich and very poor is concerned:

> We do not perceive there is any evidence that such is likely to be the result of the existing system of auctions. We happen to have some knowledge of the situation of most of the principal auctioneers here, in New York, and in Philadelphia, and we doubt if there have been twenty fortunes acquired by that business for the last twenty years.

As to the merchants believing auctions to be unconstitutional:

> If they are correct in this opinion, then the efforts of the auction opponents should be to make this infraction of the National Constitution known, and their object would be at once accomplished, without any further trouble.

On the matter of auctions tending to concentrate the whole trade of the country in a few cities:

> The Great New York Canal, the River Hudson, and all the other natural and artificial conveyances to New York city, have the like tendency, and the good people of Philadelphia, and perhaps even the Bostonians, would gladly see them all choked up, and would not find it impossible to bring forward arguments to shew that it might be a national benefit to have that operation performed, but the difficulty would lie in bringing over the New Yorker and the nation at large, to their opinions.

As to the charge that auctions are destructive to domestic manufacturers:

> It appears, however, the manufacturers are not of this opinion, since they sell a very considerable portion of their goods by auction.

On the matter of auctions injuring consumers generally, by enhancing prices:

> With regard to the consumers, then, it would be just as foolish and impolite to do away with auctions, as it would to banish the power loom, because, by the labour it saves, the hand weavers are undersold in their manufactures ... But if we admit that the consumers pay more for their goods at auction, than they would at private sale, it is no concern of those who complain of auctions, nor of the legislature which is called upon to suppress them. We contend, that in this free and happy republic, every man has a right to be ruined in his own way.

As for the auctions and the auctioneers producing gross frauds:

> That there are frauds, and gross ones too, practised by auctioneers, no one would pretend to doubt—but is a class of men to be run down in their occupation, and have their characters blasted, because some of them commit frauds ... We say then, we are ready to admit, that there are amongst auctioneers, as well as other trading classes, dishonest men, who practise frauds upon the unwary and unsuspecting; but these are crimes too often beyond the province or the power of law or legislation. The only certain remedy, is for the honest to refrain from dealing with the dishonest, and with regard to auctioneers, this corrective is so generally applied, that there are very few instances of their prospering to any great degree and for a long period.

As a general conclusion to this defence of the auction system:

> We say then, if the charges alleged by the committee against auctions and auctioneers, can be sustained, they will attach more

closely to the mercantile community who have employed them, than the auctioneers themselves; nay, the government itself is involved in the same guilt, since much of the national business is transacted in a similar way; but of all the various classes who have resorted to this convenient mode of selling, we apprehend none have furnished more employment to auctions, than the men now leagued for their destruction ... As then, we neither admit the correctness of the statements of the committee, nor the conclusions to which they would lead, if they were true—we consider the real question at issue to be not whether the auctioneers are injurious to the nation—but whether the mercantile community shall be restrained from purchasing and selling in a mode which they have found from long experience to be convenient to themselves and beneficial to the public, in order that the goods now sold by auctioneers, may be disposed of by jobbers and commission agents, at fifty times the expense—according to the committee—but as we should say, ten times the additional expense to the consumers, than is now incurred at auction.

The anti-auction committee of the New York merchants met again on the 7th of May, 1829, almost a year to the day after its original meeting. Mr Jonathan Steele read a lengthy report on the year's activities including the publication of the 'Reasons why' pamphlet, which, it was claimed, had produced a 'powerful effect on all classes'. He went on:

Our next step was to open a correspondence with the most respectable merchants in almost every town of any size in the United States. This part of our duty was extremely laborious; but the result was most gratifying. We found that the whole country was with us. Not one of our numerous correspondents defended auctions, or doubted the justice of our cause; and assurances of co-operation were received from all quarters.

Assurances it seems were not enough, for the report went on to describe in some detail the movement's attempts to obtain political influence, even to the extent of nominating their own candidates for Congress; men of 'high and independent character'.

Independence was not enough, either, for not one of the candidates was elected, although, to quote the report again:

We are proud to publish to our constituents, that, in the first, second, third, fourth, and fifth wards of this city, where the commercial and trading classes principally reside, the anti-auction candidates had a great preponderance. They polled 14,655 votes, while our opponents polled only 13,966. But this majority was neutralized by those, who, to save the labor of thinking, follow implicitly the direction of their leaders, and vote as they are commanded.

In the end of course they lost fairly substantially, but such was the strength of feeling within the movement that Congress continued to be deluged with petitions calling for the abolition of the auctions. A delegation of the New York merchants proceeded to Washington to press the interests of the movement, and there joined similar groups from Norfolk, Philadelphia, Alexandria and Baltimore, all 'zealous in the same pursuit'. In January, 1829, as a result of the pressure brought by these delegations, the Committee of Ways and Means presented a bill designed to give security to the merchants. The chairman of the committee, however, stated that in his opinion the regulation of auction frauds was a matter for State legislation. He said:

> If, however, sales at auction are the means by which frauds are committed upon the revenue, and if they enable foreigners to enter their goods at the custom house at lower rates than the same quality and description of goods are habitually entered by American merchants, there can scarcely be a question, either as to the power or the duty of congress to interpose its authority . . . . a tax upon sales at auction would neither prevent the alleged frauds upon the revenue, nor the alleged advantages enjoyed by the foreigners, unless it should amount to a prohibition; and, even in that case it would be of doubtful efficacy.

In a short session, and with a new President about to be installed, Congress steered away from the controversial issues, and the bill was not acted upon.

In the conclusion to its first annual report the anti-auction committee gave an indication of the progress made by the movement in the preceding year. It would seem to have been little in real terms despite much effort and no small expense. The final words of the report reflected the lack of progress and predicted that without a change of policy the future of the merchants and manufacturers was bleak.

> Since our association was formed, the evils of auction have materially increased, and are now more seriously felt than at any former period. While the other great markets around us have enjoyed a prosperous trade since the beginning of the present year, we have been idle; the auction rooms have been, and are now, crowded at all hours, while the private trade stores are empty. Unless we shall prevail with congress to regulate auctions effectually, our future course is down hill, and the goal is not far off . . . It will require but a few years longer to force men of capital out of the trade; and to elevate to permanent and unbridled dom-

inion a few auctioneers, before whom every retailer and manufacturer must tremble and obey.

The anti-auction movement was to reach its peak during 1829. The
hope that the new session of Congress would at last produce the
legislation considered necessary was encouraged by the success of the
New York Workingmen's Party, which had a member elected to the
State Assembly on the basis of a prospectus which included opposing
auctions on the grounds of monopoly. The Workingmen's Party was
not specifically an anti-auction party. It had stated as just one argument in its election campaign an opposition to monopolies in general,
including banks and auctions, but flushed with a first electoral success
it proceeded to press vigorously all the arguments used to achieve that
success, including some stern resolutions regarding auctions.

> Resolved: That the present auction system, which operates as a
> means of oppressing the producing classes, by introducing large
> quantities of the products of labor of foreign countries, which other-
> wise would be furnished by our own mechanics, is fraught with
> alarming evils, and should be immediately restricted.
> Resolved: That this system is most decidedly injurious to the
> mechanics interest of this city, compelling them in many cases, to
> abandon their business or dishonestly manufacture very inferior
> goods for the competition of the auction room.

Henry Niles joined in the general assault on the reputation of the
auctioneers, and the *Weekly Register* carried many items designed to
encourage the movement and to put pressure on Congress.

> The 'auction system' as prosecuted by the enemies of the American
> system, British agents and others, is a most powerful obstacle to
> home industry and honest trade, and we are happy to discover that
> it has excited the attention of the merchants, not only of the prin-
> cipal cities, but in many of the larger towns, from whose prompt
> and energetic measures a hope may be cherished, that congress
> will, at its next session, place this detestable system of chicanery
> and fraud, under such restrictions as will do away its effects.

The new pressures persuaded the Ways and Means Committee in
Congress to bring forward a new bill, the 'Ingersoll' bill, in an attempt
to restrict the auctioneers. In the event it was to be the anti-auction
movement's last chance, for when this bill failed, so did the movement
as a whole, and although the campaign continued on and off for
another decade it was not to have so much influence again. The 1830s
were to be a prosperous period in America and sufficient business was
generated to allow the merchants to survive comfortably alongside the
auctioneers. This no doubt softened the blow of the failure of their
campaign. It was commonly supposed by the merchants involved in

this auction 'war', that America, as the prime developing market of the period, was the major victim of the European industrialised countries, who were all anxious to dump their surplus merchandise on any available market. Some even believed that the auction was a device invented by the foreign invaders, aimed at speeding the process of foreign market domination at the expense of the domestic merchants—a kind of commercial colonisation.

The assumption, therefore, was that the anti-auction feeling that raged throughout Northern America was unique to that part of the world, and was not encountered in other, particularly European, parts. It was in fact stated during the course of the American campaign that the foreign importers, as virtual proprietors of the iniquitous auction system, did not suffer in their home countries the sort of domestic deprivations inflicted upon the American merchants.

That assumption was in fact untrue. There is evidence of considerable anti-auction activity in London, and the evidence shows that it was at its height in the period up to 1812, before the American movement was under way. Such evidence of anti-auction feeling in more than one country might well appear significant to the researcher casting about for the root cause of a general antagonism towards the auctioneers. With the movement confined to America, and given the economic and social conditions and relationships of the period, it is possible to make a case for the wrath of the domestic merchants being simply a matter of sour grapes due to the efficient business practices of the importers, principally the British. The realisation that a similar movement was afoot in England, and before the British traders so efficiently promoted the auction in America, could lead to a more careful consideration of the arguments proposed by the opponents of the auction in both England and America—chiefly that the auctioneers were basically corrupt.

In 1812, in London, a pamphlet was published whose author was in no doubt that such was indeed the case. In common with so many other publications of the period, the pamphlet had a title which was in effect a synopsis of the text. It was called *The Ruinous Tendency of Auctioneering and the Necessity of Restraining it for the Benefit of Trade commonly called in a Letter to the Right Honourable Lord Bathurst, President of the Board of Trade.* Many of the general complaints against auctions and auctioneers which are contained in this pamphlet are the same as those which were to be brought by the organisers of the later American anti-auction movement. The English merchants also blamed the auctioneers for poor business in the retail trades, and for much more besides. The pamphlet began:

The partial stagnation of many branches of trade, which, at this season of the year are usually most flourishing, is attributable to a

variety of events; one of those branches in which very many tradesmen and mechanics are about this period more particularly busy,
is entirely at a standstill, and this arises not so much from causes
which might be expected to operate generally and equally upon all
classes, such as the revolutions abroad, and the chartist demonstra-
tions at home, as from the crafty conduct of a body of men formerly
under a little wholesome restraint, but from whom unfortunately
all restrictions since the free trade system, or alterations of the tariff,
has been recently withdrawn, to the serious injury of shopkeepers
of that particular class to which I last allude, and also to the injury
of the revenue in more ways than one. I mean that irresponsible
body of men called 'Auctioneers', who know no laws or restrictions
in their mode of business, but such as they themselves think proper
to impose by their arbitrary Conditions of Sale ... the buyer who
finds himself taken in at a 'Rigg Sale', has therefore no redress, he
cannot return a damaged article, as he might do, at the regular
shopkeepers, "it being sold subject to all faults and errors of description" and these faults in many instances he is prevented from
discovering until too late, the defective article seldom being on view
for the inspection of the public until just before the sale commences.
But the buyer is not the only one injured by their mode of doing
business, the tradesmen whose too frequent want of trade arises
from the contemptible meanness of 'bargain hunting' noblemen
and gentlemen, and is too often compelled to send his goods to an
auction room, to meet his engagements, is also a sufferer by the
malpractices of the gentlemen of the rostrum, and seldom, if ever,
obtains a fair price for his articles, how should he, when a sale is
made up, not as it ought to be, of goods sent in for absolute and
bona fide sale, but of property belonging to the auctioneer, either
purchased at a low price of the man who wants money, or manu-
factured expressly for such kind of sales.

Having informed us that the auctioneers are taking business away
from the shopkeepers by virtue of their more entertaining and addic-
tive, as well as more efficient, method of sale, the writer moves on to
another subject which was to become a favourite of the American
movement; that of imperfect merchandise being offered for sale, and
with insufficient time allowed to view and judge the quality, or lack
of it. He goes on:

An auctioneer has no occasion to attend his room above two days
in a week, in which he suits his own convenience; he simply issues
his mandate, to tell his customers when he permits them to attend
him; and they obey his call with a degree of obsequiousness that
allows him to do as much business in three hours as the majority

of shopkeepers do in a week; there is no indulgence shewn to the fastidious; no leisure for picking and choosing; should any person there evince a desire to search after defects, he is told that he should have attended at another time. Now, in viewing goods, as it is called, the auctioneer keeps nobody to assist his customers in the examination; they must carry with them all the judgement necessary to a good tradesman, and be aware of all the arts used to conceal defects; and if by extraordinary diligence and perseverence half a dozen persons happen to discover the imperfections of any article, the auctioneer cares little about it, for the time that they have held it under examination has kept it out of the hand of a seventh, who, in his ignorance, buys upon the puffing recommendations of the juggler in chief.

As the document progresses it becomes bolder. The general criticism of the auctioneers becomes more particular as the writer mentions certain contemporary salerooms and quotes what are claimed to be specific instances of deceptions of various kinds. These references are of particular interest because both Christie's and Sotheby's get a mention. First Sotheby's:

Ruinous as this system is to trade, it is perhaps not so mischievous in that point of view, as for the grudging and groveling spirit that it engenders in that portion of society which ought to be above illiberality and meanness. What progress can we make in the work of civilisation, when we see a clergyman, a barrister, or a physician, truckling among a parcel of 'low fellows' at Squibbs's, Robins's, or Leigh and Sotheby's, for permission to get a fortunate nod at the Auctioneer, that is to enable him to save a few shillings in the purchase of his trinkets or books?

The writer distinguishes this pamphlet from others of this and the later period of anti-auction feeling by citing instances of alleged saleroom malpractice as support for his general criticisms. His mention by name of certain auction rooms does not lay any specific charge against them individually, but the context of the quotations gives an indication of the author's opinion. For example, in the critical passage quoted above he clearly feels that the premises of the three auctioneers named—all well-known salerooms of the period—were not fit places for the professional classes. On the other hand, he speaks highly of 'the late Mr Christie' in his account of the case of the 'capital clock' which follows. Considering that the pamphlet is wholly and violently auti-auction; what amounts to more than a word of praise for even a 'late' member of the fraternity would appear to be significant. The piece is concerned with inadequate viewing facilities, Conditions of Sale and to some extent the condition of the customers.

It will scarcely be out of the rememberance of many of the trade that a large handsome-looking clock was placed so high in one of our first-rate rooms, that it was impossible for any one to examine it without getting a pair of steps or a ladder to do so. A gentleman who happened to see it for the first time, a few minutes before the sale, was struck by the outside appearance, and gave a commission to a broker to buy it for him—now as the lot was not taken down whilst being sold, and as the description ran "A capital clock in case, in the style of Louis XIV"; it was bought as such. What was the surprise of the broker, when he found that it was only "outside visible show" without any "good works" or, in fact, any works whatever. And what will the reader think when he is told that the lot was left on the commissioners hands by his employer and the only redress he (the commissioner) obtained was a reference to the 'Conditions of Sale', viz.:—'Lots to be Taken Away with all Faults and Errors of Description', &c., and so much do the auctioneers rely upon their power, that I have known an auctioneer, as agent, bring an action to recover the amount of purchases at a sale, although he had not delivered the goods;—it may not be very creditable to the auctioneer to add that the purchaser who was too fond of grog, and was then already 'far gone', had just before the commencement of the sale been supplied by the knight of the hammer with a very 'stiff glass' or two of gin and water, in fact he was drunk, and his biddings should not have been taken. The late Mr Christie, who for distinction sake I shall call 'Gentleman Christie', upon a similar occasion, in his mild and amiable manner (when comes such another?) once told his porters that 'he was sure the gentleman was very ill', and begged of them to take him out of the room, and give him every attendance.

Not all the text references are so direct, and the writer obviously had one eye on the libel laws when disclosing the more sensational of the alleged malpractices. He does claim however to be able to produce the evidence, if required, for a long string of 'offences' such as operating a 'ring', defrauding the revenue, signing famous names on paintings, and making up sales of job lots and advertising them as the property of some deceased person. In almost every case his assertion is that the public at large are mere pawns in a game where the unscrupulous auctioneer is king.

Can it be regretted, that men who are for ever hunting for bargains, are for ever being cheated, and is it at all surprising that men should be so blinded by great names, (as has so recently been the case at Stowe) that they will give, for vile imitations, modern copies, and newly made up articles of art, more than originals might be bought for in a shop?—take a few examples:—

LOT
  46 Mary Queen of Scots, a palpable recent fabrication, 54 gs.—
     Lord Spencer
  55 Mary Queen of Scots; and Lord Darnley, two portraits, man-
     ufactured upon the portraits of Some Dutchman and his Vrow.
     (Lord Darnley with a profusion of beard) 60 gs.—Earl Spencer
 141 Print of the Duke of Buckingham, by Cooper, can be bought
     for 7 s. in a shop-$5\frac{1}{2}$ gs.

Obviously some of the claims made are exaggerated, but we know
that the auction was extremely popular in the first quarter of the
nineteenth century, and it is undoubtably true that many salerooms
had opened their doors expressly to cash in on the auction boom. It
is also likely in the circumstances that there were not enough genuine
goods available to keep all the auctioneers fully employed, and therefore inevitable that spurious items, particularly works of art, should
find their way on to the market. The pamphlet had a warning or two
for the unwary:

WEEKLY SALES—There are weekly sales now, in all parts of
London. These sales are principally made up by Jew brokers, who
attend what are called the 'out-door sales', in, and near the metro-
polis, and it is very rarely that genuine goods are introduced. Persons should be particularly cautious in attending these rooms, for
should the auctioneers not be the principal holder or proprietor,
the real proprietors are in the room, and they will take care that
the lots do not go under their full value, taking into consideration
that they are chiefly second-hand goods vamped up for the occasion
... Some of the auctioneers of the present day, will buy a house
full of furniture as it stands, get up a sale, put in wine, or any
article that they please, and sell the whole off as the genuine property of the recent proprietor, dead, or gone abroad. Last year Lord
Abergavenny's name, together with Sir Charles Weatherell's, were
both used to get up a rigg-sale in Berkeley Square, (Entrance in
Mount Street,) the whole of which was the property of a dealer
except a few articles of furniture that were in the house when Lord
Abergavenny died, but the auctioneer only put 'to be sold at the
residence of the late Sir Charles Weatherell'. Who we ask among
the discerning public would detect so artfully contrived a fraud?
Not three years ago, a similar sale was advertised, as property
removed from Barnards Castle, a few pots and pans, some culinary
articles, and refuse furniture, may have been the turns out of the
Elizabethan abode, but the major part of the curiosities, pictures
&c., were the property of a descendant of Moses, who with 'his
people', bid manfully against any chance buyer...

> ... And we do not hesitate to say, that since these men have troubled our city, there have been so many tricks played—such as altering names on pictures, making Shakespeare's, Elizabeth's, Cromwell's, out of other portraits, getting fictitious documents to bolster up a copy of a Raffaelle, or a Titian; ingeniously contriving some non-descript bronze; making casts of the old matrixes, and pretending they are dug up, and so very many other tricks, that it is not much to be wondered at that the more sensible sort of the higher classes become disgusted, and may consider that every tradesman is a scoundrel...
>
> ... The sales held at the mart, the Sheriff's sale rooms, and the Cosmorama of Pictures and Wines, &c., require so much space and time to describe truly, that we must unwillingly leave them for our History of the Tricks and Frauds of Auctioneers.

Tricks and frauds aside, however, it was not considered prudent to beard the lion in his den. In early nineteenth century London all manner of misfortune might await he who was so bold; better to fire a salvo from behind the anonymous pen, discretion being the better part of valour at almost any time.

> Any one who ventures to find fault in the auction room, during the sale, with the manner in which he has been drawn from his home many miles by means of delusive advertisements, runs the risk of being given in charge for interrupting the sale. Within this last month a wretched rigg-sale was got up by an auctioneer at Turnham Green, who gave no address—and another at the house of the late Mrs ——, near Ponders End—at the latter one, much dissatisfaction was displayed at the whole proceedings by the Trade, and one man was threatened to be locked up for complaining publicly of the imposition. One auctioneer once threw a Jew down his stairs, another turned one out, and was held to bail for the assault,—several of them have shown a pugnacious feeling towards such persons as tried to expose the deceptions about to be practised. Not many day since a man was perambulating backwards and forwards, before the Hall of Commerce, having a large placard and distributing bills cautioning the public against a mock auction about to be held there, and openly stating to what auctioneer the goods advertised belonged—but he soon disappeared, and the sale took place notwithstanding.

Like the man with the placard, the opposition of the anti-auction movement soon disappeared, and the sales went on notwithstanding. In both the English and American campaigns similar criticisms had been raised against the auctioneers, and serious charges of fraud and misrepresentation brought. In each case the high point of the anti-auction activity coincided with a period of general recession in business, and the domestic merchants were quick to blame the new popularity of the auctions for the poor trade. No doubt the auctions aggravated the problems of the merchants in a bleak business climate, and no doubt the merchants over-reacted somewhat with their campaign; but what of the charges of corruption. There would seem to be little doubt that many of the claims made against at least some of the auctioneers were justified. It is almost certainly true that exaggerated descriptions of merchandise were published, that gullible clients paid too much for their goods, that spurious items were 'got up' for sale, paintings were falsely signed and house sales rigged. It is also true that the auctioneers were allowed to shelter behind conditions of sale drawn up by themselves for their own convenience.

A deplorable state of affairs indeed—but reflect on this. Things now are almost precisely the same as then, with the exception of a small amount of legislation which is almost impossible to enforce, and there is little, if any, control over auctions. In fact similar criticisms of the system are quite regularly voiced, and then disappear, and the sales go on notwithstanding.

CHAPTER 6

Sotheby's and Christie's—
1745-1900

Indisputably the two greatest auction houses in the world are Christie, Manson & Woods of St James's, and Sotheby Parke Bernet & Co of New Bond Street, both founded and based in London. The way in which each of these famous names rose from their humble beginnings to become the international giants that they are today is a fascinating story; not an easy one to tell, for there are gaps in the evidence, but fascinating nonetheless.

There is no doubt that Samuel Baker, bookseller of London, he whose bob-wigged and plum-coated portrait hangs in the Bond Street offices today, was the founder of the illustrious firm known as Sotheby's. There is equally no doubt that James Christie, auctioneer of Covent Garden, whose half-length portrait by Gainsborough hangs today in the Paul Getty collection in America because his successors sold it, was the founder of the equally illustrious firm known as Christie's.

The two firms have followed a roughly parallel course over the years, competing with each other, with the two other major London salerooms who survived, Phillips and Bonhams, and with all the other auctioneers who came and went over two centuries. Whilst peaceful co-existance has long been the order of the day—no auction wars here—there is one highly controversial matter which has spanned the years from those eighteenth century beginnings to remain largely unresolved to the present day. The small matter of which one may honestly claim to be the oldest established firm of fine art auctioneers is an issue that has occupied not only generations of writers on the subject, but generations of partners of the respective firms, and certainly in no small measure the publicity departments of each.

The problem is that Sotheby's, although having a valid claim to have preceded Christie's by more than twenty years in setting up their shop, sold for most of the eighteenth century only books, Samuel Baker was after all a bookseller. James Christie, on the other hand, dealt from the start with the general run of house contents, furniture, pictures, jewellery etc., and as a result Christie's also claim precedence as the oldest fine art saleroom in the world.

The question that has been asked over and over again is whether the sale of books alone, of whatever kind, justifies the use of the term 'fine art' in Sotheby's claim to have been first. For many years Sotheby's have used on their letter heading the words 'Auctioneers of Literary Property and Works illustrative of the Fine Arts', which is an entirely reasonable statement in the circumstances; but open up the standard press release issued by the firm and you will read:

> Sotheby's, the oldest as well as the largest, fine art auction house in the world, was started by Samuel Baker, a London bookseller, in 1744.

Christie's simply ignore the claim and describe themselves in their own publicity handout as:

> the oldest fine art saleroom in the world, founded by James Christie on December 5th, 1766.

The matter is not quite resolved by another major interested party, the *Guinness Book of Records*, who simply reproduce the Sotheby release, but drop the word 'fine'. They state:

> the largest and oldest firm of art auctioneers in the world is Sotheby Parke-Bernet of London and New York, founded in 1744.

Even that is not the full extent of the debate, for the matter has been further complicated by the recent publication of a biography of Sotheby's by Frank Herrmann entitled *Sotheby's—Portrait of an Auction House*. I am indebted to Mr Herrmann for the excellence of his research which has proved invaluable in the production of this chapter. Much of the detailed information in his book was gleaned from difficult to trace records, even for someone working within the organisation, as he did. The greatest part of the material which he discovered would simply not have been available to anyone else, and his book is a tribute to his patience and perseverance.

The new complication brought forward by his research relates to the first sale of Samuel Baker, always until now believed to have taken place in 1744. The information upon which this belief was based had been supplied by the Reverend Thomas Frognall Dibdin, famous nineteenth century biographer, who recorded that there was a note on the flyleaf of that 1744 catalogue in Baker's own hand which read 'The first Auction sold by Sam Baker, 1744.' The supposed first catalogue was of the library of Dr Thomas Pellet, but we are now assured that a study of both the handwritten inscription and the style of cataloguing show it to be the work of another, possibly a less well-known auctioneer called Joseph Brigstock.

It is now thought that the founding father's first effort was the sale of the library of the Rt Hon. Sir John Stanley, Bart, described as 'containing several Hundred Scarce and Valuable Books in all branches of Polite Literature'. The 475 lots were to be sold over ten evenings in the Great Room, over Exeter Exchange in the Strand beginning on Monday, March the 11th, 1744–5. The explanation for the double year date at this period is that until 1751 the legal new year in England began on March the 25th. New Years Day was still, however, popularly celebrated on the 1st of January, and it became the usual practice, therefore, to print the legal and popular year dates in this way.

Samuel Baker's career as a bookseller began at the age of twenty-two with the publication of his first catalogue on the 19th of February, 1733–4. It was a bookseller's catalogue headed 'A Catalogue of a Choice Library of Books', and it carried the quaint phrase at the foot of the title page:

> Which will be sold Cheap (the Lowest Price mark'd to each Book in the Catalogue) on Tuesday, the 19th of this Instant February, 1733–34, at SAMUEL BAKER'S, Bookseller, at the Angel and Crown, in Russell-street, Covent Garden, and to continue every Day till all are sold.

This is another important factor in the determination of the date of the first auction sale by Baker, for it was not until 1745 that the words 'which will be sold cheap' were replaced by 'which will be sold by auction'. Little doubt then that Sotheby's was in fact founded in the year of 1745, but no change as yet on the firm's headings which still bear the legend 'founded in 1744'.

Having established a founding date, however, it is important to reiterate that Samuel Baker was essentially a bookseller. He was also a bookseller who liked to diversify, and he advertised as a stationer, as a publisher, and clearly he started to use the auction as merely another string to his commercial bow. In those early days Samuel Baker was very much a part-time auctioneer, as the frequency of his sales indicates, with just one sale in 1745, another in 1746, and a third in 1747.

Each book in those early sales was sold as an individual lot, and the sales continued for days on end, anything between twenty and forty, even fifty days being quite normal. The style of these sales must have been very different from the sales of the present day. With just a few lots being offered in each short evening session, but with the sale stretching over several weeks, the atmosphere must have been leisurely and in direct contrast to today's bustling auction scene.

Perhaps Baker's first important sale was that of the library of Dr Richard Meade in 1754. Dr Meade's collection of pictures and drawings, cameos, coins and sculpture, was sold by the principal fine art auctioneer of the period, Abraham Langford, who had not long taken over the business of Christopher Cock, whom we have discussed earlier and who had recently retired. This collection, which was sold between 1754 and 1755 in three sales, fetched a total of £10,550 18s. The library entrusted to Baker was sold in two parts, the first sale beginning on the 18th of November, 1954, and lasting twenty-eight days, the second running for twenty-nine days from the 7th of April, 1755. The two sales realised £5508 10s 11d, altogether a highly successful operation.

In view of the infrequency of the sales and the leisurely pace at which they were conducted, it is the more surprising to discover that the auctioneers were not immune to the occasional disappointment in terms of results. It seems that it was entirely possible for the auctioneer-booksellers to saturate the market with just too many books; and Baker learned his lesson with the Rawlinson library, yet another important property to come his way, which he set about disposing of on the 29th of March, 1756.

Rawlinson was a lawyer with an extensive library, so extensive that we are advised by the eighteenth century diarist, Thomas Hearne, that the four rooms which he occupied in Grays Inn were so full of books that he was obliged to sleep in the passage. The sale, which should have been a feather in Baker's cap, turned out in the end to be something less than a triumph. The first part of the sale, comprising 9405 lots of books, took fifty days to complete and realised only £1161 18s 6d. A subsequent sale of 'upwards of Twenty Thousand Pamphlets' occupied nine days beginning one year later on the 3rd of March, 1757, and realised £203 13s 6d. In a third and final session Baker disposed of Rawlinson's 'Prints, Books of Prints and Drawings' over a period of eight evenings. One hundred and three prints by Durer made £1 10s 6d, and a collection of woodcuts by the artist was sold for 2s 6d. Twenty four etchings by Rembrandt realised only £3 5s, and the sale total was a paltry £163 10s 3d.

Two notable events occurred in 1766, one a matter of fact and historical record, the other a matter of gossip and speculation. The matter of fact is that on the 5th of December of that year James Christie took over the Pall Mall rooms formerly occupied by a print-maker, and was at last in business on his own account after spending several years as assistant to a Covent Garden auctioneer. In the early years he was quickly to establish a reputation for selling anything from household goods to fine art with a notable eloquence.

An early Christie catalogue lists:

> two Nankeen Chamber-pots; Sir Isaac Newton, Pope, and Handel in bronze, finely repaired by the late in- genious Mr. Robiliac ... four flatirons, a footman, a gridiron trivet, two brass candlesticks, snuffers, hanging iron, ladle &c.

A

CATALOGUE

OF THE GENUINE

Houfhold Furniture

Jewels, Plate, Fire-arms, China, etc. And
a large quantity of Maderia (*sic*) and high Flavour'd Claret

Late the Property of

A Noble PERSONAGE

(DECEAS'D)

The Furniture confifts of Rich Silk Damafk, mix'd Stuff
ditto, Cotton and Morine in Drapery Beds, Window-
curtains, French Elbow and back Stool Chairs, a Large
Sopha with an Elegant Canopy over ditto, Variety of
Cabinet Work in Mahogany, Rosewood, Japan, Tor-
toifhell, inlaid with Brafs, etc. Large Pier Glafses, a
curious Needlework Carpet 4 yards by 5, Turkey and
Wilton ditto, fome valuable Jewels, and Plate, etc. Ufe-
ful and ornamental Chelfea, Drefden and Oriental
China, a Mufical Spring Clock and Eight-day ditto,
fome fine Bronzes, Models, Pictures, &c. &c.

Yet another sale included a squirrel cage, a barrel organ, and a coffin,
the latter, James Christie is said to have explained, 'having been made
originally for a man who had recovered from a malady deemed
usually by the medical confraternity to be fatal'.

His eloquent manner was recorded by the cartoonists of the day,
one such catching him in full flight and bearing the legend—'will
your ladyship do me the honour to say £50,000—a mere trifle—a
brilliant of the first water, an unheard of price for such a lot, surely'.
Another described him in its caption as 'Eloquence or the King of
Epithet', all these obviously picturing him on his better days when he
had managed to attract a good sale of pictures or jewellery, in which
he specialised when he was able. The very first lot in his first sale is
recorded as being 'Six breakfast pint basons and plates', and was
purchased by Sheperd for nineteen shillings. In the early days and in
between the 'fine art' he also managed to dispose of 'seven bright bay
nagtail geldings' for Thomas Rumbold, sold at prices between $8\frac{1}{2}$ and
38 guineas, and 'about 72 loads of excellent meadow hay' at Holland
House, Kensington, bought for £247 16s by the Duke of Queensberry.

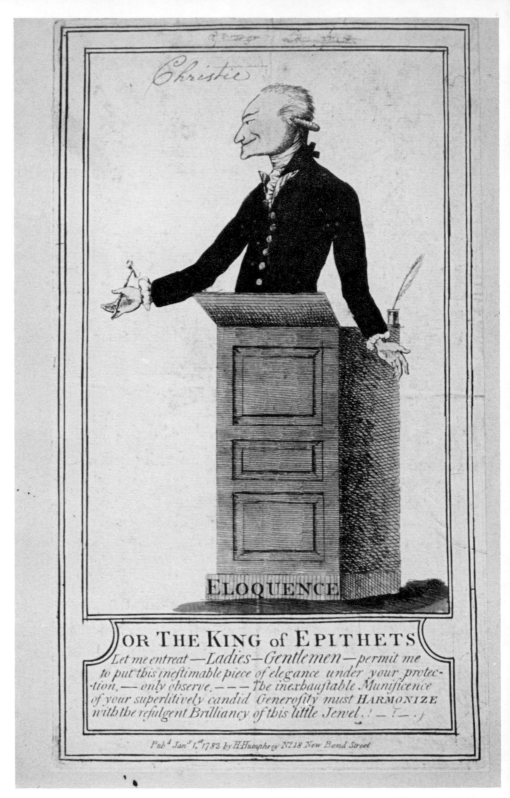

'Eloquence or The King of Epithets—James Christie at the rostrum. From a print by H. Humphrey, 1782—Photo courtesy Christie's

THE SPECIOUS ORATOR.
WILL YOUR LADYSHIP DO ME THE HONOR TO SAY £50-000
—A MERE TRIFLE.—A BRILLIANT of the FIRST WATER.
an unheard of price for such a lot, surely.

'The Specious Orator'—portrait of James Christie by Richard Dighton, 1794—Photo courtesy Christie's

His conditions of sale were on the whole conventional, 'no person is to advance less than 6d under One Pound, above One Pound, 1s., above Five Pounds, 2s. 6d., and so in proportion'. They did, however, contain one recommendation which would certainly be difficult to apply in today's saleroom atmosphere, 'in cases of dispute the lot to be put up again, or be decided by the majority of the company present'.

Christie's first sale of pictures took place on the 20th of March, 1767, and if the prices are anything to go by they must have been a pretty dubious lot, a 'Holbein' making £4 18s, a 'Titian' 2 guineas and a 'Teniers' just fourteen shillings. The earliest catalogue in the possession of the firm is said to bear no date but to state that the goods specified 'will be sold by Auction by Mr. Christie at the Auction Room, in PALL MALL, on Fryday next, and the Four following days'.

That other notable event of 1766 was a criticism of Samuel Baker, which was published by another London bookseller, Henry Dell. A poem written and published by Dell contained comments in verse on many of the members of the bookselling fraternity, including Baker, of whom he said:

> Oh!—waddling like a duck,
> To public auctions 'tis you owe your luck,
> By them enrich'd, now grown so stiff and proud,
> You're like a bashaw, o'er th'inferior croud;
> The muse could tell, but prudence stops her tongue,
> From what mean trick your vast importance sprung;
> I wish Cervantes were alive to see,
> His Sancho Pancha fresh reviv'd in thee.

I am grateful to Frank Herrmann for quoting the passage as well as his source, Terry Belanger's *Publishing History*, and am interested to note that neither Mr Herrmann or Mr Belanger have been able to find any details of 'the mean trick' referred to in the poem. Having dealt in a previous chapter with the various criticisms of the auctioneers in both England and America, it is worth noting that, as in this case, very few of even the major auctioneers of the day were to escape such criticism in one form or another. It is highly unlikely that corroborative evidence for 'a mean trick' would have been allowed to survive for more than two centuries, and I hope it is fair to say that it is almost equally unlikely that those auctioneers who themselves survived could have done so without at least one 'mean trick' to their credit.

Just one year later, in 1767, Baker decided to share the burden and the business with twenty-five year old George Leigh, and shortly after his arrival the firm's official title became Baker & Leigh. In 1768 Baker's wife Rebecca died at the age of sixty three, and it seems that from about this time Baker went into a sort of retirement. The Bakers had not been blessed with children of their own and in his later years Samuel appears to have spent some time cultivating the links with his relatives by marriage. His niece Betsy seems to have been his favourite, and Betsy—born Elizabeth Cotton—was the wife of John Sotheby.

Samuel Baker died in 1778 at the age of sixty-six and was buried beside his wife in St Pauls churchyard in Covent Garden. George Leigh had been a full partner in the firm since 1774, and now under the terms of Baker's will, his nephew John Sotheby was to be introduced into the business. Very quickly, within three months of Baker's death in fact, the title of the firm was changed again and became Leigh & Sotheby. From this moment until 1861 the ship was to be steered by three generations of the Sotheby family.

While Leigh & Sotheby attracted the more important literary properties, James Christie was going from strength to strength by selling anything and everything in Pall Mall. By 1770 he had moved into number 125, next door to Schomberg House, into which Thomas Gainsborough moved to become his neighbour. The Great Auction Rooms were becoming a favourite meeting place for the socialites of the day, the group including Gainsborough, David Garrick and Joshua Reynolds.

The friendship with Gainsborough extended to the artist painting a portrait of the auctioneer free of charge, provided that it was hung in the saleroom to serve as an advertisement for the studio next door. The portrait has in the lower left-hand corner a fragment of a landscape, designed to demonstrate the artist's versatility and to maximise the possibility of commissions.

The good times were, however, soon to be seriously disrupted by the side effects of the French Revolution, which may have hit Christie's harder than it did Leigh & Sotheby. The uproar in France played havoc with the fine art market, and picture sales were particularly vulnerable. It was said that Old Master paintings could be picked up in the courtyard of the Louvre for ten francs each, and in those troubled times Christie switched to selling a form of merchandise that was more easily transportable and altogether more discreet, jewellery.

During this period a favourite of Louis XV, the Countess Du Barry, escaped from France with a considerable treasure in jewels accumulated during her years at court. When put under Mr Christie's hammer her collection realised £8791 4s 9d, and the Countess, encouraged by this success, returned to France for more. She was, however, betrayed at her chateau by a negro servant, and the guillotine prevented any further disposal.

The events in France could well have affected James Christie's business in more ways than one. Christie had set out his stall to cater for the disposal of the fine arts and his business was aimed at a clientel drawn principally from the upper ranks and the aristocracy. One side effect of the French Revolution could well have been to persuade the English aristocracy to maintain a low profile in the circumstances. The sport of saleroom competition only served to make the general public aware of the substantial sums being offered by the few for mere trifles of ornament or decoration, and might well have become unfashionable. The Revolution had, in any event, rendered fine art prices unstable to say the least, and it is highly likely that there was an inevitable disinclination to be involved in such a volatile market.

The full effects of this recession might have been very close to disastrous for Christie, but while there is evidence that his business declined significantly, much of the evidence is of a negative nature in that there is little available information for the period at all. The brief biography issued by Christie's themselves contains no detail for the period immediately before and after the turn of the century, and other sources—books and articles—are no more forthcoming.

It was necessary to resort to the laborious process of reading through many of the newspaper advertisements of the period in an effort to assess the level of auction activity in these difficult times. In the event the exercise proved worthwhile, for a study of those advertisements contained in the *Morning Post* of 1801 revealed interesting information relevant to Mr Christie.

One fact that is clear from the research, although the explanation is not, is that Christie no longer appears to be selling from Pall Mall, but is advertising his wares from a rather less salubrious address at no. 8 Dean Street, Soho. The firm's occupation of the Dean Street premises is not recorded in any of the sources examined in the preparation of this book, and therefore no precise explanation can be offered here. The change of address might suggest that in difficult times Christie had prudently decided to cut his coat according to the financial climate, and that the survival of the business was more important to him than the preservation of an opulent facade.

An assumption of financial difficulties could be said to be corroborated by a reference in *Farington's Diary* which draws attention to Christie's difficulty in settling an account. In March, 1795, the firm had sold 'the capital, genuine, and valuable collection of pictures, late the property of that eminently distinguished artist, Sir Joshua Reynolds, President of the Royal Academy (dec'd).' The *Diary* for the 2nd of August, 1795, reads:

Mr. Drew, the solicitor—met and conversed on the subject of Christie not having yet settled for the sale of Sir Joshua's pictures. He has threatened Christie to advertise to the purchasers not to pay any money to him, etc. Christie said he would give security for the money, and pay the difference in the present price of the stocks, but could not settle the acc't in money; blamed the nobility, etc., who did not pay, particularly Lord Kinnaird.

Certainly by 1801 the style of advertising and the quality of the goods advertised appear to be of a lesser and a more diverse nature than had previously been the case. There is even some evidence that the goods were not proving easy to dispose of at all, for on no less than three separate occasions we find Christie advertising a debtor's sale which was either being continually postposed or failing to attract buyers. The advertisement first appears in the *Morning Post* of the 13th of January, 1801, and for whatever reason the same—or extremely similar—notice appears again on the 27th of January and the 24th of February of the same year. The advertisement reads as follows:

'SUPERB HOUSEHOLD FURNITURE, CHINA, PIER
GLASSES, PRINTS, CARPETS, &c., &c.
By Mr. CHRISTIE
At the Great Auction Rooms, No. 8, Dean-street, Soho,
This Day, at Twelve o'clock,
THE CAPITAL STOCK in TRADE of a
CABINET-MAKER and UPHOLSTERER,
Assigned over for the benefit of his Creditors, and which
will be sold without any reserve.
    The Stock, which is perfectly modern, comprises cap-
ital cabinet-work, in mahogany wardrobes, double and
single chests of drawers, dining-tables, to join with circular ends, secretaries and book-cases, sideboards, ladies
and gentlemen's dressing-tables, mahogany and japanned chairs, in leather, and satin horse-hair; four-
post bedsteads, rich chintz cotton furniture, with gilt
and japanned cornices; field bedsteads and furniture,
suitable bedding; brilliant pier glasses, in rich gilt
frames; Brussels, Wilton, and other carpets, some of
large dimensions; cut-glass lustres, and lustre candle-
sticks, beautiful china, in burnished gold, a very extensive assemblage of prints, in gilt frames, with a variety
of other goods'

All credit to James Christie for keeping the ship afloat in difficult times, but sad to record that the difficulties coincided with what were to be his last years. It is worth noting that the firm's advertisements at this time are in fact no more frequent or important than those of any of the other auctioneers of the period—including Squibb, Robins and Phillips. There is also a further irony in that Christie, who at one time had a financial interest in the *Morning Post*, should suddenly find himself having no influence at all with the proprietors; and even on occasion discover his advertisements tucked away at the bottom of the auction page, sandwiched between 'desirable leasehold premises in Pimlico' and an advertisement for a treatment for venereal blindness.

Confirmation that Christie and the proprietors of the newspaper were not on the best of terms comes from David Stuart, who acquired the paper in 1795, and recorded:

> Shortly after I joined the Morning Post, Christie, the auctioneer, left it on account of its low sale, and left a blank, a ruinous proclamation of decline. But in 1802 he came to me again, praying for readmission.

His prayers were not answered, and 'gentleman' James Christie died in 1803. He was succeeded by his eldest son, also James, who in 1823 was to take the firm to the King Street premises which they occupy today. There is little evidence of the firm's activities in the intervening years, but we can be reasonably sure that hard times continued for much of the first quarter of the nineteenth century. As James the elder may have discovered, however, survival was the name of the game, and the Industrial Revolution was well under way and busily producing the moneyed middle class which was eventually to prove such a boon to the auctioneers.

When times are hard it seems one resorts to selling whatever is available, and quite by chance our local newspaper research turned up what might well be Christie's first 'probe' into the country; not fine art this time, more a dabble in the speculative side of the property market. An advertisement in the *Windsor and Eton Express* on Thursday the 14th of September, 1814, places the firm once more at the Great Rooms, Pall Mall, but selling land in Buckinghamshire for development.

> Valuable Beechwoods, freehold farms and picturesque spots for cottage residency with land ... Fulmere and Hedgerley, Bucks. A valuable tract of Beechwood, called Wapsey's Wood, together with two adjoining inclosures of arable, on the High Road, near Beaconsfield, Bucks.

Leigh & Sotheby, meanwhile, had soldiered on to the end of the eighteenth century by way of their multiple literary interests. By the 1790s they had marginally increased the annual number of auction sales, they continued to issue a booksellers fixed-price catalogue of considerable proportions, and they had also grown large as publishers.

The substantial investment expended on the development of the publishing side of the business was to produce an occasional bonus for the auction department when the firm's authors consigned their private libraries to the saleroom.

George Leigh, in later life, had become a notable saleroom character, destined to be immortalised in the written word. Following the death of James Christie he had presumably become the senior London auctioneer, and his manner and disposition have been remembered affectionately. Mannerisms too have been recorded, and in particular, in Leigh's case, his use of his snuff-box. One of the firm's authors noted that when Leigh became excited he made 'adroit and whimsical exercise of his snuff-box', and antiquarian Richard Gough wrote in 1812:

> this genuine disciple of the elder Sam (Baker) is still at the head of his profession, assisted by a younger Sam (Sotheby); and of the Auctioneers of Books may not improperly be styled facile princeps. His pleasant disposition, his skill and his integrity, are as well known as his famous snuff-box, described by Mr. Dibdin as having a not less imposing air than the remarkable periwig of Sir Fopling of old, which, according to the piquant note of Dr. Warburton, usually made its entrance upon the stage in a Sedan chair, brought in by two chairmen, with infinite satisfaction to the audience. When a high price book is balancing between £15 and £20, it is a fearful sign of its reaching an additional sum if Mr. Leigh should lay down his hammer and delve into this said crumple-horn-shaped snuff-box.

No oblique criticism then for Leigh, in fact nothing but praise, and in particular from a London bookseller, William Gardiner:

> Mr. Leigh, to the birth, person, and manners of a gentleman, adds, in the autumn of life, the cheerfulness, the bloom, and the gentle, friendly warmth of spring; and, during a space of forty years devoted to the service of the publick, has attended to its interests, whatever might be the magnitude, with the utmost vigilance, impartiality, and success; and, in a profession accompanied by much trouble, perplexity, confusion, and uncertainty, has spared neither his person nor purse, to introduce regularity, method, and precision; and has preserved a character not only unstained and unsuspected, but highly honourable. His discharge of duty during the hour of sale cannot be too highly praised, whether for a gracefulness of delivery that adds interest to such a correct enunciation of his articles as each of their Authors would approve or for that polished suavity with which he moderates the occasional asperity of contending parties.

Another Sotheby arrived in the late summer of 1800, Samuel, son of John Sotheby; and the firm's title changed again, this time to Leigh, Sotheby & Son. What should have been the beginning of a period of stability for the business was to prove to be quite the reverse, however, and the next few years were to prove the most unsettled in the firm's long history. In 1804 the two elder partners had a major disagreement, and Leigh and young Samuel Sotheby moved to new premises at 145 The Strand. John Sotheby remained, held two more sales, and then retired. He died just four years later, but such was the rift in the family that his library was sold by the York Street auctioneer W. Richardson in May, 1808.

In 1816 George Leigh died after a highly successful career spanning almost fifty years. Shortly after his death the young Samuel Leigh Sotheby was introduced into the business, and shortly after that, in 1818, the firm moved again to 13 Wellington Street, which was to be its home for almost a century. By 1827, young Samuel, the most scholarly partner to date, was firmly at the helm.

There is an ivory gavel in a glass showcase at Sotheby's New Bond Street headquarters which, if it were able, might describe accurately the history of those early days. The gavel had belonged to Abraham Langford, the auctioneer who sold the fine art while Baker sold the books, and if it is possible to immortalise a hammer in verse, Dibdin did so in 1812 in *Bibliography, a Poem*:

> And down
> Th'important hammer drops.
> This instrument
> Had wielded been of old by Langford. He
> With dying breath to Baker had bequeath'd
> This sceptre of Dominion; which now decks
> The Courteous hand of Leigh.

The gravel passed out of the firm's possession through a senior clerk who moved on to become a partner with another firm of auctioneers. It was returned in 1837 by his son, and has remained with Sotheby's ever since.

The apparently uncertain financial climate of the early nineteenth century must have contributed greatly to the equally apparent inability of young James Christie to follow in his father's footsteps. He seems to have made little impression on the auction scene and left little record of his term of office as head of the firm. He died in 1831, aged 58.

His son, G.H. Christie, succeeded him, and just three weeks after his father's death took William Manson into partnership. After the ups and downs of earlier days both Christie's and Sotheby's seemed now to be entering a period of consolidation. Certainly Christie's, for the rest of the century, enjoyed a continuous run of good to average sales which were here and there highlighted by a more important event—often a picture sale—which could be used for publicity purposes, much as today.

It is at about this point in their history that the London salerooms became a focus for the public at large, with much of the interest generated by the media coverage produced by those occasional spectaculars. The publicity encouraged many new buyers into the auction rooms but also many more who remained mere spectators. In the introduction to his book on Christie's, H.C. Marillier comments on the 'lookers' in the saleroom.

> They cannot or do not buy, but they like looking on and watching things sold. As a rule they mark their catalogues religiously. But whether their attendance be on this or on a higher plane, they cannot help learning. They see displayed in turn all the works of brain and hand that men count precious. Pictures, tapestries, furniture, china, jewels, plate, the rarest books, the most historic armour. All the treasures of the East and of antiquity come before them, catalogued, dated and described with surprising accuracy considering the vast range of art which has to be dealt with. In the realm of material things there is no such liberal education to be found anywhere else, unless it be in the less invigorating atmosphere of a museum, where everything is dead and laid to rest. In the sale-room things are alive and merely changing hands; sometimes, in the case of great sales, with an intensity of suspense and subdued excitement which is quite sensational.

Joseph Haslewood, solicitor and book collector, described by Samuel Leigh Sotheby as 'my Excellent Friend', was the author, in 1828, of a document intended for the guidance of young Samuel. Entitled *Hints for Young Auctioneers of Books* it set down a sound basis for the compilation of a catalogue; going so far as to offer instruction on how best to frustrate the efforts of the 'rig and knock-out crew'. Yet another indication of the continuous attention paid to the auction rooms by the 'ring'.

Even with the benefit of these model guidelines, and despite having been established for almost a century, the firm was still far from being the automatic choice for the disposal of the finest libraries. It must have been irksome for all concerned to observe, throughout the first half of the nineteenth century, a succession of major literary properties going to their greatest competitor—Robert Harding Evans. The library of the Duke of Roxburgh went to Evans and the sale was said to rank as the most influential of the nineteenth century. It could seem also that young Samuel Sotheby had not given due attention to Mr Haslewood's 'hints', for it is also a fact that even the library of his 'excellent friend' was sold by Evans after Haslewood's death in 1833.

It was possibly the intense competition in the bookselling and auction field that was encouraging the firm to diversify yet again, this time within the auction side of the business. Sales of paintings and watercolours became more common at Sotheby's after about 1825, and included the studio sale of Richard Parkes Bonington. The elder Samuel died in 1842 at the age of 70. Although overshadowed to some extent in business by the younger Sotheby he had, in life, earned much respect, and in death a generous obituary in the *Gentleman's Magazine*. Part of this read:

> The character of the late Mr. Sotheby was strictly exemplary in all the relations of private life; and though not so happy as he deserved in realising his fortune in a very arduous profession he retired from it with the good wishes and the regret of very many who had long known and highly respected him.

Just a year after Samuel Sotheby's death young Samuel took as a partner a long-standing employee, John Wilkinson. Quite soon Wilkinson took over the duties of the rostrum—to the total exclusion of everyone else it is said—while Samuel concentrated on management. In 1847, with business improving, the firm took on Edward Grose Hodge, who was to play an important part in the later history of the firm.

The 1840s are something of a barren area in the search for information regarding the progress of the firm and its partners. In his book Mr Herrmann describes the period as the 'Dark Ages', and it is certain that if his research has proved unproductive then there is little hope for mine. Ironically, however, the same decade produced two items of extreme significance in providing a picture of the London auctions and auctioneers, as well as an image of their effect on the public and the media.

The first of these items is a nice piece of descriptive journalism which appeared in the *Morgenblatt fur Gebildete Leser*, and which is worth quoting at length.

> The London book auctions offer considerable food for thought on the subject of the misfortunes and frailty of human life for, whenever an eminent person dies, or goes bankrupt, his library is usually destined for the public auction rooms. These auction sales are also often very entertaining, and in a city like London, they take on a greater importance and a very particular interest. It might be thought strange that these sales are sparsely attended, not only by foreigners but even by leisured Londoners. The fact is that this inconceivable indifference can only be explained by the words 'ce

n'est pas la mode'. If one considers the size of London the main book auction rooms are relatively close to each other. An hour's brisk walk will take one from Piccadilly, along Pall Mall and the Strand as far as Fleet Street. Within this area can be found the premises of the principal book auctioneers, Messrs. Evans, Sotheby, Fletcher, Hodgson and Southgate. At the beginning of Spring these gentlemen announce their sales in the newspapers and publish sale catalogues. One or other of them will almost certainly hold a sale towards the end of July or August, at a time when 'the season' which exerts such an incredible influence on all branches of business, is drawing to a close. They come to mutual agreement on the dates for sales and it is only in an emergency that two or three sales might take place on the same day. Like most businessmen these gentlemen specialise. Evans has pride of place, as had his father who was well known in the literary world as editor of a collection of English ballads which filled several of the gaps left by Percy. And like this father before him Evans has been granted the privilege of presiding, as auctioneer, over the sale of the valuable libraries of noblemen and the wealthy middle classes. His knowledge of books has become almost proverbial in London. After Evans comes Sotheby who is often the choice of the aristocracy and the rich when antiques, coins, engravings, literary curiosities and other similar objects, as well as books, are to be auctioned. The other three gentlemen share among themselves the sales entrusted to them by the middle classes, and are none the less esteemed for that ... Genius is not always needed when one writes a book but genius alone can sell books at a public auction in London. For this reason I would accord the auctioneer's hammer as much respect as the writer's pen.

The auction rooms are open a few hours before the sale so that the books can be viewed. The behaviour of enthusiasts is amusing even then. They stand in front of the table or shelves where the books are displayed, with catalogue and pencil in hand. Sometimes serious, sometimes smiling, they pick up and leaf through a book then put it down with a show of disinterest. They nonetheless mark the lot number carefully in the catalogue before looking round to make sure that no one has noticed and they eye anyone else who stretches out a hand for the book in a challenging manner. Many people leave the room as soon as the auctioneer takes his place. This is not always because they have found nothing of interest. Often it is because they know themselves too well and cannot trust themselves if they stay. Hard won experience has taught them that, difficult though it may always be to exercise restraint once the bidding starts, for them it is impossible. If a man whose appearance or triumphant expression annoys you bids a shilling more than your limit, you cannot help bidding another shilling. If he then gives up you will have nothing more to regret than the loss of two shillings, or, if you are sensible enough to stop bidding you will be able to congratulate yourself on your will-power. There are even some secondhand booksellers, whose enthusiasm has not been tempered by their trade, who have to send messenger boys to represent them at sales. These lads are often excellent representatives who can calculate the bidding with a skill unexpected in boys of twelve to fourteen. They have often reduced more experienced and important buyers to despair. Usually not a year passes without at least one sale which attracts the interest of all the London bibliophiles. ... Last year the most prestigious sale was that of Lord Berwick's library which contained some splendid heraldic works, manuscripts and autographs. All the collectors were in a state of excitement because, among the documents was a deed relating to Shakespeare's house in Blackfriars which bore his signature, and as everyone knows there are only four signatures of the great playwright still in existence. When Sotheby raised the precious document the room was overflowing with interested spectators. The auctioneer himself hesitated to break the sudden silence. Finally after a short preamble he started the sale. After five minutes of bidding the sum offered had reached one hundred guineas. This seemed to be the limit for most people. On the faces of many a frown, a twist of a lip or an expression of defeat revealed the fading of hope, or an inner conflict between desire to continue bidding and determination to stop. There was a long pause before the next bid. The bidders withdrew one after another. Excitement was running high and Sotheby's voice as he announced each new bid became more deliberate. When he had said one hundred and fifty guineas for the third time everyone held his breath. Only when the hammer fell and the auctioneer solemnly said 'gone' was the silence broken and the spectators who had been motionless as statues became men again. The City Library had won the day.

The other significant occurrence of 1848 was in fact an event. Not an ordinary event, but a fully fledged spectacular, in fact the sort of momentous event that occurs perhaps once in a century, and perhaps not even then. The bankruptcy of Richard Plantagenet Temple Nugent Brydges Chandos Grenville, 2nd Duke of Buckingham and Chandos, produced a situation about as close as the English ever get to matching the events in France towards the end of the eighteenth century. In August 1848 the small revolutions in the English countryside were mostly those made by the wheels of the carriages carrying prospective purchasers to Stowe House, seat of the Duke and venue for the great sale of the contents of all the Duke's residences which was to last for forty days.

Such sales, like Revolutions, are great levellers. The public at large are admitted to view a previously private inner sanctum, and encouraged to handle and evaluate and bid for works of art and property of every kind gathered over centuries by an aristocratic family. The cause and effect of the fall of Buckingham involved the highest as well as the lowest in the land, for the inevitable end was perhaps precipitated by the visit to Stowe of Queen Victoria and Prince Albert. The enormous expense of decoration and building works undertaken as preparation for the visit when added to the Duke's less than competent money management and the debts left by his extravagant father, left him in an impossible situation; and it is said that the bailiffs were already installed, disguised as footmen, before the Queen had left.

The dispersal of the effects was a joint effort involving our two heroes. Christie's were to sell the contents of Stowe House, whilst the catalogue of sale announced that Sotheby's would sell the highly important and extensive library at their rooms in London. The combination of scandal and auction spectacular captured the public interest, and the newspapers kept the enthusiasm going. On the eve of the great sale *The Times* reported:

During the past week the British public has been admitted to a spectacle of painful interest and gravely historic import. One of the most splendid abodes of our almost regal aristocracy has thrown open its portals to an endless succession of visitors, who from morning to night have flowed in an uninterrupted stream from room to room, and floor to floor—not to enjoy the hospitality of the lord or to congratulate him on his countless treasures of art, but to see an ancient family ruined, their palace marked for destruction, and its contents scattered to the four winds of heaven. We are only saying what is notorious, and what therefore it is neither a novelty nor a cruelty to repeat, that the most noble and puissant prince, his Grace the Duke of Buckingham and Chandos, is at this moment an absolutely ruined and destitute man. Our advertising columns have introduced to the public the long list of estates, properties, and interests which are no longer his, and will not revert to his heirs. The last crash of this mighty ruin is that which now sounds. Stowe is no more. This morning the tumultuous invasion of sightseers will once more be endured, and to-morrow the auctioneer will begin his work ... And everything is to be sold. The fatal ticket is everywhere to be seen. The portrait of Charles Brandon, Duke of Suffolk, the founder of the family, by Holbein, is Lot 51 in the 21st day's sale. That every other ancestor should go to the hammer,

whether Vandyke or Lely, or Kneller or Gainsborough or Reynolds, follows of course.

When the auctioneer's work was ended at Stowe, the total for the
forty days sale was just £75,562 4s 6d, a result which could not be
described as successful. Too many good things, it seems, were just too
much of a good thing for trade and public alike. The whole sorry
affair finished up as a low spot in both the history of England and
the history of auction. Even the scheduled sale of the highly important
and extensive library was something of an anti-climax, for the most
important part of the library was never sold publicly at all. The
collection of ancient manuscripts and unpublished State papers was
sold privately to the Earl of Ashburnham after negotiations with the
British Museum had broken down. Samuel Leigh Sotheby finally
agreed a price of £8000 with Ashburnham, and the already printed
sale catalogue was withdrawn.

By a curious twist of fate the son of a gamekeeper, brought up at
Stowe, Thomas Woods, was to join Christie's and remain with them
for more than half a century. He is still commemorated in what
remains the firm's title to the present day—Christie Manson & Woods
Ltd. Two paintings by Frans Hals, portraits of a lady and a gentleman, were sold in the Stowe sale for seven guineas and ten and a half
guineas respectively. They re-appeared in a Christie sale in 1899,
catalogued this time by Woods, and realised £5250 between them.

Samuel Leigh Sotheby had changed the firm's title after his father's
death to S.L. Sotheby & Co., but in 1850 he gave credit to the work
of John Wilkinson by changing it yet again to S. Leigh Sotheby and
John Wilkinson. Samuel Leigh Sotheby was found dead in mysterious
circumstances in June, 1861. He had recently taken a lease of Buck-
fastleigh Abbey for the enjoyment of the scenery in his retirement.
The *Gentleman's Magazine* reported:

> The circumstances of the death of this gentleman are very distress-
> ing. After lunching in good spirits with his family, he started, as
> was his custom, for a ramble near the Abbey ruins; not returning
> his absence caused intense anxiety; but it was not till the next
> morning that his body was found in the River Dart in very shallow
> water. From evidence before the Coroner, it appeared that Mr
> Sotheby was subject to fainting fits, and it is supposed that he was
> suddenly seized with heart disease when near the brink of the river.

With his death the last Sotheby had gone from the business and John
Wilkinson was left in control. In 1864 he took Edward Hodge as
partner, but the significance of so many generations of Sotheby's was
not lost on them, and the title of the firm became Sotheby, Wilkinson
and Hodge.

Events within the saleroom were in the meanwhile almost as dramatic as those without. A series of sales conducted by Sotheby's for a naturalised Frenchman, Conte Libri Carucci della Sommaia— Libri for short—attracted a good deal of attention and no little controversy. Libri, it seems, manoeuvered himself into a post which gave him access to the French library system, and exploited the poor accountability that he found there by simply helping himself to whatever was rare and valuable. His dispersal sales of surplus items grew to such proportions that the cat finally came out of the bag, causing him to flee France and remove his massive collection to London.

Sotheby's took on the task of further disposals which started well in 1849 but finished on a sour note in about 1865. Libri became dissatisfied with the prices realised and brought a Chancery suit against the firm. After Libri's death in 1869, legal costs amounting to £1500 were met personally by John Wilkinson. Some of Libri's books remained and these were kept by Wilkinson in lieu of costs, but not sold during his lifetime. After Wilkinson's death in 1894 the acrimony felt by his heirs over the whole affair caused them to give Christie's the instructions to sell the books. They did so in February, 1895.

For Sotheby's 1865 was the year of the great fire of Wellington Street. Several fine collections of books awaiting sale were totally destroyed and the building was extensively damaged. The feelings of those to whom the destruction of a fine book represents much more than an insurance claim, is epitomised by the report of the son of a well known Paris bookseller, J.J. Techener, some of whose books were lost in the fire.

> My father went to London, there to receive the sad confirmation that the auction house of MM Sotheby had been entirely destroyed. The conflagration, fanned by the wind, had begun by devastating the basement store rooms; the floors of the building, weighed down by books, collapsed one after another as the fire advanced to the upper stories. The huge packing cases containing our books had been stacked in the middle of a large room on the first floor over the second basement. The floor, weakened by the fire, was one of the first to collapse; our packing cases were plunged into the immense furnace below and fed the flames, which then roared up to reach every inch of the worm-eaten panelling on all sides of the antiquated premises. Within a few hours the fire had devoured everything. Several days later, the crumbling remains were extracted from the ruins, and cartloads of charred and blackened books were taken out, together with many misshapen volumes, for the water had destroyed everything that the fire had spared. It was an irreparable loss for Bibliophiles.

It was soon, however, business as usual at Wellington Street; in fact throughout the second half of the nineteenth century it was better than usual, for by then Sotheby's were the undoubted leaders in the book auction field. The firm was fortunate also at this time in having formed an association with probably the most remarkable bookseller of all time, Bernard Quaritch.

In the auction room Quaritch was brave and resolute, and easily overcame most of the opposition. His clients were wealthy collectors and his turnover grew annually; all he needed was the capital to finance his large stocks. This he received in the form of the lengthy extended credit allowed to him by the auctioneers. In return his spirited buying kept prices high, which attracted the attention of the press and drew new business to the firm. It is difficult to believe now, but true, that this association for many years regulated not only prices but the timing of sales, which had to be convenient to both in terms of supply and demand. The association also, in large measure, contributed to the success of both the auctioneers and the bookseller.

At Christie's it was the occasional important sale of paintings which continued to capture the headlines. The merchants of the Industrial Revolution had been established long enough by now to have joined the ranks of the collectors, and their presence in the market place was an important factor in the increasing prosperity of the salerooms. It still came as a surprise to many, however, to discover that someone other than a conventionally educated member of the upper classes could actually acquire the taste necessary to form a first class collection in the specialist field of art. The sale of paintings which took place after the death of Elkanan Bicknell in 1861 was, therefore, for just that reason, a sensation.

The Bicknell sale was the first major disposal from an altogether different class of collector, and it was not until the catalogue was released that the full extent of his lifetime of careful judgement and quiet patronage was to be seen. The collection, which included many Turner's, realised a substantial £58,639 12s. Public and press alike were fascinated by the sale. One London newspaper said:

THE BICKNELL COLLECTION.—There took place last Saturday an event in London, such, as we venture to think, could scarcely in the same time and under the same conditions, have happened in any other city in the world. It was not a great national event—a royal reception, or a popular demonstration. It was merely a sale of pictures. The collection of paintings thus sold had been gathered together by a private Englishman, a man of comparatively obscure position, a man engaged at one time in mere trade; a man not even pretending to resemble a Genoese or Florentine merchant-prince, but simply and absolutely a Londoner of the middle-class actively occupied in business. This Englishman, now no more, had brought together a picture gallery which would have done no discredit to a Lorenzo the Magnificent, although his name is probably still hardly known to the general public of the very city in which he lived. He had been the patron of some of the greatest of modern artists, and had formed a collection which would have brought tourists from all parts of the world to the dingiest and most decaying of Italian towns. Offered for sale in an auction-room on Saturday ... the collection realised a sum of money only wanting a few hundreds of sixty thousand pounds. The artists whose works were thus purchased, were for the most part, too, our own. It was no mere competition of fashionable pretenders, feeling themselves secure to praise and purchase so long as 'your Raphaels. Correggios, and stuff' were in question. English money was being spent upon English art.

The Bicknell sale can fairly take the credit for the beginnings of the great price rise in what were then modern pictures of the English School. It was soon followed by yet another fine collection, put together by yet another of the merchant princes, Joseph Gillot, who had invented a press for manufacturing steel nibs, made a fortune, and invested in paintings. When his collection was sold by Christie's in 1872 it included twelve paintings by Turner, twenty-six by William Holman Hunt, twenty-nine by David Cox, seven Constables and twelve Gainsboroughs. This sale also attracted widespread attention. One contemporary report stated:

> The prices obtained surpassed any hitherto given for pictures of English landscape-painting, and the general interest was something quite extraordinary. The rooms were completely besieged, and hundreds of persons could not even get within sight of the auctioneer; while at the close of the sale, on Saturday, the street was blocked with carriages, and the pavement crowded with gentlemen and ladies eager to hear what the Turners had sold for.

The Turners had in fact sold very well, and as prices continued to rise with each successive major sale, so the public interest simply grew and grew. The *London Graphic* remarked:

> The Christie audience revels in high prices simply for money's sake, though of course some of the applause is meant for the pictures.

The Wynn Ellis sale of 1876 was something for them to revel in, 'such a sensation', said *The Times*, 'as has never been experienced in the picture world of London'. The particular sensation in this sale was Gainsborough's 'Duchess of Devonshire', and when the painting was

A Peep at Christies;─ or ─Tally-ho, & his Nimeny-pimmeney taking
the Morning Lounge

placed on the easel as its turn came up, there was a burst of applause, this time for the picture, from the crowded room. The auctioneer was Thomas Woods, who gave a brief history of the painting whose previous owners had included a schoolmistress and a picture restorer. The bidding opened at one thousand guineas and closed at ten thousand one hundred when it was knocked down to Agnew for what was then the highest price ever paid for a single picture at Christie's.

Before and after the sale there had, however, been much discussion regarding the authenticity of the painting. It is said that when Sir John Millais saw the picture in the saleroom he descended Christie's main staircase shouting, 'I don't believe Gainsborough ever saw it'. The debate continued in the press after the sale, but within three weeks was summarily adjourned by an unknown thief who broke into the Agnew showroom in Old Bond Street and cut the painting from its frame. The picture was lost for twenty-five years before eventually being recovered in Chicago.

At Sotheby's, Edward Hodge was withdrawing from an active involvement in favour of his son Tom, and although the younger Hodge appears to have displayed little of the flamboyance of the firm's founding fathers, he does seem to have been just what was needed at this point in the firm's development. Hard working and efficient, keeping tight and personal control of the business, he gave the stability and reliability necessary to allow the firm to expand into new and profitable areas. Although books remained the principal commodity, sales of coins, engravings, porcelain and all kinds of antiques became much more common under Tom Hodge.

By the end of the century both Christie's and Sotheby's were settled into a prosperous routine, with the best still yet to come. More than ready for an assault on the twentieth century, both were already embarked on the course that they were to pursue to the present day — auctioneers to the rich and famous, purveyors of the finest of fine art; the nearest in fact that any business might get towards achieving the status of a national monument, with all the privileges thus implied. That this process was well begun before the end of the century is confirmed by a report in *The Times* of the 3rd of February, 1883, which states:

The season at Christie's only warms into its wonted life and activity with the meeting of Parliament, although sales begin at the famous rooms in November, and are continued every week, without presenting much that can be expected to have very vivid attractions for any but the regular 'marchand de bric-a-brac', whose love of

---

'A Peep at Christie's'—Miss Farren and the Earl of Devon. From a colour-print by Gilray, 1796—Photo courtesy Christie's

art lies in the nutshell of his pocket. Whatever of high interest for
amateurs there may be in the hands of the great art auctioneers is
reserved for the sunny days of spring and summer, when the swallows of art and fashion have come back to their favourite haunts in
King Street, St. James's.

A far cry now from those mid-eighteenth century beginnings when
one potential buyer had enquired of 'the great art auctioneers':

> I would feel very much obliged if you would kindly let me know
> by return of post if you have a perfect Articulated Skeleton at
> £1–1–0, if not what is the nearest price.

The 'swallows of art and fashion' might not have returned so promptly
for some of those early offerings which included:

> A pedigree bedstead for accouchement which the owner
> wishes to sell to someone else desirous of an heir because
> it has twice been responsible for twins.

It is on occasion no bad thing for the successful businessman to rum-
mage about in the old tin trunk in the attic for a recollection of
humble beginnings, and a final piece of early correspondence might
also serve to encourage those who have never managed to pluck up
the courage to present themselves with their 'maybe' treasures at the
front counter of one of the major London salerooms.

> Sir,—I have an old relic it being a shoulder of mutton do you think
> it is of any value, you know what a shoulder of mutton is, it is just
> the same only hard like wood, it is been in our family a great many
> years and is supposed to have been in the purifying wells. I dare
> say you would like to see it before you could tell me if you will let
> me no about it I will bring it up.

CHAPTER 7

Auction Methods and Styles

The range and diversity of the auction business is reflected not only in the vast quantities, of merchandise despatched annually by the auction method, but by the very range and variety of the method of selling itself. The modus operandi of the world's auctioneers varies considerably from one country to another, in some cases it has varied within the same country over a long period of time, and in many cases it has and does vary from one range of merchandise to another.

In England for example the ascending bid method has been in general use for so long that it is known in some quarters as the 'English' method. We know, however, that until the end of the seventeenth century the method known as 'sale by candle' was the system in most common use, and it was not until after the period of experimentation at the end of the seventeenth and the beginning of the eighteenth centuries that the ascending bid method became the standard.

It is in fact possible today to find isolated instances of local variation in the auction method, one example being that the port of Hull uses the descending bid method for selling fish, while nearby Grimsby sells by conventional ascending bid. Other more unusual survivals remain, and during the 1930's the *Conveyancer* carried a series of correspondence devoted to the subject and entitled 'A Curious Survival'. One previously quoted survival was the 21 yearly renewal of the lease of Church Acre at Chedzoy in Somerset, which since 1490 was sold during the burning of a piece of candle, and presumably still is. Another correspondent to the series reported on:

the candle auction held at Tatworth, near Chard, where every April a supper of bread, cheese, pickles, and beer precedes the letting of Stowell Mead. Both feasting and business take place traditionally at the 'Poppe Inn' known also as the Country Hotel. Stowell Mead is famous for the excellent crop of watercress growing in the stream running through it. After supper an inch of candle is lit, and bidding continues until it dies out, the last bid before the final flicker securing the tenancy for the ensuing year.

Another contributor to the same series in August, 1932, recalls an even more obscure variation on the theme – sale by sand glass. He tells us that:

> The tolls of Burrow Bridge, which spans the Parret, near Athelney, and which is the last remaining toll bridge in Somerset, are offered for sale each year in February, and are sold to the person who makes the highest bid before all the sand in an ancient one minute 'hour glass' has run through the glass three times. The auction is still conducted on the traditional lines laid down when the bridge was built, under authority of a special Act of Parliament passed in 1824, which created a body of Commissioners, who were empowered to raise by loan bonds the money needed for its construction, which amounted to about £2,500.
>
> At the auction held on Tuesday last a bid of £800 was made shortly after the sand had started running through the glass for the first time, and no advance on this sum was offered during the time taken by the sand to complete its three runs.- the glass, of course, being inverted immediately each run was completed.

It has of course been pointed out that the candle method was a slow process, and this is also the case with a method such as sale by sand glass. Both methods could only be appropriate to sales with a small number of lots where time was not a crucial factor. The point is nicely made in another letter on the subject to the same periodical.

> Sir,- With reference to the article on this subject in The Conveyancer for this month it may interest you to know that until a few years ago the tolls of Haw Bridge over the Severn near Tewkesbury were let in precisely the same manner as those of Burrow Bridge referred to in the article.
>
> As an articled clerk it amused me to see the letting of the tolls of Haw Bridge because, as the bidders consumed free beer meantime, no advance was made on a bid until the sand had nearly run out for the third time. Consequently the auction took a long time to complete.

In France, the strict regime applied to auctioneering by government regulation has ensured that in terms of method the business has been subject to little, if any, change over the years. The control exercised by government is a unique feature of the French auction system, and in no other country in the world do similar regulations exist. French law decrees when and where sales will be conducted, and by whom; for the government retains the authority to delegate to individuals the permission to act as auctioneer. It has in fact long been the case that a lump sum payment might buy a licence to conduct auctions, and it is also a fact that this privilege, known as the 'charge', is a valuable property right under French law and may, like property, be either sold or willed to a descendant.

A regulation which has caused problems in the international world of fine art auctioneering is that which allows only French citizens the right to conduct auctions in France. It is this piece of legislation that has caused the major international auctioneers, in recent years, to establish a fine art base in Monte Carlo, where the measure of independence enjoyed by the Principality of Monaco allows more flexibility. Here a modern 'Huissier' acts as liaison between government and foreign auctioneer, arranges the sale accomodation and countersigns contracts. In this way firms such as Christie's and Sotheby's regularly conduct sales by their normal method using their own auctioneers. There is, however, one small difference in that when the bidding is over it is the Huissier's hammer that falls to declare the lot officially sold.

In Austria the Dorotheum is an auction house quite unlike anything else in the world. Founded at the beginning of the eighteenth century it is now the largest auction establishment in central Europe. It is in fact more than an auction house being partly pawn shop, bank and finance house. Sales are held every day and unredeemed pledges and household goods as well as fine art go under the hammer to the tune of over two thousand sales per annum.

Apart from Holland the ascending bid method is, and has been, the common method in most European countries. It has been the normal method in France for a very long time, with one notable exception. In the wine producing areas, when the time comes to sell the wine, it is necessary to establish a price related to the quality of the vintage. In some parts it has long been the practice to establish the price by holding an auction, not of the whole of the produce but simply of a representative sample before selected buyers. Such sales are sometimes conducted by 'candle', and a modern description of the custom is as follows:

> In the immense and cobbled courtyard, steep, slanting roofs come down over the balconies, their coloured slates laid in patterns of yellow and green and black—the traditional Bergundian roof. It is here that the wine auctions are held, usually on the third Sunday in November. The bidding for each lot, or queue, lasts until a measured bit of candle has burned down to the mark. On the Saturday before the sale, bidders taste the wine from the barrels, which are kept in the cellars beneath a small inner courtyard. The prices paid are a barometer of what the vintage is worth, and of its quality, and the buyers come from all over the world to attend the auction. Such sales have been taking place for over a century.

The descending bid method of sale has been so long used in Holland that the use of the term 'Dutch auction' immediately identifies the method. The proper operation of the descending bid system depends upon the auctioneer selecting a starting price above the figure that he would expect the lot to make. He then calls out successively lower prices at regular intervals until the lot is claimed by a shout from one of the assembled bidders. The auctioneer will then announce the name of the buyer and the bid price.

In complete contrast to the ascending bid method the first bid in this case is the final and winning bid. The onus is thus on the individual buyer to judge what represents a fair price for the article on offer, for to allow the bidding to decline too far is to risk losing the goods to a competitor. When using this method reserve prices are applied by stipulating a figure below which the auctioneer will not go. Despite the long tradition, however, the use of the method in Holland today in the field of art and antiques is limited to just one or two auction houses. Most fine art salerooms conform to the ascending bid method in more general use worldwide.

The Dutch method is today most usually employed in the commodity field, and its use in that area of trade is by no means confined only to Holland. Fish is sold by the method not just in Holland itself, but in parts of England and in Israel. The only difference between the sales in the three countries being the viewing of the merchandise. In Holland the fish is brought to the buyers and shown as sold, in Hull the auctioneer and buyers move from lot to lot among the rows of baskets laid out for inspection, and in Israel a conveyor belt carries the fish past the buyers as the auctioneer offers each lot.

A modern version of the descending bid method has replaced the calling of prices by the auctioneer with an electric clock mechanism on which an indicator moves anti-clockwise through a series of descending numbers. In a tiered amphitheatre up to a hundred buyers sit at desks facing the clock, each able by pressing a button at his side to stop the clock when the indicator reaches the point at which he chooses to bid. The clock when stopped registers not only the price but the number of the seat holder who has bid successfully. The auctioneer and his staff, located in a booth high above the selling floor, are free to simply record buyer and price, and it is said that in Holland, when selling cut flowers by this method, it is possible to complete an astonishing six hundred transactions an hour.

A method used in Japan is a form of simultaneous bidding system which is chiefly associated with the Tokyo fish market. Very early in the morning the buyers gather on the quayside to examine the day's offerings. Each lot is identified by number and the buyers make a careful record of those lots on which they wish to bid. As each lot is offered by the auctioneer those bidding display a hand signal which indicates a monetary unit. All the bidders must indicate together on a signal from the auctioneer, who will then read the bids and determine the winning bid. In practice, however, it takes a few seconds for the bidding and the determination to be made, and the experienced buyer may well find time to adjust his signal on observing the bids of others. A characteristic of this particular method is that it generates a great deal of noise as the multitude of bidders attempt to call the attention of the auctioneer to their bids. As with the previous Dutch method, the Japanese also operate a modern electronic version of the simultaneous bidding system designed for the wholesale fruit and vegetable markets. Here the buyers are seated at desks with a bidding keyboard and a slot for an identification plate. On a signal from the auctioneer the buyers will operate the equipment together, and the highest bid and bidders number will appear on an electronic board at the front of the saleroom.

Two of the more ridiculous auction methods must be the 'handshake auction' and the 'whispered bid auction'. In the first a semicircle of buyers grasp the auctioneers hand in turn. Under cover of a piece of cloth each squeezes the auctioneers fingers while orally indicating a denomination — say 'tens'. The multiple of the spoken figure is indicated by the number of fingers grasped and sometimes the number of squeezes given. At the end of the bidding only the auctioneer knows who has bid most, and the system is therefore open to abuse. The method is said to be very ancient and to have originated in China. Auctioneers using the method may be identified by their bruised hands and swollen fingers.

The whispered bid method is reportedly used in the fish markets in Singapore, Manila and Venice. In such sales the buyers approach the auctioneer and whisper their bids in his ear. In doing so they operate without any knowledge of their competitors offers, and again it is up to the auctioneer to sort them out in his head and to nominate the successful bidder. The disadvantage of the system is that it is very time consuming, its advantage being that it is extremely quiet.

For many years efforts have been made, when dealing with certain types of commodities, to devise systems which would bring together interested buyers from widely scattered areas by linking them electronically. As early as the mid-1940s a system registered as Selevision made such sales possible in the United States. In this case buyers in several major cities were supplied with a specification of citrus fruit waiting to be shipped from a Florida port. The equipment incorporated bidding machinery for each city, a device at the point of sale for selecting the highest bid, and a time clock to limit the bidding time. In Denmark fruit is auctioned in a similar way. In three cities — Copenhagen, Aarhus and Odense samples of the fruit are placed in the auction halls and buyers may bid by pushing buttons which transmit the bids to the auctioneer in Copenhagen.

One writer on the subject of the variety of goods sold by the auction method has listed more than one hundred and fifty kinds of merchandise sold in United States alone. The list is a whole alphabet of items ranging from aeroplanes to yachts, of which tobacco is one of the most interesting, having had a long and historic association with the auction.

During the eighteenth century much of the American tobacco crop was exported and there was, consequently, a tendency to pack the leaf into large parcels—called hogsheads—prior to sale. This method of packing, although convenient to the shippers, did not assist the buyers and led directly to substantial abuse of the system. The principal deceipt was the practice of packing the centre of the hogshead with inferior or damaged leaf and even twigs and stones, while conserving the superior leaf for the exterior of the package. This was in fact a double deception, for the rubbish deposited in the centre would add considerably to the weight and therefore the value of the consignment.

In the later eighteenth century several States approved legislation which established an inspectorate to regulate the business. The inspectors had the power to destroy bad parcels of leaf, and to grant export licences only to shipments from designated warehouses with satisfactory and approved inspection facilities. As time passed demands for even better quality control indicated once more a general dissatisfaction with the inspection system, and it soon became an accepted practice for the buyers to follow the inspector round the warehouse to observe the opening and proper inspection of the lots. Having made the examination the buyers were, of course, only interested in purchasing the inspected packages which had appeared satisfactory. It was therefore but a small step to the point where the goods were offered for sale in the warehouse immediately after inspection. With all the major buyers present it was logical that the method of sale should be auction, and as a direct consequence of the change many of the inspectors assumed the role of auctioneer. By the end of the first quarter of the nineteenth century the auction was firmly established as the principal method of sale, and remains so today.

As the nineteenth century progressed so also did the general disquiet with the hogshead method of packaging, and abuses of the system seem to have multiplied. There was in theory a guarantee provided by legislation which allowed a dissatisfied purchaser to submit a misrepresentation claim to arbitration within a period of six months. The effectiveness of the guarantee was however limited by the fact that the arbitration board was in America while the tobacco might well be in Europe by the time any deception was discovered.

Improved transportation and the growth of domestic consumption after the Civil War effected a necessary and radical change in the operation of the market. Much less tobacco was sold in hogsheads and the markets generally switched to the sale of loose leaf. Little has changed since then. Today the grower sorts his crop, ties it in hands and transports it to the warehouse—a large single storey building with many skylights. The tobacco is placed in shallow baskets a little over a metre square, and each basket is given a ticket which indicates the weight of the leaf and the name of the grower.

As the buyers move from basket to basket the warehouseman calls the grade of the basket to be sold while the auctioneer begins the weird chant characteristic of tobacco auctions. Bidding is usually by nods and winks and signs, and when the lot is knocked down the floor boys mark the buyer's name and the price on the ticket. In this case, and this is a most unusual feature found only in the tobacco auctions, a form of reserve pricing actually takes place after the bidding is completed; for the grower may refuse the winning bid by either simply turning over or tearing the ticket.

A major criticism of the system is that the speed of the operation tends to favour the bigger buyers and to work against the small producer. The time taken to sell each basket is on average between six and ten seconds, which means that bidding is a matter of snap judgement in most cases, and can lead to wide discrepancies in price between almost identical baskets. This is of little importance to the big buyers whose purchases at the end of a session will average out to a satisfactory figure. It is a matter of some concern, however, to the small farmer with a limited number of baskets included in the sale who might just be unlucky enough to receive a low price for all of them.

An interesting variety of the electronic bid gathering auction is that which serves the Californian citrus fruit market. Rail wagons loaded with fruit and ready for despatch are offered for sale through an agency with offices in several States. Buyers bid on a catalogue description of the merchandise, some of which is already on the move by the time it is purchased. The advantages claimed for the system are firstly speed, which is important when dealing with perishable goods, and secondly efficient distribution in that areas suffering shortages of particular goods may obtain supplies quickly by simply raising their bids.

No catalogue of the many and varied types of auction sale would be complete without mention of the one kind which is quite different to all the others in that it is fraudulant and unlawful. The 'Mock Auction' is a type of sale designed by unscrupulous operators to exploit the excitement generated by the auction technique. It is most effective when conducted before those members of the public who do not normally attend public auctions of the more usual kind.

The likely practice of the exponents of the mock auction is to take a short term lease—just a day or two—on empty shop premises in a busy city centre, hoping to attract lunch hour office workers, tourists, or just shoppers with an eye for what might appear to be a bargain. A graphic description of this type of sale was given by Lord Denham during the debate on the 'Mock Auctions Bill' in the House of Lords in March, 1959.

> I could describe the course of a mock auction sale in one sentence by using the jargon of the mock auctioneer: 'The pitch-getter gets the pitch, and then hands over to the top man, who first nails the mugs, then runs out the Hinton lots and finally gazoomps the sarkers'. Perhaps I had better construe. The 'pitch' is the audience to whom the goods are sold, and the only job of the 'pitch-getter' is to collect an audience inside the shop where the sale is to take place. When he has done that he hands over to the 'top man' or auctioneer, who then 'nails the mugs'—that is, sorts out the 'mugs' from the rest of the audience, and ensures (by a method which I will explain later) that they stay in the shop until the sale is over. Then he 'runs out', pretends to sell, the 'Hinton lots', those lots which are never in fact sold, and finally 'gazoomps', or cheats, the 'sarkers', those of the 'mugs' who have enough money on them to be worth his while. This description may not make the matter very much clearer to your Lordships, but it should certainly show you the amount of good faith there is in this type of sale.

Lord Denham went on to describe in detail the various stages of the deception, a shortened version of which is as follows:

> 1.   A 'pitch-getter' stands behind a table at the entrance to a shop on which there is a sign 'Clearance Sale'. On the table before him are fine-quality articles—cigarette lighters, alarm clocks, and so on—which the pitch-getter informs the gathered group are to be sold at 'giveaway' prices inside. 'This fine cigarette lighter will be sold for as little as one shilling' is a typical statement.
> 2.   Then, having attracted the 'mugs', he moves the table inside through the entryway, taking the mugs, or most of them with him.
> 3.   The 'top man' (i.e. the auctioneer) now goes to work on the mugs. The first thing he must do is to isolate the gullible. With that objective in mind, he offers a sealed package at auction which is quickly bid up to say, 10s.; having established this 'value', he then offers the others present the same proposition at the same price, explaining to them that only those who have shown confidence in the operation by purchasing one of the sealed packages will be permitted to participate in the balance of the sale. Although the money is collected, the sealed packages are not given to the buyers, but instead each gets a token that entitles him to one of the sealed

A late nineteenth-century association of auctioneers. Photo courtesy Estates Gazette

packages later. Thus the 'sarkers' (mugs with money or 'live' ones) are nailed down.

4.   Having isolated the sarkers and nailed them down, the top man then auctions off some genuine articles that a) mugs bid on but never seem able to buy (only the stooges get them), and on which b) the 'buyer' is always given a substantial rebate (e.g. 19s. back on the purchase of a 20s lighter). At this point free merchandise may ostentatiously be given away to the suckers to cover up the 'knocking down' of the good merchandise to the housemen.

5.   The final step is to 'shear the sheep', as it were. The auctioneer says, 'we are coming to the last lot' and indicates that he has several items in this lot but that only one is to be sold (for advertising purposes), and the highest bidder will take it. (Actually, these items are such things as a cheap wrist watch, inexpensive table lamp, etc., all having been made especially for this purpose and none of which the mugs have seen before). Lively bidding ensues, partly because the impression has been created that a portion of the money will be returned, and the item is bid up to perhaps £5. The auctioneer gives a choice of items to the winner. At this point the auctioneer stops the proceedings after a stooge has whispered in his ear, to announce that he has heard that some of those present suspect the sale is rigged and believe the opportunity to buy is being given only to house people. He then asks the sarker who has just been awarded the merchandise whether he has ever seen any of the people in the shop before. When the sarker answers 'no', the auctioneer says that the only way to disprove the untrue statement is to allow others who have bought sealed packages the same purchasing opportunity. The auctioneer's assistants try to stop him from doing so, saying that he is too 'generous', but the auctioneer is adament. So he and his assistants collect £5 from each of the sarkers, and the auctioneer says: 'all right, you have trusted me and now I am going to reward you. I am going to give you something in addition to what you have purchased', and holds up a fountain pen and pencil in an attractive cardboard box.

The 'mug' is handed a carrier bag in which the main item that he has chosen (e.g. cutlery) and his pen and pencil set are placed; then the auctioneer opens one of the sealed packages and pulls out a bottle of scent, which also goes into the bag. Each sarker is then given a bag containing his purchases, and the sale is over. When he arrives home, the sarker finds that he has purchased for £5. 10s., merchandise worth a pound or less.

Such auctions were outlawed by the Mock Auctions Act, 1961, which is 'an Act to prohibit certain practices in relation to sales purporting to be sales by auction'. The maximum penalty for a conviction under the act is a fine of one thousand pounds or two years imprisonment, or both. The Act defines a mock auction as a sale of goods by competitive bidding during the course of which:

a)   any lot is sold to a person bidding for it, and either it is sold to him at a price lower than the amount of his highest bid for that lot, or part of the price at which it is sold to him is repaid or credited to him, or is stated to be so repaid or credited, or

b)   the right to bid for any lot to which this Act applies is restricted, to persons who have bought or agreed to buy one or more articles, or

c)   any articles are given away or offered as gifts.

To protect the genuine auction—which is a sale of goods by competitive bidding—from breaking the law without realising it, the Act adds that the restriction at a) will not apply if the reason for a reduction on the bid price 'was on account of a defect discovered after the highest bidding in question had been made, being a defect of which the person conducting the sale was unaware when the bid was made, or was on account of damage sustained after that bid was made.'

CHAPTER 8

Modern Times 1900–1950

By the dawn of the new century the variety of goods being sold by auction around the world, and the numbers of auctioneers employed in selling them, had grown to the most enormous proportions. In England alone the number of licenced auctioneers exceeded sixty thousand. In London the fine art auction market was firmly established as was a central organisation—The Auctioneers Institute of the United Kingdom—founded in 1886 and now boasting almost two thousand members.

In France the fine art sales were not yet so common as in London and the main business of the auctioneers was still largely concerned with the sales after death and by order of the court. The rest of Europe was using the auction increasingly for the sale of commodities, and sales of agricultural and horticultural produce, livestock, fish and all mannner of merchantable goods were becoming common. In America the auctioning of slaves had of course ceased, and the fine art revolution was yet to come. Nevertheless a variety of merchandise was coming under the auctioneers hammer, principally the tobacco and cotton and fruit crops of the now United States.

Despite the new intensity of activity however, the period between 1900 and 1950 was to become, almost literally, an economic minefield. Competitors in the race for the glittering prizes which were to be available by the middle of the century were required to carefully negotiate two world wars and a major economic depression of considerable proportions. It was necessary to survive physically as well as economically, and to reach the finishing line in sufficiently good condition to be able to take advantage of the opportunities to come.

Between 1907 and 1908, Tom Hodge, by now anxious to retire from the business through ill health, was strenuously seeking a buyer for Sotheby's. Lengthy negotiations with Hodgson's, the other major London book auctioneers, and with Knight, Frank & Rutley, auctioneers and estate agents, finally broke down when Hodgson's were unable to agree the terms of payment. With the breakdown of negotiations a remarkable opportunity was lost to the two would-be partners, for the asking price at that time for a one-third share in what was to become the biggest fine art business in the world was a mere £10,000.

Hodge subsequently prevailed upon a friend, Montague Barlow, to identify a trio of partners to take on the firm; and Barlow duly presented himself together with Felix Warre and Geoffrey Hobson for the task. The final agreement was signed in 1910, and from then on there were four partners to share the burden.

As the storm clouds of war gathered across Europe in 1914, auction activity all but came to a standstill. Sales continued throughout the war years, but were much less frequent and mainly the forced sales brought about by bankruptcy or death. There were of course exceptions, and without any doubt the most notable sales of 1915 to 1918 were the Red Cross sales which were held at Christie's during those years. The story of the sales is an interesting one which was recorded in the report of the Red Cross Society's war activities published in 1921.

In the latter part of 1914 when the society was appealing urgently for funds, it was found that many people who could not send money were willing to contribute gifts in kind. Christie's were approached with a view to their disposing of the gifts on behalf of the society, and immediately offered their services and the use of their staff and sale-rooms free of charge. A committee of thirteen was set up under Sir Charles Russell to deal with collections, the King and Queen offered to head the list with gifts, letters were written to likely donors, and a general appeal was issued through the press in December.

The response to the appeal resulted in the production of an 1867 lot catalogue for a sale which began on the 12th April, 1915, and lasted for twelve days. Among the items sold was a seventeenth century wheel-lock sporting gun presented by the King which realised £360 10s. Five manuscript pages of 'Pickwick' were sold for £450, and a Stradivarius violin was bought by Lady Wernher for £2500 only to be immediately given back to be sold again for a further £1400. A Townsend cartoon, previously published in *Punch*, was purchased by the Red Cross Committee and presented to Christie's as a momento of the sale. The result of twelve days of selling and a good many more of preparation was a grand total of just over thirty seven thousand pounds.

The decision to hold a second sale in 1916 was to cause problems for the auctioneers. The staff at Christie's was by now so depleted that the arrangements for the preparation of the catalogue had to be considerably revised. The Red Cross Society decided to collect and store all the goods themselves in their own building, and to appoint a number of sub-committees to deal with the various categories of gifts. Each sub-committee was headed by a chairman who was expert in a particular field, and at the end of the process the various committee components were cobbled together to produce the composite catalogue.

It was at this point that the auctioneers problems began, for Christie's insisted on checking as many of the entries as possible to ascertain the correctness of the cataloguing. On top of this, as each donor's name was entered with the catalogue description, they were faced with the arduous task of checking, from every form of reference and directory that was available to them, the correct spelling of names and the correct title of each individual donor. Even after taking every care there were complaints after the sale of mis-cataloguing and mis-spelling, for it is always difficult for the individual to comprehend that what might appear a simple task when dealing with one or two references, represents in fact a monumental undertaking when dealing in limited time with several thousands.

In economic terms, however, there was little to criticise, for the sale was a great success. For this sale the King sent a panel of Chinese embroidery and the Queen a pair of bracelets. The French government donated a Sevres biscuit group, and four miniatures by Engelhart fetched £1500. A Toft dish was purchased for 650 guineas by Lady Wernher, who again asked the auctioneer to re-sell it immediately, once more outbid everyone else to re-purchase it for 600 guineas, and then presented it to the British Museum.

Another *Punch* cartoon by Townsend was put up and bought by a member of the Red Cross Committee, who again presented it to Christie's at the end of the sale. The total realised by the 1916 sale was almost sixty four thousand pounds, and this success ensured that yet a third such sale would be held in 1917.

The 1917 sale went ahead despite by now not only an acute shortage of staff at Christie's but also an acute shortage of staff at the printers, and an acute shortage of paper to print upon. Mindful of all these factors the Red Cross Committee endeavoured in their appeal to limit the number of entries for the sale by requesting that only high value items be contributed. This attempt to minimise the preparation was in the end quite unsuccessful, for on the 2nd of March, 1917, the auctioneers set forth on another twelve days sale comprising some 2132 lots.

Some excellent silver was included in this sale consisting of tankkards, jugs, goblets and a fine George the First wine cistern which was sold for £1995. Other items included the original drawings, manuscripts and the doll models for the eleven Golliwog books presented by the artist, Florence Upton, which fetched the same price. Lady Wernher again featured considerably in the buying, in this case fighting a lengthy bidding battle with Mr Morland Agnew for Frederick Walker's painting 'The Plough'. The owner of the painting had intended to leave it for the nation but at the last moment had decided to enter it for the sale. Lady Wernher eventually won the battle with Agnew, buying the picture for £5670, and immediately presenting it to the National Gallery; thus bringing great satisfaction to all concerned, including Mr Agnew, who it was revealed had intended to do precisely the same thing.

This third sale realised a total of over seventy one thousand pounds which was donated to the Central Prisoners of War Fund.

The fourth of the Red Cross sales began on Monday the 8th of April, 1918, and by far outshone those that had gone before. It comprised a staggering 2948 lots and lasted for sixteen days. The sale of jewellery alone occupied the whole of the first day and realised £35,000. The King presented a collection of prints from the library at Windsor, and many of the buyers at the sale emulated Lady Wernher in purchasing works of art and presenting them to the nation.

Max Beerbohm offered to draw a caricature of the sale in progress to be offered to the highest bidder, and the work was bought in advance of its execution by Lady Wernher and presented to the auctioneers as a momento. The total of the fourth sale was a magnificent one hundred and fifty thousand pounds which brought the aggregate for the four sales to over three hundred and thirty two thousand pounds in all.

A copy of the fourth sale catalogue, signed by all the donors and purchasers, was put up as the last lot in the sale and fetched £650. It was presented to Christie's by a group of subscribers as a souvenir of the sale, subsequently bound by Riviere and placed in a glass case in the office of the senior partner at King Street as a permanent reminder of this most remarkable series of sales.

As far as both Christie's and the Red Cross Fund were concerned, however, the four sales organised by the Red Cross Committee itself were not the end of the story. Sales were held by other bodies, under the auspices of the same auctioneers, which were to the benefit of the Red Cross Fund. The first of these was held in 1915 by the Royal Society of Painters in Water-colours, which raised a little over £2000, but by far the most important and interesting were those that became known as the 'pearl sale' and the 'gold and silver sale' which were held in 1918 and 1919 respectively. For a description of these sales and the events leading to them I could do no better than to quote directly from H.C. Marillier's book on Christie's published in 1926. He tells us:

> When collections were being made for the sale in 1918, it occurred to the Committee to appeal for pearls to be made into a necklace. This resulted in enough being received to form two necklaces, which sold for £2000. The success prompted a further idea of collecting pearls for a single great Red Cross necklace, the proceeds

of which should go to the sick and wounded. A special committee was formed to deal with this scheme, under the presidency of H.R.H. Princess Victoria, with Viscountess Northcliffe and Lady Hall as chairmen of sub-committees. Tremendous activity was displayed in advertising the appeal all over the world, and pearls to the number of 4000 flowed in in such lavish manner that the question developed into one of a number of necklaces. This somewhat nullified the primary idea, though it added to the value of the receipts. An exhibition of the pearls was held at the Grafton Galleries, and at first it was the intention to dispose of the necklaces by means of a gigantic tombola or lottery. This suggestion, of course, stirred up the anti-gambling fraternity to an extent, and produced wild outcries; and though Lord Lansdowne in the House of Lords tried to introduce a short Act legalising lotteries in the case of war charities, the Archbishop of Canterbury managed to prevent it being passed. After this triumphant vindication of the powers of virtue, the lottery project fell through, and the pearls were handed over to Christie's, who sold them to advantage with the benevolent help of the great dealers for £83,628 16s 2d., Messrs. Carrington buying the chief necklace, Lot 101, to which a large diamond clasp was attached, for the sum of £22,000 ... The seventh and last sale connected with the Red Cross funds was the so-called gold and silver sale, organised under the patronage of those excellent judges the Master of the Mint and the Governor of the Bank of England. Miss Elizabeth Asquith organised the collection committee to appeal for gifts of broken gold and silver ornaments and plate. Arrangements were made by local mayors throughout the country for gifts to be brought to the respective town halls by July 6, 1919, the anniversary of their Majesties' wedding day. Among the many valuable gifts were a silver tankard inlaid with gold, presented by the King, which was sold for £1000, and a silver teapot and stand presented by the Queen. The gifts were sent to be sold at a special shop taken for the occasion in New Bond Street, and the appeal was in full swing when it was suddenly cut short by the signing of the Armistice. The shop was then closed, and the remaining goods, amounting to 121 lots, were sold at Christie's on March 19, 1919, and realised £2385 18s 9d, one lot being put up and re-sold no less than twenty-six times. The total amount which resulted from the gold and silver collection was £53,196 10s 5d.

From the total of seven sales which took place between February, 1915, and March, 1919, it can be calculated that the sum of £413,406 13s 1d was raised for the benefit of the joint funds of the Red Cross Society and the Order of the Hospital of St John.

As one would expect however, charity sales apart, the war years were sheer financial disaster for most of the auctioneers. The fine art auctioneers were obviously the hardest hit, and only the reserves of the big four London salerooms saw them through. Much of the provincial business was restricted to the forced sales, and many of those tens of thousands of registered auctioneers simply shut up shop.

Business did get going again after the war, but well into the 1920s it was slowly does it as far as prices were concerned. Some of the finest and rarest items continued to set record prices but the opportunities for dealers and collectors were often remarkable. It is interesting to note the very large increases in value which have obtained between then and now, and Frank Herrmann in his book on Sotheby's cites some good examples taken from sale catalogues of 1922. A seventeenth century Italian flintlock rifle, the stock inlaid with buckthorn and mother of pearl—£19 10s—today's value £5500. A pair of English hand-revolved magazine flintlock pistols, second half of the seventeenth century—£135—worth today about £30,000. An entire collection of Martinware pottery comprising 151 pieces in all 'almost entirely of vases largely derived from vegetable forms, many beautifully unlaid, mottled and glazed with a wide range of colours, and practically all signed and dated'. The collection complete in two display cabinets fetched £260, or just a little less than each individual piece might be expected to realise today.

Mr Herrmann also cites a humorous incident of the period appealing enough to bear repetition, coming as it does from that time of great interest in Egyptology, and involving none other than Howard Carter of Tutankhamun fame. In a Sotheby sale of Egyptian antiquities, a fine example of statuary—a 12th Dynasty Head of Amenemmes the Third—was expected to make a very high price and was accordingly treated with great reverence throughout the viewing. Major Warre was conducting the sale, and when the head was put up Carter jokingly opened the bidding at £4000. His bid was somewhat muttered however, and Warre, seizing the advantage, raised his eyebrows questioningly and repeated, 'Fourpence did you say, Mr. Carter?' The head was sold for £10,000 to Gulbenkian.

Competition among the auctioneers became intense during the late 'twenties' as business picked up. Many of the provincial estate agents passed on their important chattels business to either Christie's or Sotheby's, and the two vied with each other to be the first to locate likely properties as soon after the death of a wealthy or notable person as was seemly. It was not uncommon for the head of one firm while on his way to an important provincial funeral, to meet the representative of the other on his way back. Such encounters prompted the comment that 'he must have been there to assist in the last rites'.

Almost always goods located in the country were removed to London for sale, but on the odd occasion when a decision was made to sell on the premises the local auctioneer was usually and deliberately involved in the organisation of the sale. The object was to avoid complaints of poaching local business, a far cry from the present when the poaching of local business is policy for the London salerooms who now wish to see less country auctioneers surviving.

It was really against all expectations that the years from 1925 to 1929 were good years for business, but the sudden boom was to come to an end in a more dramatic way than any could have imagined short of another world war. In April of 1929 Montague Barlow retired from Sotheby's. His farewell dinner was a grand affair, and an invitation had been extended to old Tom Hodge, who was forced to decline because of ill health. In his reply to the invitation, however, he made a prophetic statement regarding the continuing competition between the big two; but even from the brink of disaster neither he nor any of the revellers could foresee that the party was almost over. His letter read:

> My dear Clem,
>
> It is extremely kind of you to ask my wife & me to the dinner you are giving on the occasion of your retirement from Sotheby's. I wish I could come but I really cannot. I'm sure you understand me, & you one day may be up against the same difficulty in a modified degree. That you would like me to be with you makes me happy & is in keeping with the tradition of perpetual good feeling and regard between all members past & present, staff & principals alike, of Sotheby's. It is difficult to believe that you have been twenty years in the firm but its magnificent increase in fame, power & volume of business helps one to realise it. One now may well say that my father's and my dream of Sotheby's being the leading auctioneers of everything in the way of literature & art may materialise. We were not to see it but he relaid the foundations for the old firm & my old friends Barlow, Hobson & Warre built on them & are building. May they raise a sky scraper that will attract all the world.

From precisely this moment in time the longstanding hope of all the Sotheby partners, old and new, was to be fulfilled. The Wall Street crash in America and the slump in England were somehow to hit Christie's harder than Sotheby's. Record profits were to turn to losses overnight, and from now on it was to be Sotheby first and Christie second in order of popularity. The dramatic events of the 1930s were to turn previously unthinkable options into matters for serious consideration. The possibility of a merger between the big two auctioneers was suddenly on the agenda, with the simple objective of savings on advertising expenses. Things were that bad.

The dramatic turn round in the fortunes of the two businesses is indicated by their accounts for the early thirties. In 1931 and 1932 Christie's made a small loss while Sotheby's made a small profit, but in 1933 Christie's losses were in excess of £8000 while Sotheby's profit was in the order of £13,000.

By 1934 the accountants had analysed all the figures in preparation for a merger. A new unlimited company was to be formed. Trading was to cease at Bond Street and the King Street premises were to be enlarged to cope with extra staff. There were to be nine directors, five from King Street and four from Bond Street, and Warre was to be chairman. In the end agreement could not be reached on the division of profits. Christie's were unable to accept their new role as number two in the auction business, although the current figures clearly indicated that Sotheby's now had the lead in terms of profitability. The negotiations foundered and no further progress was made.

Despite the uncertainties however, and regardless of the wild fluctuations of fortune due to the economic climate, the fine arts had become such an important part of the auction scene that the commentators were constantly casting about for evidence that London was the leader in the world art market. The arrival for sale of one notable collection from abroad drew the comment from *The Times*:

> this is an indication that continental collectors recognise the supremacy of London as the art market of the world. High prices are realised in Paris, Berlin and New York but in no capital in the world do prices for fine pictures and art objects maintain such a consistently high level as in London.

What was considered to be the best evidence for the truth of that statement was to come right at the end of 1936, just weeks after the item was first published. The event was the sale at Sotheby's of the fine library of the recently deceased Anton Mensing, a notable Amsterdam auctioneer. The decision to sell in London was widely regarded as indicating the importance of the London salerooms, particularly when it was noted that the Dutch themselves had been selling books by auction for at least as long if not longer than the English.

By the late summer of 1939 the dogs of war were once more roaming the streets of the European capitals. Ironically, the hallmark of the later destruction of London, fire, had struck prematurely at Phillips when in July their rooms in Bond Street, their home since 1797, were consumed. The firm very quickly moved to Blenstock House, missing only one sale, and have been there ever since. Under the new German menace the arts were once more to decline, and the newly established art auction markets were to be slowly but surely reduced to rubble. Of the four capital markets Paris was to remain intact but impotent due to the rapid capitulation of France, London and Berlin were to slowly decline due to the constant attention of the Luftwaffe and the RAF respectively, and New York was to carry on in a strictly limited way.

Although domestically America escaped the worst effects of both world wars, the Wall Street crash and the great depression which followed hit the general population hard. The collapse of the stock market was a national calamity which wrought havoc with the existing social order, and the speed of the disaster has left recorded many a tale of unfortunate miscalculation to illustrate the drama of the period.

Jerome Kern, a household name as the author of many hit musical shows, was a great collector of books and particularly of eighteenth and nineteenth century English literary manuscripts. Kern's library was offered for sale at the Anderson Gallery in New York in 1929, immediately prior to the collapse of Wall Street. It is often the case that a mood of apparent boom and buoyancy precedes the final dramatic fall, and so it was here. Prices at the auction were astronomical, leading one observer to write:

> the sale was a most dramatic event and had an influence on book prices for years, and possibly for the rest of time. Everybody lost his head and the prices were fantastic.

The incredible final total for the sale was one and three-quarter million dollars, and the equally incredible consequence was that Kern invested the proceeds on the booming stock market and within just a few months had lost everything. With hardly time to recover from her economic difficulties before Europe was plunged once again into war, it is hardly surprising that even in America, so far removed from the holocaust, the auction merely pottered along dealing principally with the necessities of life rather than the extravagances of the art world.

In London and the provinces the auction rooms carried on with what business there was and with the staff that was left. There were no gala occasions, and most of the business was conducted by the most senior partners, those whose age had spared them a place in the front line. At Sotheby's and Christie's it was time to look again at the possibility of a merger. Once more the figures were trotted out and the calculations contemplated. Once more it was agreed that the Bond Street premises would be sold and the new company would operate from King Street, beginning in October, 1940. Again, in the end, nothing came of it, and the two firms soldiered on with the old guard in command.

The two of them did, however, come to one particular arrangement. They decided that in the event of the premises of either firm being damaged in the blitz the other would provide suitable accommodation for the victim. When Christie's premises were virtually destroyed in 1941 Sotheby's immediately offered assistance, but the firm had already been offered temporary accommodation close by, and eventually moved into Lord Derby's house behind Oxford Street for the duration.

The other member of the London quartet, Bonhams, had been forced to move before the war by the expiry of their Oxford Street lease. They had set up shop in Burlington Street but Hitler's bombers forced them to move once more by destroying, within the space of just ten days, not only those premises but their secondary room at Whitfield Street. The firm spent the remaining war years at Newman Street where the business was run by Leonard Bonham's sister, Helen Maddick, who recalls that the Germans pursued them even there. She tells of the approach of a flying bomb during one of the weekly sales:

> I was in the rostrum and Mr. Lewsey, who had been with us for many years, was in the clerk's desk. We heard this buzzing thing coming over and the only two that were still upright afterwards were Mr. Lewsey and me because we could'nt throw ourselves out of the rostrum. Everyone else dived under tables and furniture — you could'nt see a soul. When it went off you saw people's heads appearing, some looking rather shaken, others looking rather sheepish, and some absolutely terrified; and we were still sitting there.

When the war was over the rebuilding began, quite literally in the case of Christie's, for only the facade of their King Street premises remained, and this was taken down brick by brick in order that the building could be reconstructed in its original form. For all the major auctioneers, however, rebuilding the business to the former levels of interest and excitement was to take a little longer than it would take to re-assemble the buildings. Understandably, between 1945 and 1950 auctioneering, particularly in the fine arts, was at a low ebb, and quite often prices realised for not insignificant works of art slumped to the levels of fifty years earlier—certainly very little progress was made.

As always however, as in any recession, someone was making money, and in one particular area of trade quite a lot of it. As always, and certainly in this case, the auctioneers were involved in this money-making process, the like of which will probably never be seen again. Some of the dealers involved became millionaires in a very short space of time, and the auction ring flourished in a way that makes the pickings of even the modern operators seem like so much petty cash.

The business was war surplus, the rapid disposal of billions of poundsworth of precision equipment and stores no longer required by the armed forces. Such sales were very often an outdoor operation conducted at airfields and factories and warehouses all over the country. Many of the larger provincial auctioneers assisted in the disposal, particularly those near to the major depots. Records of the sales are scarce, but reminiscences abound. Much of the detail has become a sort of folk history of the period handed down from those who actually participated; and some of the stories are almost unbelievable.

The fact that many of the dealers in war surplus acquired their wealth quickly does not suggest a high level of efficiency on the part of the auctioneers. Whether it was a case of an inability to cope with the sheer volume of goods, or simply a lack of expertise in cataloguing such a diverse range, there is a good deal of evidence to suggest that misdescription was the rule rather than the exception.

I am fortunate indeed to have a client who was actually involved in some of those buying operations and who in fact made a few pounds out of the business himself. His own personal version of events, gathered from his own experiences and largely in his own words, is as follows:

At the end of the last war, the then Ministry of Disposal decided to sell by auction the vast stocks of surplus war materials—everything from socks to aeroplanes—which were lying at the various supply depots all over Britain and abroad. Those appointed to do the selling were mostly country auctioneers whose principal previous experience had been the sale of livestock, agricultural machinery and land, together with the occasional chattels disposal. Faced with huge quantities of highly technical equipment and stores their performance was, to say the least, somewhat less than competent.

The range of goods was so diverse and the quantities so large that the auctioneers did not appear to make much effort to get a sensible return for the seller. Catalogues would include single lots described as 'a field of bicycles', five thousand beds might be sold off in lots of five hundred at a time, and literally thousands of pairs of boots and shoes and blankets, hundreds of tons of aircraft and radio spares, would be lotted in such large amounts that the value of each lot was almost impossible to estimate, and only the largest dealers with ample storage could be involved in the serious buying.

Buyers at the sales included scrap dealers, farmers, textile merchants, radio and electrical dealers from London and other major cities, as well as buyers from the aircraft industry. Some of these had experience of war surplus dealing from the first world war and were up to all the tricks of the trade. Viewing of the goods was usually the day prior to the sale, with two days allowed in the case of major disposals. When the view was over the big dealers would convene a meeting in the lounge of a convenient hotel and a chairman would be appointed to run the business. All those present would then disclose which lots interested them, and perhaps three members of the group would be nominated to do the bidding. A private room was hired for use after the sale in which was held the knock out, the previously elected chairman acting as auctioneer. At every sale there were a number of minor dealers or 'small-fry', who were advised which lots the ring would be bidding for. They were further advised not to oppose the ring bidding on those lots, and told that they would be looked after if they attended the later knock out.

When the small-fry had been paid off to an individual valuation determined by the chairman the real bidding began in earnest. Each highest bidder would, as usual, put the difference between the price he paid and the price at the sale into a kitty which, as usual, was shared out at the close of the business. It was also possible for individuals to make killings and sometimes fortunes by cashing in on gross cataloguing errors which they alone had discovered—or even when they had not.

There are many examples including a sale at an aerodrome at Hartlebury where one lot in the catalogue was described as a large quantity of empty boxes situated in an adjacent field. The lot was sold for £75, but it transpired that the approximately two thousand boxes were in fact filled with platinum tipped sparking plugs. As platinum was even then valued at about £90 an ounce, the miscatalogued lot was worth many thousands of pounds to the lucky or shrewd buyer.

In a sale at Stafford a large quantity of steel dropping canisters were offered as a lot. These were the type of containers that had been used for dropping supplies to troops and resistance workers in occupied Europe. They were about six feet long and made in two halves bolted together lengthways. A local dealer hit on the bright idea of unbolting the two sections and selling them to farmers as animal feeding troughs. In the event it turned out to be a better idea than he had thought, for when the canisters were opened each one was found to contain a new high quality radio set and spare parts. Within days he was beseiged by dealers from all over the country, all anxious to outbid each other to obtain the highly prized radios.

The client who recounted these stories was, as I have said, personally involved in the business at the time, and as an example of the amounts of money which were made he has quoted to me the details of a deal which he himself made in February, 1952. He attended a sale, again in Stafford, in the middle of a spell of particularly bad weather. Most of the lots were strewn about in open fields and as a consequence of the weather very few people attended the sale. Mr G., as I will call him, was determined to make the difficult journey however, for in the catalogue was a lot described as 450 cylinder liners, a commodity for which he had a ready market. Without even viewing the lot he duly purchased it at the auction for £120, which considering that his buyers were willing to pay £10 each for the 450 liners left a very good profit in prospect.

Imagine his surprise, and delight, when he discovered on arriving later to collect his purchase that instead of 450 liners he had bought 450 boxes of liners, and that each box contained a batch of 10. His buyers—Rolls Royce and the Israeli government—were able to take all 4500 liners between them at the going rate, and Mr G. for his £120 outlay plus transport netted a cool £45,000. When trying to put that sort of profit margin into perspective remember that at the time a good quality detached house would cost about £2000.

While the country auctioneers were trudging around the fields trying to get a bid for half a million pairs of knickers, Peter Wilson was in New York trying to buy Parke-Bernet. He began negotiations on behalf of Sotheby's as early as 1947, but without success. That negotiations began so early is however a clear indication that Sotheby's saw the golden opportunities ahead for the fine art auctioneers.

In July, 1949, the hundred year old restrictions on auctioneers were lifted. The Auctioneers Act of 1845, which imposed the obligation of obtaining a licence, was repealed by the Finance Act 1949. Now anyone could become an auctioneer, and many were to do so.

At the close of the first half of the twentieth century the auction world was preparing to take its share of the affluence just around the corner. Of the European capitals London was struggling but determined, Berlin was divided and out of the running, while in Paris the customers were still wandering about the old Hotel Drouot, which fifty years after poor Uzanne's plea was just as dirty as ever. If ever New York had an opportunity to become number one in the art auction world it was now, but while London simmered New York failed to boil, and the chance was lost. In the next decade the winner of the art auction capital of the world competition would be announced.

CHAPTER 9

Towards the Present Time

The period between 1950 and the present day is the time when the seeds of the art-auction connection, planted so hopefully by the pioneers of the major salerooms so many years before, blossomed to such brilliant effect that the fine arts began to totally dominate the auction scene. As time passed the thickness of the icing on the auction cake grew and grew, and when the slicing up was completed it was Sotheby's and Christie's who had taken it almost all, leaving only crumbs for the rest to share.

There were three main ingredients in the rich mixture that was produced, and first and foremost of these was the new and fast growing market for fine art. As the memories of war receded the feeling grew that the nuclear weapons that had so effectively shortened the last war would forever prevent any possibility of another. The technology developed to aid the war effort was available to the new industrial producers, and the wealth generated was greater than at any time before.

Just the scent of a new opportunity was enough to stimulate ingredient number two, as the men from Sotheby's and Christie's took to sailing the Atlantic in search of new international links in a rapidly shrinking world. The invasion of New York by the London salerooms began as early as 1947, and although initially repulsed, persistance was to pay off in the end.

The third ingredient was a vital one and a real bonus for the ambitious London auctioneers. Rapid technological growth was leading to highly efficient media coverage of major events, and to the speedy commercial development of the small screen with the big appetite—television. The growth of business, and of profits, permitted the big two in particular to make the most of the opportunities provided by the media, and their proximity to the major media sources allowed them to develop the special relationship with the press and television which has led to the interchange of expertise that we see today.

In 1957 there was to occur at Sotheby's a sale which was to bring together all the ingredients in abundance, a sale to epitomise the new and modern style of the fine art auctioneers, and above all a sale

which was to launch Sotheby's in particular, but the London salerooms in general, into a spectacular orbit. It was a sale of Impressionist paintings, drawings and sculpture which had been formed into
a collection by William Weinberg, a banker recently deceased. The
items had been acquired for disposal in London by a high level ex-
peditionary force headed by Peter Wilson which had travelled to Mr
Weinberg's home in New York to examine and negotiate for the quite
remarkable collection.

The press publicity which accompanied the sale was of an unprecedented nature, and while even Christie's would reject a claim that
the sale did them any good directly, there is no doubt whatsoever
that the sale and its attendant publicity set the future course of fine
art auctioneering not just for the London salerooms, but nationally
and internationally as well. Quite unusually Sotheby's commissioned
an advertising agency to take care of publicity and public relations
for the sale, and even more unusually an invitation to the viewing
was sent to Buckingham Palace. On the day before the sale the Queen,
with Prince Philip and Princess Margaret, arrived at Bond Street to
view the pictures. They were shown round by Anthony Blunt, then
Keeper of the Queen's Pictures, and the interest shown by the Royal
Family was the crowning glory to the pre-sale build-up.

The publicity campaign had begun five weeks before the sale with
a huge press conference, and coverage had extended through national
and provincial newspapers in France, Italy, Germany and Holland.
The American press was of course keenly interested, and the event
was also reported in Canada, Australia and New Zealand. Television
was to have a dual role in the proceedings, for as well as providing
some impressive publicity—'Panorama' devoted the best part of a
programme to the sale—closed circuit television was used for the first
time to relay events in the main and overcrowded saleroom to two
secondary rooms used to accommodate the overflow audience.

Few of the newspaper reports failed to mention the significance of
such a major American collection finding its way to the London
salerooms. The American *Christian Science Monitor* said simply: 'London
has become the centre of the art market'. The *Sunday Times*, however,
pointed out that much of the collection, although having resided in
America, had in fact been assembled from European sources, principally from Holland. The collection included paintings and drawings
by Seurat and Degas, bronzes by Daumier, but above all a group
of paintings, drawings and watercolours by Van Gogh, most of
which had been used in the filming of the Irving Stone novel *Lust
for Life*.

Many of the newspapers speculated on the results of the sale and
some of those doing so were not exactly the sort of journals that one
might expect to be much interested in such an event in normal cir-

cumstances. The *Times Educational Supplement* expressed the hope that some of the pictures might find their way into museums for the benefit of the public at large, and the *Glasgow Herald* found space to comment on the prior sale of Weinberg's art reference books. The long list of newspapers and periodicals which reported on the sale in one way or another included the *Financial Times*, *New Yorker*, *News Chronicle*, *Punch*, *Washington Post*, *Le Figaro*, *Birmingham Post*, *Sunday Times* and *Daily Telegraph*. As well as television news coverage there were numerous broadcast references by BBC radio in London and CBS radio in Washington.

After such acute media interest it is fortunate indeed that the sale itself was not an anti-climax. It was in fact a great success, and the report in *The Times* summed it up:

> The flower of the intelligentsia, divided fairly evenly between the opulent and the impecunious, crowded Sotheby's rooms yesterday in such numbers that business had to be dealt with in three rooms at one and the same time by means of closed T.V. circuit. Dealers and collectors from Europe and across the Atlantic were naturally present in force, including Lord Rothschild and Baron Elie de Rothschild, and there was an unusual amount of spirited bidding from private individuals. The scene was extraordinarily animated, adorned by half a dozen feminine hats—perhaps chosen to vie with the charming confection worn by the Renoir lady of one of the paintings—and if any pins were dropped during the more tense moments of the morning, the sound did not reach the ears of your correspondent.
>
> Nor surprisingly did the perpetual comings and goings of television operators and press photographers, present in greater numbers than ever before seen in an auction room, distract the attention of the company or mar its obvious enjoyment—an enjoyment which occasionally found expression in delighted ripples of laughter as the hammer was about to fall and a further bid of £500 or so came at the last moment ... the total for the 56 lots was £326,520 ... It was a memorable occasion, not merely because it made auction room history or because it will be many years, if ever, before a small personal collection of nineteenth-century masters of comparable quality comes on to the open market, but also because it would appear to provide overwhelming evidence that London has fully regained its position as a highly efficient world centre for the disposal of works of art from either side of the Atlantic.

The Weinberg sale gave Sotheby's a great deal of experience in the finer points of organising a complex international sale of the kind that was to come increasingly their way in the years ahead. It was also to prove to be an early example of a business technique which they were to use to great advantage in the future, that of completely demoralising the opposition by virtue of their well publicised success. In this case Parke-Bernet were furious that the collection had not come to them.

Christie's were not to know that a benefit would eventually come their way as a result of this watershed of a sale, for they were in fact in some difficulty at the time. They had somehow managed to lose their place as the favourite auctioneers of the rich and famous and were drifting along in something of a backwater. In 1958 the company was re-organised and the chairman replaced. The new broom technique dictated that the King Street premises were repainted, that a series of board-room lunches were inaugurated to which were invited collectors, curators, journalists and politicians, and that a full-time representative was installed in New York to help stimulate international growth.

Thus Christie's stepped into the international arena and set off in hot pursuit of their major rival. They had a lot of ground to make up, but the stakes were high and the winning post some way off.

One of the greatest auction houses on the other side of the Atlantic was Parke-Bernet, with premises on Madison Avenue in New York. Parke-Bernet were the auctioneers that Sotheby's had been looking at since 1947, and having observed the New Yorker's ups and downs, had been waiting for the right moment to pounce. Pouncing was in Sotheby's opinion infinitely preferable to having to start from scratch by opening a brand new saleroom in New York, with the extra disadvantage of then having to compete directly with the established American auctioneers.

By November, 1961, it seemed that the chance of a takeover was gone, for Parke-Bernet had managed—against the odds it seemed—to convince the executors of the estate of Mrs Anna Erickson that New York was the place to sell one of the finest small collections of Old Master paintings in America; a collection which included the legendary and magnificent Rembrandt 'Aristotle Contemplating the Bust of Homer'. Representatives of both Sotheby's and Christie's had made repeated trips to New York, where the collection was housed, during the negotiations for an auction venue, and had Sotheby's succeeded in wresting the prize from Parke-Bernet at that time it might well have marked the end for the American auctioneers.

In the event New York was the venue and the sale on the 15th of November, 1961, was a spectacular success. The sale total was 4,679,250 dollars with the star item, the 'Aristotle', making just half of the total at 2,300,000 dollars. The then president of the Parke-Bernet Galleries, Leslie Hyam, said after the sale:

We simply had to have the sale. This was a prime battle, a prime test. If our competitors had taken the Erickson, they'd have taken the cream from the top of everything for the next five years. The publicity which we enjoyed would have gone overseas for the benefit of the other side. But the results, I think, justified our position that in the United States, the wealthiest country in the world, there are no limits to what people will pay, under competitive conditions, for the finest things.

Although not having put in the same length of service as its major overseas competitors, Parke-Bernet was nevertheless able to boast a respectable pedigree. It was one Thomas E. Kirby who in 1885 opened in New York the 'American Art Association', which was eventually to become Parke-Bernet. Kirby had arrived in New York from Philadelphia where he had won a considerable reputation as an auctioneer. He had also won the support of an influential group of backers, and both he and they were determined to launch the lavishly appointed auction house which they believed New York was ready for. Lavish it certainly was as an observer of the new premises reported at the time.

His large, high display rooms were hung with velvet; his corridors were mirrored and marbled; every pre-sale display was arranged by an artist in interiors; the auction room itself was hung in red velvet, was opulent in gilt plaster; his catalogues were beautifully printed authorities, to be saved as source books about antique furniture, paintings, rare books and objects of virtue.

The firm progressed nicely in its comfortable surroundings until the mid-1930's when disaster struck in the biggest possible way. The staff at the time included all the essential ingredients for the later success of the firm for Hiram Parke was there as well as Otto Bernet and the Englishman Leslie Hyam. The troubles began with the death of C.F. Bishop, who had bought the American Art Association from the Kirby family and amalgamated it with the Anderson Galleries of Park Avenue to make it the biggest auction house in the United States, with a turnover in 1935 of ten million dollars.

Milton Logan, an employee who had found favour with the late owner, was also favoured by the two impressionable women who were the principal beneficiaries of Bishop's estate, his widow and his private secretary. Logan prevailed on them with an offer of just 175,000 dollars for the galleries, which was immediately accepted. Even at such a bargain price, however, Logan could not raise the money and brought in an old school-friend and insurance salesman, John Geery, who cleverly secured the transaction with just 10,000 dollars in cash, a 65,000 dollar loan and promissory notes for the balance of 100,000 dollars.

At the end of 1937, just weeks before the new partners took over, the entire professional staff of forty, led by Hiram Parke and Otto Bernet, walked out. As a last resort, fearing what was to come under the new management, a consortium of the staff had offered the two women more than that promised by Logan and Geery, but they had been turned down. When Logan and Geery took over they immediately set about systematically swindling their clients by paying out considerably less than the amounts paid for goods, but even in spite of this the business went steadily down-hill.

The old staff, meanwhile, in temporary premises down the street, struggled on in difficult circumstances and waited expectantly for the collapse of the new regime with the hope that they might recover the old premises and salvage what was left of the business. They did not have too long to wait. Without trained staff and lacking personal experience of the business Logan and Geery were soon in financial difficulties.

The beginning of the macabre end came when Geery discovered in the files an insurance policy for one hundred thousand dollars which the firm had taken out some years before on the life of the book expert, Dr Rosenbach, while he was on a mission for them in Europe. Geery immediately took out insurance on Logan's life in the sum of one hundred and fifty thousand dollars with Lloyds of London. No sooner had Geery paid the premiums than the firm finally went bankrupt, and at once the old team—now Parke-Bernet Inc.—moved back into the old purpose-built accommodation.

With events now moving very rapidly Logan and Geery were arrested on charges of grand larceny, and released on bail. On an evening in February, 1940, the two of them took a car ride along East River Drive with a friend of Geery's, John Poggi, seated in the back. It was Poggi who from the rear seat cracked Logan's skull with a lead filled pipe, and the two of them, Poggi and Geery, dumped him out of the car and left him for dead. Logan, however, was not dead and managed to attract the attention of a passing police car. Geery, learning some hours later that his partner was in the hospital with a police guard and likely to recover, went into the cellar of his house and shot himself.

It was in 1949 that Parke-Bernet took over the present accommodation at 980 Madison Avenue, and it was in 1953 that there began an intensive campaign on behalf of the London auctioneers to poach business from the United States in general and from Parke-Bernet in particular. Both Sotheby's and Christie's now had permanent offices in New York, and their representatives conducted a verbal publicity battle with Parke-Bernet's Leslie Hyam, with all concerned extolling the virtues of their own service while damning the facilities of their opponents.

John Herbert, for Christie's, stated that without doubt 'London is the undisputed centre of the art market', and he claimed that one of the best reasons for selling there was 'the knowledge that its auction house experts have acquired during the past 150 years'. He was inclined to finish with the real clincher, the commission rates in London, which were 'approximately half what is demanded in America and France ... It pays to sell in London ... There is a three per cent sales tax in New York and a ten per cent Federal tax on certain kinds of goods'.

Sotheby's played their part in the campaign by claiming through Peter Wilson that 'in recent years all the most important sales of paintings have been at Sotheby's', and by reminding potential sellers that 'there is no import duty on works of art of any kind over 100 years old coming into Britain; nor on pictures or books of any date. There is no government or any other tax on sales by auction. There is no export duty out of the United States.' The Sotheby sermon usually concluded 'payments of the proceeds of sale in London can be made, without formality or delay, in any currency (including US dollars), or in sterling, as desired.'

Hyam's counter argument for Parke-Bernet and the American art market was simple and to the point, 'the idea that sellers get higher prices in London is British propaganda. With relatively few exceptions, the outstanding works offered here have gone to American buyers.

Wherever the outstanding works ended up, it was without doubt the publicity value of the major dispersals which was the greatest asset as far as the auctioneers were concerned. Here was a clear case of a mackerel to catch the sprats, for we must not forget that the largest part of the auctioneers volume of business comprises goods in the lower price range, and that those goods are brought in by efficient publicity. Hyam certainly did not overlook the smaller fish in the form of the foreign tourist-collector wishing to visit an auction in an unfamiliar country. A Parke-Bernet 'bulletin' for 1962 contained a 'Phrase Book for Foreigners', part of which read:

'Q. I come from Lille (Stuttgart, Issy-les-Moulineaux). I am a collector of paintings (paperweights, autographs of Balzac) and I wish to purchase one (some)

A. You may purchase it (them) at a reasonable price at a public auction (public sale). Let us go in. Here is the elevator. Take us, if you please, my friend, to the sale room.

Q. Good afternoon. Have you a Rembrandt (paperweight, letter of Balzac) for sale?

A. Not at the moment, sir. We are selling today English furniture.

Q. I am (am not) very fond of English furniture. My uncle says that Hepplewhite (Sheraton) is more refined than Chippendale. I

read somewhere that the English were forbidden to use anything
but mahogany.
A. Mahogany lasts longer. Come, sir, here we are in the sale room.
That is the auctioneer, who is chanting loudly from the rostrum
... Do you wish to bid on this night chair (stool, washstand)?
Q. I bid six hundred dollars.
A. The auctioneer is very excited. He sees your bid. Look, he has
knocked the chair down to you.
Q. How amusing it is here. See. The lady in the fur hat bought a
large bed (sofa, settee).
A. She is smiling at you, and is standing up (beckoning, waving).
The attendant courteously makes way for her. She is doubtlessly
wealthy (very rich). Let us follow.

Despite their success with the Erickson sale, Parke-Bernet's defiant
independence was to be shorter-lived than anyone might have reasonably imagined at the time. Sotheby's were absolutely determined to
gain control as quickly as possible in order to consolidate their position
as world leaders. The pressure finally paid off in 1964.

By August of that year it was over, but not without an extensive
public relations campaign and a good deal of intermittant sniping
from both sides through the media. The first salvo in the final battle
for control was fired by Sotheby's in the form of an article carried by
the *Sunday Telegraph* on the 5th of July, 1964, part of which was as
follows.

> Sotheby's struck the most humiliating blow last week at their Amer-
> ican rivals in art auctioneering. After a £1,000,000 sale on Wednes-
> day they blandly announced that their season's turnover for works
> of art sent from the United States alone already exceeded Parke-
> Bernet's entire takings in the year—approximately £3,800,000.
> Sotheby's is likely to be £13,000,000.

The article also referred to a direct threat from Sotheby's that failure
to acquire Parke-Bernet would cause the London auctioneers to establish their own auction gallery in New York in the following year. The
threat of imminent invasion caused the American press to become
highly excited and to report the promise of reprisals as well as asser-
tions that the premier American auction house would be defended to
the last man.

However, most of the Parke-Bernet directors went off on holiday,
and when the last man had gone Sotheby's were left to quietly consolidate their shareholding in the firm. A reporter for the *New York
Herald Tribune* who was also an officer in the US Air Force Reserve,
Earl Talbott, was able to comment on the end of this modern 'auction
war' as follows.

We had just returned from performing a stint of military duty, guarding the ramparts against all enemies of the republic, foreign and domestic, only to discover that in our absence the British had landed and made off with Parke-Bernet ... Majestic in defeat, that outpost still kept proud vigil at Upper Madison Avenue, its turrets empty but its battlements unscarred; a mute testimonial to the potency of a great alien weapon, the ten per cent commission. Nonchalantly whistling 'God Save the Queen', to throw any lurking enemy troops off the track, we negotiated the post portcullis without incident and rounded the almost empty corridors.

Someone remarked that most of the garrison had gone on leave, a piece of intelligence that we weighed with slight scepticism. Inwardly scoffing, we could only offer a fervent prayer that Sotheby's, the new seneschal, subscribed to the Geneva Convention, prescribing the treatment of prisoners of war.

An interesting domestic feature of the late 1960s was the inauguration by Sotheby's of a training scheme designed in the first place to solve their problem of how to find enough qualified staff to deal with their expanding business. In the end the exercise became more of an object lesson in demonstrating the prestige associated with the Sotheby name. Not only were they able to attract enough suitable candidates to fill the course places, but were very soon in a position to require those applying for entry to pay for the privilege of being tutored by the masters of the art. Even so, and without any guarantee of employment on completion of the training, the courses were constantly oversubscribed.

The original plan for the first year of operation was that nine selected students should each be paid £800 to undertake a ten month course of training followed by a three week trip to a European city important in the arts. The lucky first-year nine were the only ones who were ever paid for their training, for at the end of the first year the firm had decided to make the scheme self-financing by charging the students for their education. By the third year the operation was so successful that despite having moved to larger premises the intake had to be limited to fifty students.

The training given covers all aspects of the auctioneers trade and includes some practical experience in Sotheby's London salerooms. It is recorded that of the 49 students enroled on the 1980 course, 20 came from the United States, 7 from the United Kingdom and the rest from Italy, Germany, Switzerland, Austria, Argentina, Canada, Finland, France, Iran and Lebanon. The course continues to be popular, the fees increase annually, the current cost of the twelve month course is £3500.

Perhaps the most important as well as the most controversial matter to hit the world of art and auctioneering during the 1970s was the re-introduction for the autumn season of 1975 of the old Roman 'buyer's premium'. The purpose of introducing a ten per cent charge on the buyer was very simply to effect an overall increase in commission charges without penalising the vendor by raising the seller's charges to twenty per cent. The auctioneers were of course well aware that to raise selling charges to that sort of level might easily build up resistance among vendors and discourage them from dealing with the salerooms. Far from being prepared to contemplate a reduction of business, the London salerooms saw in the introduction of the premium a rare opportunity to consolidate and eventually increase their share of the art market.

To this end the first effect of the new charge to buyers was to immediately reduce the charge to sellers to only ten per cent. Thus at a stroke profitability was improved and so was the prospect of new business attracted by the new low charges. It is doubtless this facet of the move which caused the fine art trade generally to raise such a hue and cry on the matter of the premium, for any move which makes the salerooms more attractive to sellers automatically diminishes the dealer's prospects of obtaining his stock from private sources. Consequently the trade is forced to purchase from the salerooms to obtain stock and obliged to pay the premium which it so despises.

From the London auctioneers point of view the introduction of the buyer's premium was a neat piece of business made all the more effective by the fact that both Christie's and Sotheby's announced their intention to introduce it within a week of each other. The stated reason for the almost tandem announcement being that Christie's, having decided to go ahead with the scheme, notified Sotheby's before declaring their intention publicly. Sotheby's assert that it was necessary to follow suit as quickly as possible to avoid giving any advantage to their great rivals.

The timing of the two announcements drew an allegation from the art and antiques trade of collusion between the big two, and the threat of litigation hung over the London salerooms from the inception of the premium until the end of 1981 when hostilities were suspended. The threatened High Court action was then dropped ostensibly because of the very substantial cost of proceeding further. A settlement was effected between the representatives of the fine art trade on one hand and Sotheby's and Christie's on the other, with each paying a proportion of the costs already incurred.

It is worth noting that Phillips announced initially that they would reduce the commission rate to ten per cent in line with the others, but would not charge the premium. By so doing they were taking a calculated risk which required them to pick up as much business from their competitors as would increase their turnover in sufficient proportion to offset the lost commissions. In the end it did not work. The new business generated initially gradually tapered off and after three years Phillips came fully into line by introducing the premium.

Very many of the provincial auctioneers, both large and small, were also forced to come into line once the big two had established the new system. Most country auctioneers found it difficult enough to compete with the London rooms on an equal commission basis; to attempt to survive whilst charging the seller a higher rate was a prospect many found too daunting. There are of course still a few provincial salerooms which do not charge the premium and who proudly announce the fact in their advertising. It is almost invariably the case, however, that those who resist the change are principally estate agents and valuers who do not rely wholly on the auction for their livelihood, but treat it merely as a lucrative adjunct to their business.

In the international auction world the power of the premium as a business proposition has had a most significant effect on the pattern of world auctioneering. With commission rates in France and America going as high as thirty per cent because of the inclusion of government and federal taxes, the London auctioneers were bound to increase the value of their international business with the introduction of the premium. With their reputation high to begin with, the extra benefit of a lower charge to sellers produced an irresistible combination which has accounted in no small measure for the astonishing growth of the two major auctioneers.

The best remembered sale of the 1970s will be the epic house contents sale conducted by Sotheby's at Mentmore in Buckinghamshire. The record breaking total of £6,390,000 realised in the 18 session sale was not in fact destined to be a record for long, and the biggest sale total of the decade was to be achieved only a year later when the Von Hirsch sale amassed almost three times that figure, a staggering £18,500,000.

Mentmore will remain long in the memory, however, because of the intense publicity associated not only with the sale itself but with the original protracted negotiations between the executors and the Department of the Environment in which the government were offered the house and its contents for £3,600,000 in lieu of death duties. Mentmore was an obsolete and rambling Victorian monument built by Joseph Paxton in the 1850's and long past its prime when inherited by the 7th Earl of Rosebery in 1974 along with other properties and some £4½ million in taxes.

Even before the negotiations with the government had broken down Sotheby's were called in to begin cataloguing the contents for sale. In

January, 1977, the Department of the Environment decided not to make an offer for Mentmore and the sale was scheduled for May. It was important that the sale—if there was to be one—should take place before the 30th of May, for the very good reason that up to that date death duties were payable only on the agreed probate valuation, whereas to wait until later would render the estate liable to tax on the full realised value.

At the eleventh hour the public outcry at the governments decision, fuelled by press reports of the wanton dissipation of priceless national assets caused the Department to reconsider the situation, and Sotheby's to indicate that they would require a not inconsiderable fee for the cataloguing should their efforts prove abortive. This frenzied last minute activity did the Sotheby workforce no good at all, but achieved for the sale the most valuable free publicity ever obtained by any sale before. In the nick of time a government 'spokesman' announced that the saving of Mentmore for the nation was 'politically and economically impossible'. The sale went ahead as scheduled.

The five volume catalogue at thirty pounds a set was sold out three weeks before the sale despite the fact that 11,000 copies had been printed. The sale itself was conducted in a two thousand seater marquee in the grounds, and American style bid-callers were used to scan the sea of faces on behalf of the auctioneer. In the best house sale tradition the general public exhibited a severe case of auction madness by bidding sometimes hundred of pounds for the general bric-a-brac and residual contents of the kitchens, out-houses and servants quarters. Many lessons were learned from the experience of Mentmore—not least that government departments are unerring in their failure to spot a bargain even when it is staring them in the face.

We have seen how parallels and similarities abound throughout the long history of the auction, and a feature of the record breaking Von Hirsch sale of 1978 draws a controversial comparison with an earlier controversy relating to the old problem of expertise and advice. In the part of the sale devoted to mediaeval antiquities, where a mere 97 lots made about as much as the entire Mentmore sale—£6,368,150—a twelfth-century English gilt altar candlestick base was knocked down for £550,000. On the morning after the sale it was revealed that the lot had been purchased on behalf of the British Rail Pension Fund, and the revelation raised a furore in the British press.

It seems that having noted the rapidly escalating prices of works of art, as well as having been subjected to pressure from individuals within their ranks to participate in the buoyant market, the trustees of the fund approached Sotheby's to ask them to act as the fund's advisors. It would be difficult to imagine a more absurd piece of business than this. The custodians of large sums of money gathered from the contributions of the working class investing large amounts on works of art on the advice of the premier auctioneers, who had the most vested interest in maintaining spectacular price levels. The disquiet that was strongly felt at the time is not dispelled by Mr Herrmann's account of these events in his book on Sotheby's. He expresses an internal viewpoint in his account, and lists some doubtful arguments in support of the venture. He says:

> Why Sotheby's? people asked. The answer given was that they were known to be the most prominent firm of fine art auctioneers, the most internationally based, with the largest number of experts on their staff, and the biggest turnover. The very multiplicity of departments, in fact, militated against prejudices in favour of any particular sort of object on any given moment, be it Old Master paintings, primitive art or ancient atlases. Many months passed in which the objectives of buying suitable articles were considered and established, and the procedures for so doing were laid down. The person appointed to manage the selection process was Annamaria Edelstein, who had worked in the antique trade for some years before editing Art at Auction for several issues. The combination gave her a useful insight into the art market, internationally. She worked completely independently though in consultation with the firm's experts. Before suggesting specific acquisitions there was the most scrupulous vetting process which included a detailed comparison with similar objects displayed in museums or recently sold elsewhere. A completed proposal form with the suggested price tag was then put up to a progression of committees. Such suggestions might be for objects coming up for sale at Sotheby's itself, at Christie's, in Paris, Zurich, Monte Carlo, New York or from dealers, and even occasionally from private collectors. A budget was fixed at about three per cent of the annual funds available, and in November, 1974, the British Rail Fund made its first purchase, an English translation of a seventeenth-century book on architecture. It had once belonged to Thomas Wentworth, Earl of Stafford, and later to none other than Sir Thomas Phillips. As it happened, the early purchases could not have occurred at a more opportune moment. Prices were depressed and there were few buyers for really important objects in the market. Some of the items bought in the first two years already looked like considerable bargains two or three years later when similar pieces again came up for sale. The fund operated for something over five years. By the time it closed in 1980 it had bought in excess of 2,000 objects at a cost of £40,000,000.... The fund's managers had expressly stated that they would not dispose of any piece for at least a generation—many of their known liabilities would not, in fact, arise until well into the next century.

That brief passage, while setting out to be a reassuring statement, begs a number of questions on the propriety of such an arrangement. There is nothing in the statement of reasons 'most prominent auctioneers—biggest turnover—largest number of experts on their staff' to guarantee the kind of objectivity needed to benefit the fund. 'The multiplicity of departments' were all Sotheby's, so a lack of internal bias was of no consequence to the fund. The person appointed to manage the selection process 'worked completely independently' but consulted with Sotheby's experts. Suggested prices for possible acquisitions were presumably set by Sotheby staff, who must surely have had a quiet chuckle on finding themselves setting the reserve price with the vendor and the bidding price for the fund.

The whole arrangement was reminiscent of an earlier twentieth century controversy involving the previously mentioned art dealer, Joseph Duveen, which in the same way raised the question of the relationship between purchaser and seller and adviser when the adviser was an interested party. Duveen specialised in selling major works, usually authenticated by his partner Berenson, for substantial sums to wealthy collectors. He had a vested interest in following the progress of the paintings he had sold and when they appeared again on the market he often purchased them for resale. This tactic maintained a price level and safeguarded his expertise, but could on occasion prove expensive.

Duveen found the answer to the problem in the early 1920s assisted by the United States Revenue Act of 1917, which had introduced tax reductions for charitable donations. He preserved both his reputation and his bank balance by persuading his clients to present in some cases entire collections to museums, or even to endow new museums. The arrangement was attractive to many of his clients who benefitted from the tax concessions as well as gaining public recognition for their magnanimity. It was also perfect for Duveen whose expertise was unlikely to be questioned in his lifetime.

As Mr Herrmann remarked about the Sotheby connection with the British Rail Pension Fund, 'only time can tell whether this adventurous exercise will have fulfilled its purpose'. Of course by then no one will remember.

CHAPTER 10

Some Modern Criticisms

We have seen how in the early nineteenth century, in both England and America, the auctioneers came in for a good deal of criticism regarding the way that they conducted their business. Some of the early pamphlets on the subject of the auction actually detailed how the system could be abused by unscrupulous operators, and how those abuses might damage the normally good relations between the general public and the merchants.

There is some justification for saying that little has in fact changed since then. Some particular abuses which occurred in the early days may have been replaced by new and more sophisticated varieties, but there is no doubt that abuses do occur and probably always will, at least so long as the small amount of auction legislation remains so difficult to apply. There will always be those who will attempt to gain a financial advantage by misrepresenting goods sent for sale and there will always be those at the other extreme who will try to buy cheaply by operating a dealers ring. The only real effort to control such activity will have to be made by the auctioneer and his staff, who may struggle manfully to regulate the business as best they can.

The present legislation is, however, no deterrent to the smart operator in the saleroom, and every minute that passes after the fall of the hammer multiplies the difficulty of discovering evidence of malpractice. Imagine then the difficulty of obtaining satisfaction if the auctioneer himself should be seeking financial benefit in ways other than by the straightforward management of his business. The prospects for the clients of such an auctioneer would be grim indeed, and of course there are and have been those who have become involved in the auction business simply to make a quick killing.

Such auctioneers—often ex-dealers—might sell mostly goods which they own themselves in the sales they operate, they may misrepresent items hoping to knock them down to unsuspecting members of the public, they may bring down the hammer quickly on genuine goods which they wish to buy in for themselves, and they might even fail to pay out the proper bid price to clients after the sale. The reputation of such firms eventually diminishes to the point where they can no longer function profitably as an auction room, but usually by then quite a lot of damage has been done, and so have quite a few of the local population.

While there is little to be done about the really unscrupulous operator except to regret his occasional appearance on the scene, in the case of misrepresentation and the dealer ring there would at least appear to be some remedy in that sound judgement on the part of the saleroom staff should be able to guarantee reliable cataloguing and establish protective reserve prices.

In a perfect world that would be the end of the problem, but sad to say that even the expensively staffed London salerooms have so far fallen short of that degree of perfection. Ironically, their efforts to justify the wealth of expertise which they employ has led to a different kind of abuse in which the general public are encouraged to believe that their expertise is in fact infallible. However, on the several well documented occasions when a catalogue description has been challenged after a sale, and when the burden of the evidence has seemed to be against them, the London auctioneers have relied on their superior financial resources to dissuade a dissatisfied client from challenging their inflexible attitude in the courts.

Of course expertise is simply opinion based on scholarship, and both the opinion and the degree of scholarship are bound to vary from individual to individual—except that in the case of the major auctioneers it should not be seen to be so, for unerring expertise is what the London salerooms sell, and is the illusion which becomes a reality in the annual balance sheet.

Within the fine arts generally it is the picture sales that have consistantly produced the spectacular results over the years, indeed it is the publicity obtained from such sales—from Old Masters to Impressionists—that has been a significant factor in the growth of the London salerooms in particular. It is also in this area that the greatest ambiguity exists in relation to expertise, and an area where even the expert is advised to tread carefully; for in commercial terms the difference in value between just an unsigned painting and an unsigned painting attributed with some authority to a great artist can be astronomical.

If we look at the table of conventional terms used in picture cataloguing not only by the London salerooms but in principal by most auctioneers, we will see a well regulated scale designed to give confidence to the buyer in a difficult field.

THE CHRISTIAN NAME(S) AND SURNAME OF THE ARTIST	In our opinion a work by the Artist
THE INITIALS OF THE CHRISTIAN NAME(S) AND THE SURNAME OF THE ARTIST	In our opinion a work of the period of the Artist which may be wholly or in part his work

Those are part of a table of terms published in a Christie's South Kensington sale catalogue, and bearing such conventions in mind most of the smaller auctioneers will tend to err on the side of discretion when cataloguing paintings. That is they will not give a full cataloguing—christian names and surname in full—where there is any doubt at all about authenticity, for to do so is to virtually guarantee to the prospective buyers that the painting is by the artist named. By simply describing the painting and the signature on it—initials of the christian name and the surname—the auctioneer draws due attention to the item but leaves the final decision on authenticity to the competing buyers.

In the case of the major auctioneers, however, the appropriate expert will be expected in as many cases as possible to apply a full catalogue description even to unsigned paintings in order to attract the highest price and, just as importantly, to encourage vendors to place goods with them rather than the lesser salerooms. The London rooms may therefore err on the side of optimism when cataloguing, and although this involves an element of speculation at times, it is unlikely to lead them into difficulty, for in the event of a buyer disputing the description subsequently he would need to produce his own acceptable expert prepared to support a contrary view.

A major factor related to expertise is of course the financial consequence. The expert who judges that some likely canvas is not in fact the masterpiece that it was thought to be by others may reduce the potential value of the item by many thousands of pounds. Conversely, by fully attributing some other painting to a well known artist the expert enhances the value of what might have been just another unsigned canvas by a considerable margin.

Even the judgements of the best authorities are questioned from time to time, and opinions considered inviolate are one day overturned. The man said to have been the greatest authority on Old Master paintings in the early part of this century has only recently become suspected of having allowed his financial interest in a painting to colour his stated opinion of it. Bernard Berenson was the most respected connoisseur of his time, but as the result of the publication of a biography *Being Bernard Berenson*, by Meryle Secrest, the *Sunday Times* undertook an investigation of claims made in the book, and on the 3rd of February, 1980, published a full page article on the subject. Although the matter is not directly related to the auction business, Berenson's opinions could well have been influential in many saleroom transactions during his long career. In any event the current speculations are the perfect example of how financial pressures and associated temptations might build up on even the highest authority in the land. The article says:

in the past few weeks Berenson's reputation has been rudely challenged. A major biography, just published, claims that Berenson
was prepared to use his scholarship corruptly: to 'improve' the
attribution of pictures or condone their 'prettification' so that their
value rose; to authenticate others whose origin was doubtful; and
to share in the resulting profits. The charges have created a storm—
Berenson partisans are passionate in his defence.

But final judgement on Berenson's involvement in art deals rests
in a basement vault of the Metropolitan Museum, New York.
There the papers of Joseph Duveen, the swashbuckling art dealer,
with whom Berenson worked for 32 years, are held until the year
2002.

Before they were finally locked away, however, I was allowed to
examine the bulky files. Letters, telegrams, and thousands of detailed accounts cast an astonishing light on some of the biggest art
deals of the century. They also reveal much about the life of
Berenson who once admitted that any biography of him would be
a 'chronique scandaleuse'.

The article goes on to examine the financial implications of Berenson's
partnership with Duveen and includes details of some well known
paintings, together with the partners financial interest in them and
Berenson's recorded opinion as well as the current expert opinion:

On numerous occasions Berenson adjusted his assessment of Old
Masters where he and Duveen had a financial interest in their
sale ...
Madonna and Child...
Described by Berenson, 1907, as 'entirely executed by assistants of
Verrocchio'. Bought by Berenson and Duveen for £12,000, 1922.
Sold to Benjamin Altman for £33,000, 1924, described by Berenson
as 'a perfect and pristine Verrocchio'. Currently in Metropolitan
Museum, New York as 'work-shop' (painted by an assistant)
The Madonna of Humility...
Discovered by Berenson, bought by Duveen, 1928, described by
Berenson as a masterpiece by Masaccio. Sold to Andrew Mellon
after a Duveen restoration for £50,000, 1938. Now in National
Gallery, Washington, who regard it as 'ruined' and 'not by
Masaccio'.
Madonna and Child...
In 1912 Berenson advised owner that it was 'work-shop' Verrocchio
(painted by assistants of the artist). Bought by Duveen and another
dealer in 1913 for £17,000, and sold to Clarence Mackay for
£100,000 with letter from Berenson describing it as a 'monumental'
Verrocchio. Repurchased and sold again by Duveen and Berenson,
1935, described again as a genuine Verrocchio. Now in Metropoli-

tan Museum, New York, as 'style of Verrocchio' and withdrawn from view.

The Cimabue Triptych...

Bought by Berenson on Duveen's behalf for £1,000 in 1919. Sold, 1920, to Carl Hamilton, for £35,000, described by Berenson thus: 'This picture is as surely by Cimabue as scholarship can ascertain'. Now in National Gallery, Washington as 'by a follower of Cimabue.'

Of course mistakes occur, the imprecise nature of the criteria decree that it must be so; modern technology helps today's expert, but the quantity of goods and the quality of the staff together with the demands of the system will conspire to defeat perfection. A percentage of error is of course acceptable as well as understandable, what is surprising is that it appears that none occur in the London salerooms, or at least hardly ever. Nobody ever makes a mistake, at least very few are ever admitted, hardly any are ever corrected, there is little recourse for the vendor who loses a small fortune through mis-cataloguing or for the buyer who discovers later that his purchase is not what it was meant to be.

I was with a friend—a Hungarian picture dealer—one day, looking at two watercolours that had been purchased privately the day before. One of them was a portrait of an army officer of the 1914-18 period and the other was a pleasant English landscape in the manner of the nineteenth century artist, Copley Fielding. The two pictures had come from the same source, were similarly framed, both unsigned, and when viewed together were obviously painted by the same hand. My friend informed me that he was so impressed with the landscape that he intended to take it into London for appraisal, while the virtually unsaleable portrait would be committed to the nearest dustbin and the frame used for another picture. I was determined to hear the end of the story, and subsequently discovered that the picture had been accepted by a London saleroom, catalogued as by Anthony Vandyke Copley Fielding and sold for four hundred guineas. Perhaps it is not important, but at least two people know for certain that the picture is not what it was claimed to be when sold.

A television programme in the 'London Programme' series recently cited a similar example of dubious expertise in graphic detail. It showed a painting of a Venetian scene supposedly by Edward Pritchett, an artist well known for such views, and sold in a London saleroom with a full catalogue attribution. Viewers were then shown another similar painting, sold by the same top auctioneers in another picture sale, and again with a full cataloguing. The process was repeated for a third time and the climax came when all three paintings were put on the screen together, side by side. While all were of a similar subject, there could be no doubt, even to the layman, that the same artist could not have painted all three pictures. Obviously the cataloguer had catalogued the subject and not the artist. In at least two of the cases he should have used initials of the christian name only to indicate that the painting was in the style of the artist, but clearly in this case two buyers at least had paid an inflated price for paintings that were not the work of the artist to whom they were attributed.

These examples show that mis-cataloguing does occur, and possibly far more often than most people would imagine. In many instances the mistake never comes to light, and in those that do the matter is hardly ever resolved in a satisfactory way. Obviously the major sale-rooms have no wish to see their expertise tested before the public gaze, for that might destroy the illusion of infallibility; but there is in fact another good reason for allowing sleeping dogs to lie, and it is this. Once a painting is sold with a provenance accorded by an appropriate expert it becomes not just a work of art but an investment. When resold at a later date the painting might reasonably be expected to have increased in value, sometimes substantially. This will not be so if there is any doubt about the authenticity of the picture, and the investment could be lost.

It is almost always the case, therefore, that having made his purchase the buyer has as much interest in maintaining the accuracy of the catalogue description as do the auctioneers. Because of the large sums of money involved in the purchase of even minor works of art it could be disastrous to bring the opinions of the major auctioneers into serious question. Such action might diminish the confidence of the institutions and collectors who often rely on the auctioneers to advise them on major purchases. Taken to its logical conclusion such action could seriously undermine the basis of the whole art-auction world, and there are just too many vested interests to allow that to happen.

In the London salerooms there are a number of people working in each specialist department and their level of education and experience and therefore expertise will vary. The initial response to an item brought in for appraisal might also vary according to who is available from the department to examine the item, and whether he or she is a junior or senior assistant.

I have a personal experience of how an opinion can vary at the same auction room at different times. About ten years ago I took to Sotheby's in Bond Street what seemed to be an engraving by Rembrandt. The assistant at the front counter removed himself and the engraving into an inner sanctum and after a brief interval returned with the sad news that it was merely a copy, and not a particularly good one at that. As a confirmed non-expert on Rembrandt engravings I accepted the opinion and entered the engraving in a local sale where it was sold for a few pounds.

That might have been the end of it except for the fact that I met the purchaser of the engraving at another sale some months later, whereupon he insisted on informing me of his good fortune with a Rembrandt engraving. He had, of course, no idea that I had been the seller, but he had in fact taken it back to the same counter at Sotheby's in Bond Street, where it was immediately accepted as genuine, catalogued, and sold for more than three hundred pounds.

Examples abound of an undercurrent of inexpertise which exists even in the major salerooms, and some of the problems associated with valuation and opinion are further aggravated by the television companies, who in recent years have cashed in on the keen public interest in antiques with the 'discovery' programmes. In these programmes the expertise displayed by the television presenters has become even more significant than that of the saleroom staff. There are two reasons why that is so, the first being the form the expertise takes, which is determined by the very nature of the medium. Television is an immediate but transient influence whose statements are not answerable at once or even very soon after they are made, and even if a contrary opinion to a programme statement is eventually aired there is no guarantee that it will reach even a small proportion of the viewers who watched the original transmission.

Because of the very large audience which a programme will reach—and that is the second factor which makes television opinion so influential—there are likely to be literally millions of viewers who regard the statements made on television as statements of fact. Opinion on pedigree and estimates of value are the highlights of many of the antiques programmes, and are readily given by the resident expert. Unfortunately, the higher the valuation of an item the more interesting the programme becomes in purely television terms, and many of the estimates tend therefore to be on the high side.

As far as television news programmes are concerned it is almost always Christie's or Sotheby's, perhaps occasionally Phillips and once in a while Bonhams who get a mention either for a high price just realised or an exceptional forthcoming sale. Some auction events are of course genuinely newsworthy but the value of the free publicity obtained is incalculable, and a very important factor in the increasing supremacy of the London salerooms.

The programmes of the 'antiques roadshow' type are compulsive and entertaining viewing for many, but have little to do with the day to day workings of the antiques business. Many of the participant presenters are from the major salerooms or galleries and the style of presentation usually suggests a thoroughly spontaneous degree of expertise which the viewing public will accept as normal. They will be unaware—because they are not informed—of the preparation and rehearsal which goes into each programme. They will be unaware of the mass of insignificant rubbish which must be examined before the final assortment of selected items is ready for the screen, and they will be unaware of the opportunities that exist for editing the final version of the programme before it is transmitted.

All of these factors might influence the impression the programme makes on the viewers, were they aware of them, and while unawareness would not be important in the case of a purely entertainment programme, it is important in the case of the antiques shows which are directly associated with a multi-million pound international business with big rewards for the big operators.

The television connection is undoubtedly the best thing that ever happened to the major auctioneers. Television is the most influential and therefore the most significant single factor in advertising today. The auctioneers achieve a lot of publicity on the small screen for which they pay nothing, and not less than ninety per cent of that free publicity is won by the London salerooms.

There is a branch of the media which has sought to redress the balance by showing up the anomolies in the auction system. During 1980 the *Sunday Times* published several articles which catalogued the errors and misfortunes of some of the major auction houses, and again it was mostly the London salerooms that had the benefit of a different kind of publicity. It seems that sometimes the auctioneers had not done their homework on the matter of ownership of quite well recorded items. On the 14th of December, 1980, the paper reported:

Russian icons are bad news for the world's leading auctioneers, Sotheby's and Christie's, this weekend. Sotheby's has been told by a leading Russian art historian that an icon the firm sold at auction for the then world record price of £25,000 is in fact one of six stolen from his Moscow flat. The message came to the London auction house in a telex last week ... It was in December last year that the icon—a 16th-century Novgorod Processional double-sided example of St. Nicholas and the Virgin Mary—was sold in London. Mikhail Kudriavtsev, a historian on the staff of the Institute of Scientific and Architectural Research in Moscow, says it is his and he wants it back.

Kudriavtsev said: I am astonished that a reputable firm like Sotheby's could have accepted my stolen icon for auction without consulting me. I am listed as the owner in numerous catalogues and it has been publicly exhibited as on loan from me at international exhibitions. It has also been reproduced in numerous books, most recently Novgorod Icons, published in Britain by Phaidon ...

Christie's is facing a more complex problem over icons, representations of Christ and the saints ... The question being raised by another Russian art expert is this: are some of the world's most expensive icons fakes? He is Vladimir Teteriatnikov, formerly the chief restorer at Moscow's Institute for Conservation ... He is planning to publish a book on icon fakes. He particularly questions the validity of some in the famous George R. Hann collection, sold by Christie's in New York in April this year for £1,200,000.

Just a few weeks later the question of ownership was raised again, this time with Sotheby's Belgravia saleroom at the centre of a new controversy. The *Sunday Times* again published the story under the title 'Who owns the maharajah's golden throne?'

A magnificent golden throne from the palace of an Indian maharajah, languishing in the basement of Sotheby's Belgravia branch, is at the centre of an extraordinary row involving international art dealers, the Indian government and one of India's most glamorous socialites.

The throne and its footstool, covered in almost pure gold and dating from the 1840's, is valued at up to £80,000. It was put up for auction at Sotheby's relatively obscure branch last Thursday amid art trade speculation that it may have been smuggled out of India without an official export licence. Sotheby's admitted that it had no documentary proof that it had left India legally. Reputable dealers, not wishing to become involved or incur the wrath of the Indian authorities, did not bid and the throne was 'bought in' by the auctioneers for £36,000. Although there is strict legislation to prevent export of items over a century old, the flow of works to western art markets continues. Smugglers have found it easy to bribe Indian customs officials to ignore their consignments.

Sotheby's was clearly embarrassed by controversy after the abortive auction. David Battie, a director, said he did not know the name of the owner. 'He could be an eskimo for all I know', he said. 'We dealt with an agent but were given assurances that the thing wasn't exported illegally.'

A remarkable example of how the 'experts' can be fooled occurred in 1980, but was not reported by the *Sunday Times* until 1981. Headed 'How to make pots of money in prison' the article revealed that:

Dozens of fake ceramic works of art, supposedly made by the world renowned Cornish potter, Bernard Leach, and sold at auction houses including Christie's and Bonhams, have been traced to the pottery class at Featherstone prison near Wolverhampton.

Five auction houses, Sotheby's, Christie's, Phillips, Bonhams and Lawrence of Crewkerne, as well as several top dealers, believed that the vases, bowls and dishes were genuine. ...

Bernard Leach, who died three years ago aged 92, is rated one of the most influential English potters since the 18th century. Top price for his work stands at £4,200. His techniques, inspired by years in Japan, emphasised the value of simplicity. He encouraged other potters to learn his methods even publishing "secrets" about his glazing, a service that several prisoners found helpful.

Unknown to the prison, inmates working at the two Featherstone kilns used photographs of the master potter's work and produced dozens of vases, pots, dishes and bowls—all with the familiar Leach seal and stamp on the bottom. Prison authorities were delighted at prisoners enthusiasm for their new hobby and on one occasion actually watched the production of 14 pots, which were, unbeknown to them, all signed B.L. ... A London dealer and ceramic specialist, Richard Dennis, was one of the first to spot that there was something "rather wrong" with a number he had bought......
Another London dealer, Dan Klein, was asked by a client to bid for a "large stoneware oviform vase by Bernard Leach" at Christie's last July. But after acquiring the vase for over £1,000, he noticed that it was damaged, and asked Christie's for a price adjustment.

'They said we could have it for £400, a terrific drop. We thought how fair of Christie's', said Klein. 'A Bernard Leach pot for that amount. With hindsight one realises they went back and told their customer it was cracked. After all, they weren't to know that it had cost nothing but prison clay so their client could afford to drop the price'.

A Christie's spokesman, clearly amused by the affair, said: 'Actually, we're not in a position to comment'. Philip Rouse, of Lawrence's recalled selling three fakes. 'They were remarkably well done. At first I thought they really were Leaches and sold them as such'.

At Bonhams Eric Knowles remembered handling four of the Featherstone products before he learned what they really were. 'They were excellent', he said. 'I can now see that the prisoners only mistake was to put too many on the market too quickly.'

A good example of one that got away via some inexpert cataloguing is given in Frank Herrmann's volume on Sotheby's. In a chapter describing an important sale of Old Master paintings in 1959 a detailed account is given of the sale and its centrepiece, the 'Adoration of the Magi', by Peter Paul Rubens. The great excitement generated by the sale of this massive—12 ft $9\frac{1}{4}$ ins × 8 ft $1\frac{1}{4}$ ins—altar-piece overshadowed everything else, including the remainder of the catalogue, and a sequel to the story of the sale was not to be revealed for quite some time. Mr Hermann writes:

Another aspect of the Westminster Sale of Old Masters only came to light thirteen years later. In fact, it involved lot 13, a large dirty canvas depicting a scene from the First Book of Samuel of Abigail making her offering of loaves to David. Edward Speelman, a prominent West End picture dealer, had looked at the painting and had come to the conclusion that, although it was simply catalogued as 'by Rubens', implying that it was a work after or in the style of the master, it was indeed by Peter Paul Rubens himself. In order not to alert any other dealers to his discovery, Mr Speelman asked a fellow dealer, Steven Pollock, to bid for the picture on his behalf. Pollock bought it for £1,500 and is recorded as the purchaser in the printed price list. The picture was cleaned and revealed as an astonishing masterpiece. In the first instance Dr. Ludwig Burchard, one of the great Rubens scholars of his time, and later Michael Jaffe, confirmed its authenticity. It was initially sold to a private collector in Germany but was later brought back to England.

It is reported that a similar piece of mis-cataloguing by the same firm may have allowed an important painting by Watteau to be purchased for a fraction of its value in the mammoth Mentmore sale in 1977, but the famous case of the Holbein painting is probably the greatest example of how persistant mis-cataloguing can cost a client a fortune and the nation an asset, while making a lot of money for a dealers ring.

It was not until the 21st of September, 1980, more than a year after the sale of the Holbein, that the *Sunday Times* team was able to publish a full account of the picture's progress from a country saleroom to its controversial sale at Christie's and the doubtful circumstances of its export from Britain to America. The report began as follows:

A Holbein painting, formerly in the royal collection, has left Britain with an export licence misdescribing it as a minor Italian work. It was bought at Christie's by a London dealers ring for £3,500 and sold to the J. Paul Getty Museum at Malibu, California, for a sum said to be around £250,000.

Christie's themselves, who miscatalogued it twice, say they would now list it as a Holbein with a reserve of not less than £100,000.

Exactly how the circular shaped work, inscribed with the monogram of Henry, Prince of Wales, left Britain in April this year so grossly undervalued, and falsely described, is one of several questions the government wants answered. The *Sunday Times* last week told what it had discovered to Mr John Nott, secretary of state at the Department of Trade, and the minister for the arts, Norman St. John Stevas. They are launching an inquiry. "The facts", said Mr Nott yesterday, "are appalling".

The Getty Museum was aware of the ring arrangement at Christie's sale. Both the "ring" and the museum had scientific evidence that the picture was Flemish and could be traced to Antwerp, Holbein's circle and the years 1515 to 1530. Nevertheless the ring applied to export it as an Italian picture.

The picture was first spotted by Tony Haynes, a Coventry-based picture dealer, when it was included among the furniture at an auction sale organised by Bruton, Knowles of Gloucester. Arthur Negus, the B.B.C.'s antiques expert, is a partner in the firm and helped catalogue the lots. Negus looked at only one side of the oak panel and catalogued the carved initials PH (for Prince Henry) as a 'hatchment", an arts term meaning a tablet with armorial bearings. "In my 77 years I've never catalogued a painting" said Negus, when we told him he missed spotting a Holbein. "I'm terrified of pictures. Oh dear, oh dear".

Haynes recognised the royal monograph and the quality of both the picture and the oak panel on which it is painted. He bought it for £2,700, and after a few days research was convinced he had a Holbein. He took it to Christie's, asked them to research it and then sell it for him. Christie's handling of the matter was surprising. Firstly they included it in a sale without Haynes's knowledge, with a reserve of only £300. Haynes, alerted on the day of the sale, telegraphed them to withdraw it. When the auctioneer announced the withdrawal, a caucus of three dealers left the room.

The article goes on to tell how the painting was once again catalogued by Christie's, but only after Haynes had received a letter from them stating that they had consulted Sir Oliver Millar, Keeper of the Queen's Pictures, who could find no reference to the picture in the royal inventories. Haynes still had a feeling that something was not quite right, but he let the sale go ahead. The report continues:

Haynes's hunch was right. He had, we discovered, been the victim of a well-heeled art 'ring'. The picture was knocked down to Anthony Speelman, a prominent West End dealer. But he was in partnership with Richard Herner of the well-established firm of Colnaghi, of New Bond Street, and David Carritt, who now runs his own art business in St. James's with the Hon. Timothy Bathurst.

Art 'rings' are illegal when a syndicate fails to inform the auctioneers in writing before a sale that it intends bidding together. Speelman, Herner and Carritt did not inform Christie's. When we approached Richard Herner of Colnaghi's he said: 'There's a rumour going round that we've made a tremendous coup by selling the picture we bought for £250,000. I can't tell you exactly what it was purchased by Getty for. Our group was Anthony Speelman, David Carritt and myself. Nobody else. Now its rather dangerous talking about this. Art dealers have been buying in partnership for years. Therefore I don't think that anybody could be accused of acting in a nefarious way because that's how they always behave. As for the idea of giving the auctioneer a letter of what we're doing, well, that would be absurd. It would be like playing poker with your cards on the table'. David Carritt said he believed it was a Holbein from the outset. 'I didn't know that Burton Frederickson of the Getty Museum had bought it, I've no financial interest in it. Whether one of my company interests has, oh God, that I simply don't know'.

Frederickson, curator of the immensely rich museum, told us he saw the painting at Christie's and recognised it might be of value ... He arranged after the sale that it should be examined by John Fletcher at Oxford, who reported on May 25, 1979. 'It seems to open up a new and important facet of Holbein's work', commented Frederickson.

He refused to say how much Getty paid and could not explain how the Holbein left Britain on April 12, 1980, described as 'Circle of Giulio Romano'.

It must of course be said that the major salerooms give a satisfactory service to most of their clients with accurate appraisals and good prices. There are of course bound to be errors, and sometimes the size of the catastrophe, as in the case of the Holbein, is immense. It is a measure of the strength of the 'illusion', however, that the major auctioneer can stride away from such a calamity as if nothing much had happened. For so very many of the lesser salerooms, faced with a similar situation, a wry smile and an 'oh dear' might not be quite enough to save their reputation and their business.

It is easy to see that the aspiring art collector with ample funds but little personal knowledge or experience of the art market must follow a path which is fraught with danger. One of his greatest difficulties will lie in the detection of forgeries, for the forger's influence in art is as old as the history of art itself. The Stockholm Museum has in its possession an Egyptian papyrus which is a do-it-yourself manual for fabricating precious stones from coloured glass, and the Fogg Museum of Harvard University—which specialises in examples of the forger's art—has a statuette of Amen-Ra, dating from about 600 BC, but whose style and crude inscription suggests a much earlier period. The piece was undoubtedly intended to deceive.

Such are the problems of provenance that it is virtually impossible for any major collector, museum, or indeed auctioneer to escape the occasional error of judgement. The British Museum has made many dubious purchases which have been later regretted. One such instance occurring in 1818 with the acquisition of a 'contemporary' bust of Julius Caesar which turned out to be less than a hundred years old.

The task facing collector and expert alike is highlighted by reports that in the field of Impressionist painting very often even the painters themselves, during their lifetimes, were fooled by works which were not their own. It has been said that a fake Cezanne once deceived Cezanne himself. It has been said that Picasso in later life signed paintings which he believed to be his but which were not. It has even been said that Corot occasionally added his signature to the output of needy fellow artists in order to improve their standard of living.

As if that were not enough the situation can become even more confused by the intervention of the 'expert'. While much expertise is reliable it is a fact that in many cases expertise will vary, and it is not uncommon to find that the reputation of some young up-and-coming expert is made at the expense of another elderly or recently deceased sage whose prior opinion of some major work is overturned. It could be said that the collective noun for a group of art experts should be a 'confusion', and a classic example of the consequences of bringing together such a group is contained in the story of the Van Gogh paintings.

The Dutch art historian, Dr Jacob Baart de la Faille, is the author of several books on Van Gogh, and in one catalogue of the works of the artist he included as authentic a collection of thirty paintings which had been placed at his disposal by the Gallery Otto Wacker of Berlin. With the good doctor's authority and expertise behind them all the paintings were quickly sold, although it was noted that many of the pictures were strangely similar—for example there were four 'Cypresses', three 'Olive Trees' and four 'Self-Portraits'.

It may well have been disquiet over these similarities which subsequently led de la Faille to issue a statement to the effect that 'after exhaustive study' he felt 'compelled to append a supplement' to the catalogue which effectively re-designated the thirty works as 'dubious forgeries'. The uproar that followed from the purchasers of these highly-priced 'forgeries' led to a police investigation which culminated eventually in the gallery owner, Otto Wacker, being brought to trial charged with 'persistant fraud'.

The 'confusion' of expert witnesses at his trial, which included Dr de la Faille, Vincent Wilhelm van Gogh—nephew of the artist—and art critics Hans Bremmer and Julius Meier-Graefe, quickly set about confounding the court with their differences of opinion. Bremmer advised the court that in his view there were hundreds of fake Van Gogh's in circulation, and the artist's nephew confirmed that after Van Gogh's death the large residue of unsigned and unfinished paintings found strewn about his house were hawked about the streets on carts.

The bombshell, however, was delivered by the venerable doctor who, during the course of the hearing, proclaimed that he had once more changed his mind and testified that 'in respect of five of the thirty paintings I withdraw my opinion that they are spurious'. The conclusion of this amazing episode was that Wacker was sentenced to twelve months imprisonment which was increased by seven months on appeal. The whole sorry affair was summed up by Frank Arnau, an expert on art forgery, who in reviewing the expert testimony recorded a number of optional conclusions:

a) all the pictures were genuine; b) some were genuine and some spurious; c) all were spurious; d) some were spurious and some genuine, but the genuine were those declared to be spurious and the spurious those certified as genuine.

Perhaps the last word on the subject is contained in a statement made to the court by Julius Meier-Graefe, writer and art critic, who said:

Anyone who buys pictures and pays enormous prices for them on the strength of expert opinions alone deserves to meet with disaster.

CHAPTER 11

The Ring

The twentieth century domination of the auction by the arts and antiques market led directly to a significant increase in the activities of the 'ring'. That is not to say that in those earlier auctions no group of dealers ever organised themselves in order to gain some financial advantage on the day's proceedings. In our examination of the history of the auction from the earliest times the one thing that is clear is that nothing of any consequence is new. Dealers rings may well have operated in those Roman auctions or in the slave markets of Delos. We know that they operated in eighteenth century Paris for we have the evidence of Mercier who described the workings of the Bande Noire or Black Gang of the salerooms.

The Auctions (Bidding Agreements) Act 1927 became law on the 1st of January, 1928. The Act was the first attempt in England to legislate against the dealers ring or 'knock-out' which was known to operate in many auction rooms throughout the length and breadth of the country. Before this time it was not illegal for a group of dealers to conduct their business in this way; in fact the Act said so in a General Note:

> Apart from this Act there is no objection to such an agreement as is mentioned in this section. At common law an agreement between two or more persons not to bid against each other at an auction, even if amounting to what is commonly termed a 'knock-out' is not illegal nor does it invalidate the sale.

What then is the ring, how does it work, what is it designed to achieve and why was it necessary to legislate against it?

A ring is a group of people—usually dealers—who gather at an auction and together make an agreement nominating one person in the group to bid on behalf of them all for the items that they are collectively interested in purchasing. The effect is to substantially reduce the element of competition, thus allowing the group to obtain the goods at prices lower than those which would otherwise prevail. Ring members will then at a later stage resell the items amongst themselves at a knock-out—a much more exclusive version of the auction. The outlawing of the ring by the 1927 Act has made its operation more difficult to observe. Although there is no doubt that rings continue to flourish in every part of the auction scene, their activities are of necessity more discreetly organised than in the past, or at least they should be.

Some twenty years ago every Thursday morning in the London suburb of Ealing, about a dozen local antique dealers gathered in the ABC restaurant having previously viewed the local sale due to begin at eleven o'clock. Each dealer would have marked his catalogue to indicate all the lots in which he personally was interested. By comparing catalogues a composite could be produced showing the grand total of all the lots which the group sought to acquire collectively, and then a member or members of the group would be nominated to conduct the bidding.

Obviously the purpose of such an arrangement is to reduce the competition and thus the price of the lots, but it follows that to maximise the efficiency of the arrangement it is necessary to ensure that all the dealers who might be interested in the goods are safely contained within the ring. If all else fails any renegade dealer left out will, like any member of the general public who interferes, have to be discouraged by the group.

As the sale begins the ring sets about acquiring its composite shopping list and at the same time actively discouraging any competition. It might seem reasonable to suppose that as the group would almost always acquire a large part of its list against nominal opposition that it would accept the odd failure with good grace—not so. It is in the long term interest of any ring to discourage competition at all times. Other potential buyers failing to beat the ring time after time may well decide that future attendance at the sale is a waste of their time—and that of course is the ring's ultimate triumph.

You will be excused for wondering how the ring can afford to eliminate the opposition by outbidding them on every occasion. Total discouragement of competition must at times involve bidding more than the group wishes to pay, perhaps even more than the item is worth, and must defeat the object of the exercise as well as the competition.

It has however been conceded that the ring will acquire the majority of the items cheaply as planned. As far as the few items where competition is fiercer is concerned, it is agreed by ring members that a small financial sacrifice for the sake of future dealing is a very good investment, particularly in view of the fact that losses incurred will be shared by the group and more than compensated for by the profits. This will be better understood by a consideration of the knock-out.

Our Ealing dealers, having eliminated most of the competition and completed their purchases, will by mid-afternoon have re-assembled in the restaurant. Placing themselves discreetly at a corner table they will move to the final stage of their conspiracy. Each item purchased on the group's behalf will be put up again for sale among those present. Remember that by refusing to compete against each other in the bidding it is entirely likely that most items have been purchased more cheaply than at least one or two members would have been prepared to pay. Each member of the dealer group will have his own special interest within the range of items purchased and it is therefore certain that someone within the group will be prepared to offer more for each item than the price paid in the sale. The exception to the rule will of course be the one or two items bought against the more determined opposition.

As each lot is put up again the bidding will continue, starting at the price just paid in the real auction. Those who are interested in the item will bid against each other until it is knocked down to one of them. The difference between the price paid at the real auction and the price paid at the knock-out is the amount that the group have saved by operating the ring. The benefit of that difference will now accrue to the group as a whole rather than to the owner of the goods and the auctioneer.

In the case of the Ealing ring that difference would have been placed in the centre of the table. For example if item A had been knocked down for £50 in the real sale and the bidding had continued at the knock-out to, say, £70, the difference—that is £20—would be placed in cash on the table. The knock-out would continue through the catalogue until all the items purchased had found a buyer among the members. At the end of the session each item would be allocated to one of the group, each member would have a list of his purchases for the day, and a fairly substantial sum of money would rest on the table.

The items for which the ring had overpaid would be course need to be dealt with, and in this case the bidding within the group would start at a figure below that paid in the real auction and continue until the best price had been obtained. In the event of the best bid remaining below the price paid the ring buyer would add the item to his list at the real auction price, but subtract the difference between his bid and the higher price from the money on the table.

Despite such minor irritations a successful ring should net a substantial sum to be divided among its members at the end of the day. Having taken his share each of the dealers can, by reference to his list of purchases, ascertain precisely his saving on the day's work and assess at once the benefit of belonging to a ring. The intrepid individual who had joined the ring but made no purchases at the knock-out would simply have earned a good days wages as payment for his non-intervention in the auction, although non-participation in the knock-out is usually frowned on by other members.

The operation of a ring cannot fail to give an advantage to the dealer group as it will almost invariably diminish the price that the seller receives. The consequences of numerous rings operating unhindered could be serious for the salerooms which function efficiently by the generation of keen competition. The individual saleroom that consistantly allowed itself to be dominated by a dealers ring would soon find its business diminishing with the prices. Vendors would not be long discovering that prices were not up to the mark and would switch their input to another auctioneer.

What protection did the 1927 Act seek to give to the vendor and the auctioneer. The Act states:

> If any dealer agrees to give, or gives, or offers any gift or consideration to any other person as an inducement or reward for abstaining, or for having abstained, from bidding at a sale by auction either generally or for any particular lot, or if any person agrees to accept, or accepts, or attempts to obtain from any dealer any such gift or consideration as aforesaid, he shall be guilty of an offence under this Act, and shall be liable on summary conviction to a fine not exceeding one hundred pounds, or a term of imprisonment for any period not exceeding six months, or to both such fine and such imprisonment.

What effect did the Act have on the operation of dealers rings. The evidence of the Ealing group which I have described and which I observed personally as a young man would suggest little if any effect at all. The group operated quite openly in the late 1950s and the local auctioneers must have been only too well aware of its influence. Being aware and yet doing nothing suggests that the auctioneers had no faith in the legislation, and in the event their lack of faith was justified. A rash of publicity during the 1960's relating to the activities of various rings appeared to suggest a growing contempt for the ineffective legislation and led to calls for a revision of the 1927 Act.

The debate which prefaced the amendments of 1969 revealed the limitations of the original Act. In the House of Commons on the 6th of November, 1968, Anthony Crosland, then President of the Board of Trade, stated in reply to a question regarding prosecutions under the Act that an inter-departmental investigation had concluded that the basic trouble was not the letter of the law but the difficulty of discovering evidence. In the same chamber on the 2nd of May, 1969, whilst debating the new Auctions (Bidding Agreements) Bill Mr Edwin Brooks said, 'it is well known that the legislation dates back to the 1920's, and that under it, only one prosecution has ever been mounted, and that was as long ago as 1928'.

By the time that statement was made the new Bill, with its tougher penalties, was well on the way to becoming law, but it is interesting to note that it was not a direct concern over the inefficiency of the law which initiated the debate leading to the amended Act of 1969, but rather a famous scandal involving a celebrated ring, a valuable painting, a Sunday newspaper and the National Gallery.

This extraordinary story demonstrates well the inter-related factors of an unworkable law and a flourishing ring, but also draws attention to another matter which caused some considerable consternation at the time, not least to several Members of Parliament in the ensuing debate. That matter was the apparent unwillingness of the authorities to take action against those involved in spite of the evidence presented to them, and their failure in the event to take such action in time.

There appeared to be some justification for such a charge at the time but now more than twelve years later a careful study of all the available documentary evidence leads to a somewhat different conclusion.

The story really begins at the end of 1967 with the death at Aldwick Court in Somerset of Mr T.R. Bridson. Eighty-nine years old when he died, Mr Bridson had latterly lived a solitary life at his Aldwick Court home which was literally crammed with antiques of all kinds. The first to view this treasure trove were the representatives of the Gloucester auctioneers, Bruton Knowles, who were called in to organise the disposal of the contents by auction. Among the team that set about cataloguing the effects was the well known television expert and director of the firm—Arthur Negus.

The sale took place on the 26th of March, 1968, and the subsequent controversy was to surround just one lot in the sale, a painting catalogued by the auctioneers as 15th Century Siennese School. The picture was painted on a wooden panel, and the reverse of the panel bore an inscription which attributed the painting to Duccio, a thirteenth century Italian Master. The inscription was ignored by the auctioneers in their catalogue description.

The sale was considered to be a fairly important provincial event and as such was well attended not only by local dealers and collectors, but by a considerable contingent representing the London trade. The dealers who travelled to the sale included several who were interested in the painting, but two in particular who were well qualified to judge early Italian paintings. One of these was a London based American art dealer named Julius Weitzner and the other Malcolm Waddingham, a London dealer noted for his independent expertise in the field. Both were keen to acquire the painting in the sale, and each was aware of the other's interest in the lot. Waddingham, however, was due to travel abroad on the day of the sale and was therefore unable to attend personally to bid for himself. Waddingham was to claim later that in the circumstances he entered into an arrangement with

Weitzner who is said to have agreed that they should buy the painting jointly, in partnership.

The painting was sold for £2700 on the morning of the sale on the 26th of March, and firm evidence of the ring's involvement was to be observed later the same day. Mr Ian Nicholson, an accountant for a London firm of fine art dealers was attending the sale in a private capacity, and at 1.15 p.m. on the 26th of March was taking lunch at the quaintly named Paradise Motel not far from Aldwick Court. He was able to observe Weitzner and a group of London dealers, all of whom he knew by sight, entering the motel together. Nicholson also claimed that he overheard Weitzner requesting a private room so that he and his companions could conduct some business.

Only those dealers directly involved could confirm that the knock-out took place there and then, but there is no doubt that the eventual outcome of the settlement was to transfer sole ownership of the painting to Julius Weitzner for the sum of £7000. The £4300 difference between the price at the auction and the price at the knock-out was presumably adequate reward for those involved in the conspiracy— with one notable exception.

It seems that on returning from his travels Malcolm Waddingham, who believed that he had a private arrangement with Weitzner, was initially delighted to learn that Weitzner had successfully acquired the picture, but subsequently infuriated by Weitzner's interpretation of their agreement. Waddingham claimed that he was shown a list bearing the names of those dealers in the ring including his own. He claimed that he was offered a sum of money in settlement which assumed his inclusion in the ring arrangement and ignored the agreement that he believed he had made with Weitzner alone. Waddingham vigorously denied any involvement with the Aldwick Court ring, he insisted that he had never participated in ring activities, and he refused to accept the settlement money.

So distressed was he by the affair that as well as seeking legal advice he insists that he wrote to each of the dealers whose names he could remember having been on the list he was shown disclaiming any interest in the Aldwick Court ring. It may well have been the publicity given to the matter by Waddingham which brought it to the attention of the Society of London Art Dealers, for it appears to have been they who reported to the Board of Trade that a ring might have been at work at Aldwick Court.

The fate of the picture, soon confirmed as a Duccio, was clearly in the hands of Julius Weitzner who lost no time in seeking a new owner for the painting. His negotiations with the Cleveland Museum in America and his need of an export licence if the picture was to be sold abroad, as well as the interest expressed by the National Gallery in London in acquiring the painting, were all factors which brought the matter to the urgent attention of the House of Commons. The 'Duccio affair' was directly responsible for the ensuing debate on 'dealers rings' and the amended legislation of 1969.

The painting was eventually purchased by the National Gallery from Weitzner for £150,000. The wide-ranging and lengthy debate which took place inside and outside Parliament as a result of all the circumstances of the Duccio affair, appears when considered at a distance to have posed a number of questions, some of which were not answered at the time. Those questions include—did the auctioneers act properly in cataloguing the painting in the first place? Did a ring operate at Aldwick Court, and if so what did its operation cost the estate of the original owner of the painting? Did the Board of Trade investigators, once alerted, drag their feet and thereby lose the opportunity of obtaining a prosecution? Was the existing legislation inadequate, and if so could it be strengthened in order to eliminate dealers rings once and for all?

The answers to the first two questions seem to be relatively straightforward, at least at first glance.

There is no evidence to suggest that the auctioneers involved behaved in any way improperly in their conduct of the sale or that they did not at any time display other than the good faith associated with reputable professionals. On the second question there is direct evidence that a ring was operating at the sale in that at least two individuals were prepared to make statements to that effect in the newspapers and elsewhere.

It would be convenient to allow the matter to rest there and to assume that evidence of a ring would automatically attribute the losses incurred by the original owner of the goods to an illegal association at the sale. Such an assumption would in this case be misleading. The fact remains that after buying the picture for £2700 at the sale, the ring members resold it among themselves later the same day for just £7000; it was much later that the figure of £150,000 was agreed with the National Gallery. It follows that if the question were asked 'what price would the painting have reached at the original auction had all the dealers bid competitively', the answer would have to be 'no more than the £7000 paid at the knock-out, and perhaps even a little less'.

Clearly only £4300 of the loss to the Bridson estate can be attributed to the dealers ring, and so it was the eventual sale of the painting to the National Gallery which gave the affair its notoriety and which attracted the attention of the press and Parliament to the matter. How then was it possible for Weitzner to get away with the picture for £7000 at the knock-out, earn himself a staggering £143,000 from the sale to the National Gallery, leave the dealers ring to take the burden of the public indignation and Parliament searching desperately for remedies to an illegal practice which had in fact played only a minor role in this particular scenario.

Such a coup as this is exceptional even in the speculative area of art dealing, and credit is due to Weitzner's expertise in recognising the painting's potential, but why were there no other equally expert dealers at the sale and why was there no representation from the National Gallery or for that matter any major museum? For an answer we must look at the method employed by the auctioneers in producing the catalogue of sale after receiving the instructions to dispose of the Aldwick Court contents.

The quantity of previously unseen antiques which confronted the auctioneers when they first surveyed their task should have alerted them to the possibility that items requiring specialist appraisal might be present. No provincial auctioneer employs permanently experts who will be required only occasionally, although most will engage specific expertise as and when required. In this case Bruton Knowles were asked directly at the time whether they had in fact engaged a specialist to catalogue the paintings found in the house. Their answer was that they had done so, but they declined to name the expert.

The unknown expert, in the case of the Duccio painting, had miscatalogued it by two centuries. The catalogue description—Fifteenth century Siennese School—indicated that the cataloguer disagreed with the inscription on the back of the panel which attributed the painting to Duccio. That disagreement was crucial to the outcome, for those people interested in thirteenth century Italian paintings who simply received a catalogue through the post would have found nothing in it to encourage them to travel to the sale. The description could also have misled many of those who did view the picture for themselves but who were not thoroughly expert on paintings of the period, for they would note that the inscription on the reverse had been ignored by the auctioneers and assume that the cataloguer had taken expert advice to support his alternative description.

Had the cataloguer believed that the painting was of the period of Duccio but had not wished to commit himself to that particular artist, he could have done so by way of a conventional cataloguing technique. By simply heading the description Duccio he could have indicated that the painting was in the style of the artist and possibly of the period of the artist without committing the auctioneers to guaranteeing the attribution. Such a description might have encouraged interested parties to visit the sale to form their own opinion. Had that been the case then not only might a significantly better price have been obtained in the first place, but the ring might have found it difficult to operate at all.

The question of whether in 1968 the Board of Trade missed an opportunity of achieving the first successful prosecution under the Act was a question which was hotly debated during the build-up to the Act's amendment in 1969. When the Board of Trade investigation into the sale at Aldwick Court was concluded the papers were sent to the Director of Public Prosecutions, thus indicating that there may have been a case to answer. The papers were returned, however, because more than six months had elapsed between the alleged offence and the laying of evidence—the six months rule applying to the Act.

At this point the patience of certain Members of the House became exhausted and fingers were pointed at the Board of Trade investigators who were accused of a lethargic approach to their enquiries. Such was the feeling generated by the whole affair that there were calls in Parliament for a Public Inquiry to investigate not only the Aldwick Court sale and its consequences but also the Board of Trade examination and its failure to obtain a prosecution. There was even an attempt to establish a doubtful precedent by calling for the proposed amendments to the Act to be back-dated to the date of the sale—26th of March, 1968.

Retrospective legislation is something which finds little favour with Members of Parliament, and the proposal was eventually withdrawn. It was, however, stated many times during the debate that in this case such retrospection might well serve the interests of justice, indeed the move would have found support but for the implications of such a precedent in other areas of the law.

In the face of the evidence the allegations that the Board of Trade investigators did not make a sufficient effort to obtain a prosecution do not seem to be well founded. If there was any kind of a conspiracy which in the end prevented the matter from reaching the courts the evidence suggests that the partners in that conspiracy were the very individuals, groups and journalists who either observed personally or were informed of and reported upon the events of the 26th of March.

In order to clarify the situation it is necessary to examine the record of the debates and the questions asked in Parliament, and to put in chronological order the various statements and events which gave the affair such notoriety.

We must remember that the sale took place on the 26th of March, 1968. It was well known that the six month rule applied, and therefore that any evidence to be laid had a deadline of the 26th of September. The record shows that on the 29th of May, 1968, the President of the Board of Trade was consulted by two Members of the House on the possibility that a ring was operating illegally at art auctions. At this point there was no reference to the Aldwick Court sale or indeed to any particular event. The Board of Trade enquired into the general allegation but could find no evidence to support it.

The first specific reference to Aldwick Court seems to have been made on the 2nd of August, 1968, when the Member of Parliament for Reigate wrote to the President of the Board of Trade on the matter. Following a meeting with the Member the Board made additional enquiries in the course of which it wrote to the Society of London Art Dealers on the 6th of August. Bearing in mind the time limits it might seem significant that the Society's reply stated that it might be prepared to give some information but could not do so before the end of September. The Society replied on the 30th of September when it made a specific allegation regarding the sale at Aldwick Court, although no evidence was given relating to those involved.

The evidence recording the events surrounding the sale and naming the witnesses to those events was not to be forthcoming until released as an article in the *Sunday Times* newspaper on the 27th of October, 1968. Prior to publication, on the 24th of October, a representative of the newspaper laid certain information before officials of the Board of Trade. On receipt of the information the papers on the case were despatched to the office of the Director of Public Prosecutions.

It was of course much too late to obtain a prosecution, but there is no evidence at all to indicate that the investigators were given the necessary information in time. There is no doubt that the evidence was known to certain individuals who could have made it available in time had they so wished. In the event it seems that nobody was prepared to come forward until the time limit had comfortably expired.

What then has the law achieved in its endeavours towards eliminating undesirable practices in the auction rooms of England. In the early 1920s, before there was any legislation at all, the ring had grown powerful in all branches of the business. It is said that in those days the Armenian dealers in oriental rugs invaded Sotheby's New Bond Street galleries and organised their ring to such effect that the auctioneers encouraged a lone renegade dealer to stand against the group to ensure reasonable prices. The brave Mr Benlian, as he was called, was allowed extended credit by the auctioneers to reward his courage in ignoring the loudly voiced threats and gestures of violence from the main group of his countrymen.

The 1927 Act had little if any influence on events. It might have persuaded those operating in the London salerooms to adopt a lower profile, but there is every indication that out of town in the years between the original Act and the Amended Act of 1969 the rings tightened their hold on the country sales.

In the early 1960s the growing public interest in antiques and the very high prices achieved by major works of art resulted in more media coverage of the auction scene. The bigger coups pulled off now and again by one or other of the country rings became much more widely reported and attracted the attention of public and politicians alike. It was a series of such coups culminating in the Duccio affair that led to the amended legislation.

Despite the effort to tighten up the law in 1969, the Amended Act has fared only a little better than the old one. The original Act managed one attempted prosecution in forty-three years. It was unsuccessful. The amended legislation was to be in force for eleven years before it notched up the first victory in the history of the auction.

The story of the successful prosecution involves a small, well established country ring and confirms Anthony Crosland's words of 1968 when he said that the difficulty in obtaining a prosecution lay not in the letter of the law but in the difficulty of discovering the evidence. Again it was the *Sunday Times* which carried the report of the operation that began as a detective thriller and almost finished up as a plot suitable for a 'carry on' farce.

The report was entitled 'police film the day an antiques knockout became a punch up', and told how for two years police had been keeping watch on a particular auction room in Camarthon. The monthly sales had been attended regularly by detectives who had obtained their evidence by arming themselves with miniature video cameras and microphones while posing as saleroom porters and electricians.

Having located the secret venue for the knock-out, the cocktail bar of the Ivybush Royal Hotel in Camarthon, the officers were anxious to complete their evidence by filming a knock-out in progress, but were twice thwarted in their efforts by minor mishaps while filming. During one session a fight broke out between dealers and the proceedings were abandoned as the group was attracting too much attention. On a second occasion instructions relayed over the pocket radio of one of the disguised police officers were overheard by some of the group who again abandoned the session under the impression that a raid was imminent.

The police operation was eventually completed when the dealers, engrossed in the detail of their transactions, failed to observe an increasing presence in the room until the Detective Chief Inspector in charge announced that he was in fact a police officer and not an electrician in a white coat as had seemed to be the case.

One of the dealers is reported to have said afterwards: 'I'd been surprised to notice a middle aged man and woman snogging on a sofa in the bar. The strange thing was that when we moved to another part of the bar they moved with us. I suppose they must have been the police. When the police arrived they told us they had been bugging our meetings since April. They showed us photographs they had taken at previous meetings. We were all shocked, settlements go on everywhere, even in the best auction rooms in Britain. Why pick on us'.

As a result of these enquiries eleven men were questioned by the police and eventually brought to trial. On the 10th of July, 1981, nine of the accused were convicted of giving or receiving inducement or reward to abstain from bidding at the auction. They were each fined £500 plus costs, and banned from all auction rooms in Britain for six months.

Thus was the first successful prosecution in fifty four years achieved, and Mr Justice Waterhouse stated at Swansea Crown Court that the case showed that the statute was not dead and hoped that the convictions would serve as a warning to other dealers. While the statute may not be technically dead, it could hardly be described as the ultimate deterrent, and it is perhaps too much to hope that just one success in fifty-four years will be sufficient to deter those who make a good living from the rich pickings available. Mr Justice Waterhouse did after all say in the same statement that the evidence indicated that price rings operated on a wide scale. There were many mischiefs associated with them. They depressed prices and intimidated potential buyers.

The quiet calm of the present day auction scene is then something of a deception. The basis of the deception, however, lies not only in the determination of ring members to operate as discreetly as possible, but also in the equally determined 'look the other way' attitude of some of the major auctioneers if there is the suggestion that a ring might have operated on their premises at a particular sale. That is not to say that the same auctioneers would not take a firm line towards preventing ring activities—such measures as setting adequate reserve prices, displaying prominently the provisions of the Act, even warning suspected individuals—but once the deed is thought to have been done it is usually felt that there is little to be gained from pursuing the matter save adverse publicity for the saleroom.

As recently as the 2nd of March, 1980, the *Sunday Times* revealed that dealers rings were operating in the London salerooms on a regular basis. Part of an article entitled 'How these men ran an auction ring stated:

> Jewellery sales at Sotheby's and Christie's, the leading auctioneers, are regularly attended by dealers 'rings'—illegal arrangements whereby dealers act in collusion to hold down prices artifically.
>
> The *Sunday Times* has been able to establish the names of 10 dealers who have taken part in such arrangements. Three of them were at last week's sale of fine jewels at Sotheby's in London, and one of them has confirmed that he has taken part in a number of rings.
>
> At the same time three other members of the profession have unprecedently broken ranks to give a detailed account of the way

in which such rings operate at the expense of the public. They reveal that the rings have established a pervasive influence at the very top of the multi-million pound antique trade.

The auction houses themselves are reticent on the subject but express their concern in private. A director of Christie's said yesterday that rings had become 'much more subtle'. No auction room was immune from what he described as 'a loose conspiracy of like-minded people who are all trying to get a pearl, or a cache of pearls, cheaper than they would get them normally' ... A senior employee at Sotheby's had very much the same view. Talking of the operations of a dealer's ring he said: 'It's not only at Sotheby's. It's everywhere. I think we try and control it more than the others'. He said of the leading dealers in the ring: 'They are a cheeky lot, cocky even'.

There is no doubt that the rings continue to flourish in every part of the auction business, in London and in the country, and possibly throughout the world. The enormous turnover of the art auctioneers will continue to grow annually, and yet the legislation controlling auctions will remain much as when in 1968 Anthony Crosland spoke of the difficulty of discovering evidence of malpractice. As long as it is possible for the ring operators to pick up easy money with little or no prospect of retribution, it will be true to say that the ring is alive and well and living very close to wherever auctions are taking place.

CHAPTER 12

Now and Forever

The auction scene today worldwide, is busy and varied. In England most large towns, and some small ones, boast a local auctioneer who is usually the local estate agent as well, and who sells furniture and effects on either a regular or an occasional basis. Agricultural markets are strong and use the auction extensively for the sale of cattle and poultry, as well as all manner of farm produce and agricultural machinery. The sale of property by auction is becoming more common, there are several large and well established firms dealing in the sale of motor vehicles exclusively by auction, and in a climate of industrial re-organisation the auctioneers of manufacturing plant and machinery are doing big business.

In France the continuing policy of strict legislative control allows little change or flexibility. The system remains essentially the same, although Octave Uzanne would be pleased indeed to learn that at last the old Hotel Drouot has had a much needed face-lift — but only very recently. In the Netherlands the horticultural auctions are still the fastest in the world, while in Holland today the bidding is a bit up and down because they use more than one system.

In America the auction rooms are called auction galleries, and while the salerooms in the major cities such as New York and Los Angeles operate in much the same way as Sotheby's and Christie's for the very simple reason that they are Sotheby's and Christie's, many of the country auctioneers do not. There is probably more variety in the modern American auction scene than there is anywhere else in the world. A typical country auction operation is run by the Douglas Galleries of Massachusetts who sell anything from art to household goods. They will sell the house and its furniture, the farm and its equipment and implements. The firm holds about sixty sales a year grossing about a million dollars, and the service is personal, informal and friendly.

A different kind of auction which is unique to the United States is the travelling sale. This is a type of itinerant auction which moves around the country seeking out in particular auction-starved townships with no local saleroom of their own. C.B. Charles Galleries of Michigan is typical of the breed and conducts twenty to thirty sales a year around the countryside. Unlike most conventional auctioneers the gallery owns a high percentage of the goods which it offers for sale, inevitable perhaps in view of the element of travelling; but there are other differences.

The sales are aimed specifically at the private buyer, not the 'trade' and a most unconventional consequence of that particular policy is the 'by request' sale . At these sales the attendant buyers may request that items from the catalogue be put up in random order to avoid delay to the interested bidder. The system gives advantage to the auctioneer in that he is able to catalogue more items than he could sell in a day by the normal method, knowing that he will only be asked to offer those lots that his audience is interested in purchasing. Holding their sales in good hotels and motels the Charles Galleries organisation claims to be able to set up or dismantle the whole show in just eight hours with its highly trained road crew.

Another variation on the 'conventional' auction theme is that some American galleries will only accept bids from clients who first obtain a bidding number which is issued before the sale against a cash deposit. Where this system applies the saleroom will usually insert an extra condition of sale in the catalogue. This may read as follows:

> Bidding will be by number only. No bid will be accepted without the bidder having first obtained a bidding number from the cashier. To obtain a bidding number, a cash deposit of at least $100 is required. Additional deposits may be requested on special items at the time the item is sold at auction. However, a deposit greater than 25% of the bid will not be required. Deposit will be applied against purchase or will be refunded at the conclusion of the sale at the bidder's request. It is bidder's responsibility to collect unused deposit.

America has a 'National Auctioneers Association' and an estimated 25,000 auctioneers active throughout the country. In some States those wishing to enter the profession must pass a qualifying examination, some require a guarantee of good faith by the deposit of a Bond, while in others it is simply a matter of paying the prescribed fee and setting up shop. The National Association is in favour of a uniform licencing law throughout the United States, along the lines of the twenty or more States which currently demand a period of training and an examination.

In recent years many Schools of Auctioneering have appeared. Using established auctioneers as tutors many of them run a two-week course covering all aspects of the auction business. In good American tradition the Jim Graham School in Florida offers 'The Professional Auction Chant' and 'How to Determine Values', as well as 'Bidders Body Language' and 'True Self Confidence'. The International Auction School of Massachusetts can provide 'Clerking and Cashiering' as well as 'Estates Liquidations' and 'Sales Management' supplemented by 'The Art of Salesmanship', and the inevitable 'Self Confidence'.

The influence of Arabian oil revenues, crucial in the world economy today, is inevitably felt in the auction business. Apart from the obvious factor of wealthy Arab business men with the resources to obtain whatever takes their fancy from the fine art salerooms of the world, some quite unusual sales are taking place in the unlikely setting of the Middle East itself. The oil-rich Arab rulers have sought to bring their previously under-developed countries into the twentieth century in record time with construction and development on a grand scale. Now as major projects are completed and construction slows down, the large quantities of surplus equipment are being disposed of 'on the premises'. *Business Week* reports:

> To dispose of the surplus machinery, Mideast contractors are now trying a well-tested method for moving used goods—American style auctions. Parks-Davis Auctioneers Inc., a privately owned company based in Richardson, Texas, held the first such auction in Kuwait last February, grossing about $4 million for a Canadian contractor. Encouraged by those results, Parks-Davis has held two more auctions—in Kuwait and Abu Dhabi—and attracted crowds, even though temperatures were above 110F. The Kuwait sale on May 26 (1979) attracted some 800 people.

At the other end of the temperature scale in Canada, the Christmas eve, 1979, edition of *Macleans* magazine carried the story of an auction of a different colour. Under the title 'Big bucks for an old fishin' hole' it said:

> So coveted a game fish is the Atlantic salmon that, even in this day of diminished fish stocks and a troubled economy, affluent anglers continue to spend small fortunes to pursue it in Eastern Canadian rivers. That was amply illustrated in Fredericton one day last week when a mixed group of businessmen, dark-suited lawyers and cardigan-sweatered fishing-lodge operators gathered for the ultimate in piscatorial pursuit: an auction of exclusive fishing privileges on some of the best inland salmon waters found anywhere—choice stretches of New Brunswick's Restigouche and Miramichi rivers … By the final fall of the gavel the New Brunswick government had harvested $155,900 in annual income, a figure that will have grown to $226,055 by the time the leases expire in 1989. Not bad for two hours work—and a far cry from the first auction in 1883 when the take was just $2,775.

The same Canadian magazine carried another story at about the same time which more than any other demonstrates the extraordinary power of the auction as a sales method. Even in these enlightened times the auction's hypnotic effect overcame normal common sense in the frozen north when the entire Yukon township of Clinton Greek went under the hammer. When the town's sole financial support, the asbestos mine, closed for good, the entire population moved out and an enterprising auctioneer moved in to sell the derelict domestic and commercial properties at bargain prices.

One buyer, Stephan Herrmann, finished up with two four-bedroom houses, the 'Malamute Saloon', a six-bay garage and a trailer complex, all for just $6500. 'I guess I just freaked out with the auction's excitement' said Herrmann, who has yet to discover how to get his moneys-worth out of his frozen assets. 'What the hell if I bought more than I wanted? I got a bargain and had a ball.'

With plenty of customers like that the bigger auctioneers are also having a ball—in some cases quite literally. *Canadian Business* reports:

> When Sotheby's, one of the world's largest, with $412 million in sales in 1978–79, launched a Toronto gallery last fall, it did so in grand opening-night style. A team of financial and public relations experts flew in from the company's 40 locations worldwide to help orchestrate the premiere splash. Engraved invitations were sent to 2,000 of the city's most prominent collectors, dealers and celebrities. For three hours waiters in mustard-coloured jackets cruised the renovated warehouse gallery, balancing silver trays of exquisite tulip stemware filled with a mixture of sparkling white wine and champagne. A pianist seated at a grand piano provided a background of Cole Porter tunes. The guests feasted on smoked sturgeon, seasonal vegetables and cold roast sirloin.

Such a report perfectly demonstrates the strength and the confidence of the London auctioneers in the world art market. In the field of fine art auctioneering not only has London become the capital of the world, but Christie's and Sotheby's and in a lesser way Phillips, have in the best British tradition done their best to compensate for the demise of the British Empire by colonising large parts of the auction world. In volume of international fine art business it is virtually Christie's and Sotheby's versus the rest, with the big two well out in front, and while each of the major auctioneers work independently they appear to go to some lengths not to get in each others way.

In the United States for example it is Sotheby's who operate a system which sends teams of experts out into the countryside on what are advertised as 'Heirloom Discovery Days'. These appraisal sessions are usually organised under the umbrella of a local charity and the objective is to identify and value works of art and return to New York with the loot. The system is basically the same as that organised in England by Christie's through their South Kensington saleroom—and here called 'probes'.

Sotheby's English provincial efforts at bringing home the bacon have, in contrast with their American policy, been aimed rather at acquiring strategically situated satellites around the country. By buying up reputable and successful auction rooms and adding Sotheby to the title, they are able not only to deliver the choicest cuts to Bond Street but to dispense the remainder of the prime business in situ, leaving little but a carcase for the other local auctioneers to pick over.

In these provincial situations such is the indiminishable power of an organisation like Sotheby's that they may unconcernedly make slightly dubious decisions which the smaller auctioneer would not get away with. One particular aspect of provincial policy has caused a flurry of correspondence in trade papers and magazines across Europe. The periodical *arts antiques auctions* published in Brussels, reported in April, 1981:

> A fine row is brewing in the British trade press as the result of a letter written to the 'Antiques Trade Gazette' by Michael Adler of Hadlow Antiques, Tunbridge Wells, Kent. Mr Adler quite simply objects to Sotheby's attitude to his complaint that he had driven for six hours in bad winter weather to a viewing in Torquay, only to find that the lot he had come to see had been withdrawn. Mr Adler states, 'Still present were Mr Vaughan and Miss Millar of Sotheby's head office, who showed me the lot which they had arranged to transfer to a Bond Street sale. I suggested that it was a little late in the day to start shuffling lots, that the time was before they were catalogued. Miss Millar was generally sympathetic and understanding; Vaughan, however, exhorted me not to tell Sotheby's how to run their business'. Mr Adler's complaint that the auctioneers's actions showed a degree of indifference to their buyers drew an apology and an explanation from Sotheby's Managing Director, J.M. Linell, who said, 'Our two experts were in Torquay on other business and, while viewing the sale shortly before Mr Adler's arrival, noticed that one of the lots had been undercatalogued. It was a very rare type of watch which previous experience has shown is likely only to realise its full value in the context of a sale with international competition. We spoke to the owner, explained the situation and in the circumstances there seemed to be no alternative except to withdraw the lot.

Another correspondent from Plymouth, however, subsequently claimed, 'This is not the isolated incident that Sotheby's reply would suggest; it is a regular occurrence at their Torquay rooms, where hardly a sale passes without the auctioneer reading out a list of with-drawn lots'.

Of course in the end the 'fine row' will blow over, and who would wish to deny the London salerooms the success achieved from two centuries of participation in the auction—and what success! Growth of annual turnover in the last two decades sets Sotheby's and Christie's quite apart from other auctioneers, and in a way from other business, for regardless of world economic growth or decline, through sunshine, storm or crisis they continue a relentless progress towards total dom-ination of the auction.

The 1980–81 worldwide turnover total for Sotheby Parke Bernet was £317 million, an increase of 34% on the previous year and a figure more than twenty times the company's 1964 total of £13,350,000. Christie's latest figures of over £177 million show an increase on the previous year of 16% and a staggering hundred-fold increase over their 1957 turnover of just £1,760,000.

Much of this amazing growth has been achieved by way of a care-fully planned programme of expansion overseas. The most surprising aspect of that expansion programme being that none of the domestic auctioneers in the major cities of the world have been able to halt this relentless progress. Inevitably, as the empire grows, so the bandwagon becomes unstoppable, as the rapidly rising figures show.

It was Sotheby's successful take-over of Parke-Bernet that whet the firm's appetite for overseas expansion, and 1967 saw them breaking out in all directions. The first of the now regular Gleneagles sales was held in that year, as were a series of five sales held for the first time in Canada. A Paris office was opened in 1967, and 1968 saw a rash of new offices in Melbourne, Beirut, Florence and Canada. It was the turn of Johannesburg, Zurich and Munich in 1969, and a Hong Kong office and saleroom followed in 1973. The Dutch auctioneers Mak Van Waay of Amsterdam was purchased in 1974 and offices in Milan and Stockholm were opened in the same year. 1975 saw the opening of an office in Brussels, 1976 in Dublin and 1978, a vintage year, in Rome, Frankfurt and Geneva.

At home Sotheby's have not been idle. In 1967 they leased Hodg-son's rooms in Chancery Lane from the Hodgson family, specialist book auctioneers there since 1863, and their book department has been based there ever since. In 1971 the Belgravia saleroom was launched as a specialist secondary room dealing exclusively with the sale of nineteenth and twentieth century works of art, and their ex-cursions into the country during the 1970s have resulted in the Soth-eby title being added to Bearne's of Torquay, King and Chasemore of Pulborough, Beresford Adams of Chester and Humbert's of Taun-ton.

Christie's with almost half a century of experience in being a step or two behind their major rivals, have been almost equally busy diversifying in foreign parts. Their latest move into newly converted salerooms in what was the Maritime Museum in Amsterdam supersedes the previous arrangement of renting accommodation outside the city. Christie's now have overseas offices in New York, Los Angeles, Florida, Mexico City, Buenos Aires, Vancouver, Paris, Geneva, Zurich, Dusseldorf, Munich, Hamburg, Rome, Milan, Turin, Madrid, Vienna, Amsterdam, Oslo, Stockholm, Brussels, Sidney, Melbourne, Venice, Tokyo and Rio de Janeiro.

At home Christie's name has been added to the old-established Glasgow firm of Edmiston's since it was taken over in 1979, and their secondary London saleroom at South Kensington, previously Debenham Coe, is highly successful and expanding. It is from South Kensington that the periodic 'probes' emanate, reaching out into the countryside via teams of marauding experts who, from the comfort of a good hotel, will advise the local yokel population on the value or otherwise of their treasured possessions. The probe operation is akin to rolling out some gigantic vacuum cleaner which sucks up all the valuable art objects which have become mislaid in the provinces and restores them to their rightful place, under the hammers of the London auctioneers.

The probe has a triple benefit for the auctioneers. Of course the object is to make a profit and in most cases the owner, pleased to learn that his goods have some value, is more than happy to allow them to return with the team for sale in London. Secondly, the publicity achieved by the appraisal team has a long term effect on the local population who may forever believe that such expertise exists only in London, and last but not least the local auctioneers in the probe area will become so totally demoralised by the success of the Christie mission that they will require to be restrained from entering a monastery or joining the Foreign Legion.

The auction as a trading system is based on competition. It sets prospective buyer against prospective buyer and allows a tantalisingly brief moment of time for each transaction to be consumated. When the sale goods are especially rare and desirable items the auction becomes irresistible to most human beings, and has therefore established itself as a fundamental ingredient of the commercial system. As a basic business method it is adaptable, and has been adapted over the years by astute practitioners to meet the prevailing social needs and conditions of the times. It has assisted the ancient Roman war machine and the slave traders of the old South, it has irritated the nineteenth-century American merchants beyond endurance and encouraged the twentieth-century Sotheby shareholders to reach for another gin and tonic.

The special strength of the auction is that it is not just a fair-

weather system, to be enjoyed in the odd moments of economic stability. The auction is also effective in a crisis, and can be used to
speedily liquidate large surpluses of unwanted goods, equipment and
property. Items bought as an investment on the crest of the wave may
be disposed of quickly in a struggle to keep the ship afloat, and the
auctioneer benefits every time.

The recent economic difficulties in Britain have resulted in a con-
traction of the industrial base with the associated release of redundant
plant and machinery. This has led to a dramatic increase in the
turnover of the lesser publicised auctioneers of factory equipment, and
clearly demonstrates how the auctioneers can make a profit from
adversity. On the 25th October, 1981, the *Sunday Times* reported
under the banner 'Scots hopes under the hammer':

> The auctioneer's hammer comes down next month on the Talbot
> Car Plant at Linwood, which once employed more than 8,000
> people and represented the best hopes for the regeneration of the
> West of Scotland. 'The sale of the decade' it has been dubbed and
> Talbot UK hope to move everything from huge British Clearing
> double-action presses, to sewing machines, office desks and bunches
> of spanners. It should make them around £10m. For Peter Harri-
> man and his colleagues from the London-based auctioneering firm
> of Henry Butcher, the Linwood sale will be the culmination of six
> months of hard work. 'Turning the factory into a shop window' in
> the words of one of the Butcher team ... Peter Harriman takes a
> professional pride in the operation. 'This is the biggest sale any
> company ever had', he says. 'Bigger even than Mentmore'.

'Bigger even than Mentmore', well perhaps, if all the expectations are
fulfilled. 'The biggest sale any company has ever had', that in fact is
not true, but then that's the auction business — exaggerated claims,
the big build-up. Of course many people have fallen for the big
build-up and fallen under the spell of the auction over the years, but
they cannot say that they were not warned. In 1813 a pamphlet
published in New York and entitled *The Ruinous Tendency of Auctioneering and the Necessity of Restraining It* clearly stated:

> It will be in vain for government to trust to virtue of the people to
> resist the allurements held out to tempt them into the arena of
> some one of the numerous and increasing progeny of auction marts
> ... If selling by auction were nothing more than a mode of sale,
> tending merely to change the disposal of any given article of goods
> from the present person in trade to other hands, it would be idle
> to make it a matter of serious complaint ... but auctioneering
> is not a mode of trade; it is, in fact, a mode of destroying trade.
> It is a game at which none but knaves and fools can play, and

in which the smallest portion of honesty is an inconvenient encumbrance.

On the other hand Leslie Hyams, when Managing Director of Parke-Bernet in the early 1960s, was heard to say: 'We are too honest to make any money, we have prestige, but none of us has any wealth.' Many dealers and merchants would dispute such a statement, however, preferring to believe that all auctioneers are wealthy, that their work is easy and that they are inclined to favour and protect the seller at the expense of the buyer. Of course most auctioneers will feel that the trade are constantly seeking to keep auction prices down, and some sellers will be certain that the auctioneer favours the trade buyers for the simple reason that he relies on their regular attendance at sales.

These differing viewpoints lead directly to the variety of claims made regarding the auction. It is both honest and corrupt, it is injurious to trade and also a benefit, it favours the buyer, and also the seller, but most of all it favours the mean and grasping, idle and affluent auctioneer. On the other hand, if there is another hand, those in the business know that the auction is hard work with high overheads, and that the ninety-nine per cent of auctioneers who are not Christie's or Sotheby's or the bigger provincial rooms do not find it easy to make ends meet.

All of these statements are of course true. The auction is all of those things and more, and it must be so for the auction has a history as long as history itself. It also has a flourishing present and no doubt an amazing future in the field of ... but that's best left for another time.

Bibliography

Cassady, Ralph, *Auctions and Auctioneering*, 1967.

Ash, Peter, *The First Auctioneer: origin of sales by auction*, Estates Gazette (Centenary Supplement), May 3rd 1958.

Westerfield, R.B. *Early History of American Auctions*, 1920.

Jones, F.M. *Middlemen in the Domestic Trade of the United States*, 1937.

Selincourt, A. de (trans.), *The Histories of Heroditus*, 1954.

Braybrooke, R. (Ed.), *Diary of Samuel Pepys*, 1828.

Uzanne (Octave), *The Hotel Drouot and auction rooms in Paris generally, before and after the French Revolution — The Connoisseur*, 1902.

Sanders, T.C. (trans.), *The Institutes of Justinian*, 1927.

Hay, D., *The Italian Renaissance in its Historical Background*, 1970.

Bancroft, F., *Slave Trading in the Old South*, 1959.

Gibbon, E., *Decline and Fall of the Roman Empire*, ed. William Smith, 1854.

Fuller, A., *Economy and Society in Western Europe 1300–1600*, Open University, 1971.

Converse-Huegy-Mitchell. *Elements of Marketing*, 1958.

Brough, (James), *Auction*, 1963.

Lichine, A., *Wines of France*, 1956.

Herrmann, Frank, *Sotheby's: Portrait of an Auction House*, 1980.

Williams, E., *The History of the Caribbean 1492–1969*, 1970.

Lester, J., *To be a Slave*, 1968.

Frederick, J.H., *Agricultural Markets*, 1937.

Botkin, B.A. (Ed.), *Lay My Burden Down: a Folk History of Slavery*, 1945.

Henson, J., *Father Henson's Story of his own Life*, 1962.

Bathurst, H., *The Ruinous Tendency of Auctioneering*, 1848.

Marillier, H.C., *Christie's 1766–1925*, 1926.

Ketchum, W.C., *Auction: the guide to bidding etc.*, 1980.

Pascal, Pia, *L'hotel Drouot.. et avant, L'Oeil magazine*, May, 1957.

Pamphlets etc.

An Examination of the Reasons why the Present System of Auctions ought to be Abolished, Boston, 1828.

Reasons why the Present System of Auctions ought to be Abolished, New York, 1828.

The Auction System of Horticultural Marketing in the Netherlands, 1959.
Annals of the Congress of the United States, 16th Congress, 2nd series.

Magazines
Macleans, Big bucks for an old fishin' hole, 24th December, 1979
Business Week, American-style auctions for a Mideast surplus, 11th June, 1979
Canadian Business, Bidding up the auction business; inflation is good news for auctioneers, March, 1980
Macleans, The auction block runneth over, 1979
Niles H., Niles Weekly Register, Vols. 35 & 36, 1828–29

Newspapers
Sunday Times, Hang on, that was my icon, 14th December, 1980.
—— Who owns maharajah's golden throne, 1981.
—— How to make pots of money in prison, January, 1981
—— Holbein 'smuggled' out by dealers ring, 21st September, 1980
—— Scots hopes under the hammer, 25th October, 1981

Extracts and Advertisements
The Times
The Morning Post
The Daily Advertiser
The Windsor and Eton Express

Index